THE SIDETRACKED SISTERS' HAPPINESS FILE

THE SIDETRACKED SISTERS' HAPPINESS FILE

Pam Young and Peggy Jones

Edited by
Sydney Craft Rosen

WARNER BOOKS

A Warner Communications Company

Warner Books, Inc., 666 Fifth Avenue, New York, NY 10103

A Warner Communications Company

Designed by Richard Oriolo

Printed in the United States of America

First Printing: April 1985

10 9 8 7 6 5 4 3 2 1

Library of Congress Cataloging in Publication Data

Young, Pam.
    The sidetracked sisters' happiness file.

    1. Home economics.   2. Housewives—Time management.
I. Jones, Peggy.   II. Rozen, Sydney Craft.   III. Title.
TX158.Y64   1985   640'.43   84-40654
ISBN 0-446-51334-2

Dedicated to Fred with more love than ever

SPECIAL THANKS

Special thanks to DANNY, MOM and DAD, MICHAEL, PEGGY, CHRIS, JOANNA, JEFFREY and ALLYSON. Without their love and support, this book would not have been possible.

Table of Contents

Family Album

Afterword

Acknowledgments

We want to acknowledge Dee Anne Cloke, our best friend and co-worker. Dee Anne is the happiest, most beautiful person we know. She kept us going when times were hard and we weren't in the mood to write.

She has been, undoubtedly, the most successful Happiness File tester and without her enthusiasm, inspiration, and advice, this book could not have been finished.

We also want to acknowledge Sydney Craft Rozen, our editor. She has saved us, more than once, from literary humiliation. Sydney is a brilliant editor and a wonderful person. Our friendship has grown over the seven years that we have worked together, and we hope the combination of the three of us has created a warm and sensitive book about happiness.

Special thanks also to Fredda Isaacson, senior editor and vice-president of Warner Books, who knows us so well that her articulate editing makes us sound better. She has shown us that an executive can combine incredible intelligence, graciousness, and family feeling, and she is a warm example of what happiness is all about.

THE SIDETRACKED SISTERS' HAPPINESS FILE

Introduction

Writing a book about how to be happy hasn't been easy because we haven't been happy every day, but we've had to write anyway. In fact, we had to ask for an extension on our manuscript deadline because we hit a couple of really rotten months where we weren't happy at all, and our writing reflected our circumstances.

As sisters, we both agree that our families are our first priority, and they reflect that caring. When something goes wrong at home, it throws everything else out of balance. As effective as the Happiness File has been in our everyday lives, we still have to say that it was powerless to make us happy in the face of a life-and-death situation in our immediate family. (That experience is explained in depth in a later chapter.)

Our system is not a cure for *unhappiness*; it was designed to help the already happy person become even happier by organizing free time, directing strengths, controlling weaknesses, and breaking down life's common obstacles into manageable actions. The system can also help you achieve your goals by defining them and handling them one step at a time.

We will share with you our unique way to tap the subconscious part of the mind for self-improvement. We have discovered how to bring negative feelings gently out of the closet to neutralize them. Our techniques do not require a professional counselor, nor do they involve hypnotism or any synthetic approach to mind study. Right under your very nose is the doorknob to happiness. Turn it, open the door to something that has been there all the time, and that will follow you all the days of your life. It will change as you change (for better or worse); use it as the barometer to your success. It is your home.

We are not psychologists, but we are authorities on the subject of happiness. That doesn't mean we've never been sad, depressed, bored, or anything else that is the opposite of happy. We have cried and clung together, and although we have faith, we've both experienced gripping fear. We love life, but each of us has wanted to die.

Our methods for getting more out of life are not scientific. We have developed a system based on our own experiences; its credibility lies in our success. We are masters at turning challenges into opportunities. We have a growing business that has generated millions of dollars, a business born out of our ability to turn our totally disorganized homes into harmony and order. Our first best-selling book, *Sidetracked Home Executives*, told of our remarkable journey from pigpen to paradise. Since then it has become very clear to us that what goes on at home directly affects what happens everywhere else. If you're living your own life with commitment to the values you consider worthwhile, you will be in a position to be an influence on your family. If your family feels your love and understanding, it will be reflected in their relationships at school, in the workplace, and in the community. When that power is multiplied by others with the same spirit, it can build a country dedicated to a love of humanity that can bring peace to the world.

Experience has taught us that there is a winter and a summer to everything. We've learned to bask in the summers and enjoy their generosity, and in the harshness of the winters, we've been able to hang on to enough faith to assure ourselves that "this too shall pass" and that everything will be all right.

If you are in the midst of a serious emotional depression, or if you are overwhelmed by unhappy circumstances, we urge you to get professional help.

If you're like most of us, you are probably basically happy, but you'd like to be even more so. As sisters, we have always felt a freedom to be ruthlessly honest with each other. Because of our closeness, we have discovered truths about ourselves that might have been locked inside us by pride and ego and the false belief that we're alone. Having each other is almost like having an in-house therapist.

We think that everyone has the same basic needs. We all crave love and appreciation. We want hope and encouragement, rewards for doing good, and forgiveness when we have done something wrong. We all need a dream, a purpose for living. Self-improvement is a lifetime path, but it's a pursuit that doesn't lead to a place where everything is perfect. When you reach what you thought was your final destination, you will find that you have farther to go. There will never be an arriving, only a continuation of the quest; so you'd better have fun on the way.

PART ONE

One

The Golden Halo

June 16, 1983—Hollywood, California:
We were in Hollywood to receive the Golden Halo Award
for our television series, *Cleaning Up Your Act.* We had come
a long way from our wasted days as slobs to this day of
recognition and honor. The fact that it was June 16 added to
our celebration because it marked a special event from our
past. On June 16, 1977, six years earlier, we had decided to
get organized, and that decision had changed our lives.
Eventually we wrote two books on the subject, outlining
the 3x5 cardfile system that took us from pigpen to paradise.
Kac Young, a producer, turned the books into a weekly
television series, which led to the Golden Halo Award.

The award was given by the Southern California Motion
Picture Guild for programs exemplifying inspiration and
wholesomeness. There were about 1,000 people there, and
the place was crawling with stars. Television cameras and
reporters were there to interview the big names. We knew it
wasn't the Academy Awards, but to us it might as well have
been.

After we received the certificate (which looked like a college diploma) we left the auditorium with Kac, and headed toward her lovely home in the Hollywood Hills, where we were to be her overnight houseguests.

"Let's stop and get this framed," she said.

"Framed?" "Now?"

We both thought it was premature, that it would take too long and that the frame place was probably out of the way. Before we could finish thinking up excuses, Kac's bronze Mercedes was parked in front of the frame shop, and she was out of the car. The salespeople knew her by name. We were impressed with how she seemed to know just what the parchment needed. We tagged along like toddlers following their mother through a dime store.

"Frame it or forget it!" she quipped. Kac was wise. Our minds flashed back to our private nests of keepsakes: stashes of certificates, awards, ribbons, and newspaper clippings, never framed because our good intentions were too good. Like the L'Oréal commercial, "Sure, it costs more, but I'm worth it..." our problem was that since we couldn't afford the best, even if we did deserve it, we'd wait...and wait...and wait. Kac was willing to do it now and settle for less, knowing it could be changed later if need be.

As the clerk began to tally the cost of the project, our guilt thickened. It wasn't just important papers we had neglected: there were baby books, set aside after delivery, with only brief notations of vital statistics. Where had our babies' first seven years gone?

Our kids ranged in age from seven to seventeen and we had absolutely no written record of what had happened after we brought them home from the hospital. Our only hope of passing on the memories of those precious times would be our dependence on words. Like the wandering minstrels who recorded historical events in song rather than script, we relied on our storytelling ability to pass on the family heritage. Such primitive recollection doesn't go very far, though, when you register your child for school and enrollment officials want the little tyke's inoculation records. "Yes, he's had all his shots" isn't good enough to comply with state health regulations. We both felt guilty when our kids had to be reinoculated.

And what about the wad of hair from our babies' first haircuts? We thought of it after the cuts, salvaged the strands from the trash, and put them in our books, with the intention of coming back at a better time and arranging them each into a neat, ribbon-tied lock. It never happened and the hairs were everywhere.

Dental records, growth charts, vocabulary developmental logs... Spare us. If anyone had tried to follow the lives of our children, based on the information in their baby books, it would appear that each one had died after the first haircut.

The noise from the computerized cash register spitting out the receipt for the frame brought us back to the present. "That'll be $12.97." As our friend took care of the transaction, we glanced at each other with looks that said we were both thinking the same thing: *Hmmm . . . $12.97 . . . It looks pretty good for that.* Why had we thought it would cost so much more or be such an enormous project? The entire event had taken less than fifteen minutes.

It was a lovely southern California day. There we were in a gorgeous car, wending our way through a maze of beautiful homes we knew must belong to movie stars. Our award lay between us on the leather seat. It now had been dignified by a frame. Hanging on the wall, it would be a continuing reminder of this day. If it had been left to us, our award would have taken its place in the family graveyard of crushed cylinders back home, joining the diplomas, certificates, and awards we had earned over the years. Like the hairs in the baby books... so were the days of our lives... scattered, tangled, and disorganized.

Near the top of the hill and commanding a view of the valley below, Kac Young's home nestled against the trees. Her garage door opened automatically and we zipped in. As it closed behind us, we knew what Ali Baba felt like when he disappeared into his secret hillside retreat. The two-car garage was tastefully finished. A foreign convertible sports car waited on one side for its weekends in the sun. Sports equipment lined the walls, evidence of fun and activity.

Kac shared the house with her two "children," a Siamese cat named Summer and a sleek black cat named Lucy. She greeted them with a surprise carton of moo shu pork, which they sniffed with discrimination. Convinced it wasn't Szechuan, they began to nibble, and she was free to show us to our room.

The pink-and-lavender bedspread and pillow shams introduced the guest room's decorating theme and matched the draperies, which complemented the lavish floor coverings, which accented the decorative wall panels that beckoned the guest into the spacious bathroom for a continuation of the theme. The toilet tissue harmonized with the facial tissue, and a chorus of scrupulously chosen accessories echoed the brilliant execution of thoughtful composition.

It made us wonder how we had ever had the nerve to invite overnight guests into our homes. They'd have a choice of zipping into a Garfield sleeping bag on the couch in the living room, wrapping up in a Strawberry Shortcake comforter on a frilly twin bed, or dozing in between Star Wars Action Sheets in a wagon-wheel bunk bed.

Guest room . . . ha! We didn't even have guest towels. All of our towels were yard towels, useful on trips to the beach and after runs through the sprinkler, but totally unacceptable for company.

With the confidence of a gracious hostess, Kac instructed us to "freshen up" before dinner, and left us alone.

"I've always wondered what they mean by that."

"Yeah, I know. Whenever they say it in the movies, they always close the door, and you never get to see just exactly what they freshen."

"I wonder what we're gonna have for dinner."

"I don't know, but I could've gone for some of that moo shu pork."

"Didn't it smell good?"

"Yeah!"

"Let's just wash our hands."

We decided not to get the guest soaps wet and instead used the lavender-scented bar in the shower. Blotting our hands carefully on the orchid fingertip towel, we were careful not to spoil the satin monogram.

We left our bedroom and timidly ventured down the hall into the generous gourmet kitchen. The moo shu pork was gone, but something wonderful was stirring. There was nothing we could do to help with dinner, Kac assured us, as she led us to a sunny garden terrace for champagne. We were celebrating.

She pulled the frosty bottle from a silver ice bucket and festively popped the cork. As she poured the champagne into graceful fluted glasses, she said, "Congratulations!" In unison we both said, "Congratulations to you, too!"

She smiled. "Just think of what you've accomplished in the last six years."

We both agreed: "Yeah...back in our slob days we couldn't get the dog to do what we wanted."

For an instant we felt as if we had finally arrived, but then she said, "So what are your plans for the next six years?"

We were quiet.

Six years . . . We felt lucky to know our plans for the next six days. Expecting an intelligent response, Kac was shocked to find out that we had no plans. Her future was as clearly defined as NASA's space program, while ours was as uncertain as an Amtrak schedule.

Throughout the evening we kept returning to the subject of goals. Kac said she found time and money for self-improvement, home-improvement, investments, and business opportunities. We went to bed depressed.

The next morning we were to travel by train to San Bernardino, where we were going to teach a seminar on organization during the weekend. Kac was up early. We heard the muffled sound of her office phone ringing, then a flurry of tapping as she quickly typed something. We knew her day was off to a productive beginning.

An hour or so later Kac knocked at our bedroom door. "Good morning," she said. "Breakfast is almost ready, and here's your dress . . . I knew you were worried about it so I took the liberty of sending it to my cleaners. They do marvelous work."

"You did? . . . Thank you," the spiller said.

We examined the silk. Through the miracle of stain removal, the dress, which had had a greasy chicken breast dropped on its lap at the awards banquet, was restored. We thought of how many nice things we had ruined because of stains that we'd allowed to set.

After a tasty breakfast of omelets, orange juice (freshly squeezed, of course), toast, and coffee, we packed our bags and prepared to leave. As we hugged and said our thank-yous and good-byes, Kac presented us with a yellow envelope filled with photographs. In it were pictures from the banquet the day before. When had they been developed?

In the cab we talked about Kac as we shuffled the colored pictures back and forth.

"She amazes me."

"Me, too."

"Have you ever taken a camera to a banquet?"

"I've never taken a camera anywhere. Have you?"

"Yeah, we got one as a wedding present, so over the years I've been able to take some wonderful pictures."

"Really? Where are they? I've never seen them."

"I haven't either. They haven't been developed yet. They're in a big wooden salad bowl on top of the refrigerator."

"You're kidding . . . How many rolls are in there?"

"Oh, I don't know. There must be about eighty, I guess."

"Schwooo!"

"I wrote on most of them, so I know what I've got."

"Boy, some of those rolls would be sixteen years old."

"I know."

"It's gonna cost you a fortune to get them developed."

"Yeah, I oughta take our income tax refund and just get it done!"

The cab pulled up in front of the Los Angeles train station.

"That's $27.50," the driver demanded. We simultaneously bushwhacked through the tangle of stuff in our purses in search of the cash we knew we had. Before we had left Portland, Oregon, for Los Angeles, we had stopped at our bank to get money for the trip. We used the drive-up window with the vacuumatic teller feature and got the cash we needed. Unfortunately for the bank, we had inadvertently kept the jar. We were already late, and by the time we realized that we still had their container, we were at the airport in long-term parking. We heard a click and saw the taxi meter jump to $28.50. Quickly we gave the man $30 and left without a receipt.

The Los Angeles train station was magnificent, like a huge marble cathedral. High, columned archways towered over us. Everything was white: the floors, the walls, the ceilings, the counters, the drinking fountains, even the pigeons were white. They flew freely in and out of the depot. We had never seen wild birds in a municipal building, and we were intrigued by their flight patterns and amazed at the blasé attitude of most of the people. The terminal was as clean and white as Marie Osmond's teeth. Little helpers with long-handled whisk brooms and dustpans tidied up after the passengers and pigeons.

"They're like the Mouseke-Maintenance people at Disneyland."

"Mouseke-Maintenance?"

"Yeah, the people who love Walt Disney and would have been Mouseketeers, but they can't sing or dance so they join Mouseke-Maintenance and dedicate themselves to keeping Disneyland clean."

"Oh."

We each got a chili dog and lemonade and waited for our gate number to be mumbled.

"Sissy, do you think we'll ever be as organized as Kac?"

"I don't know."

"Do you think it's wrong to teach a class on organization when you've got a salad bowl full of undeveloped film back home?"

"No . . . It'd be wrong if we were teaching a photography class!"

"It's not just the film; it's everything."

"Like what?"

"Like the school levy. I let them put signs all over the yard, VOTE YES TUESDAY, and then I didn't."

"I didn't, either. Every time I vote I feel guilty because I don't read the information that comes in the mail, and I end up voting for the guy with the nicest name."

"I do that, too."

"Sure, like who would you want for governor: Nick Vegas, William Robertson, Orville Potdweller, or Clapper Stalone?"

"Oh, William Robertson, of course...unless it said William (Bill) Robertson...I hate that."

"Yeah. Me, too. How do you suppose Tip O'Neill ever got in?"

"He got elected as Thomas P. O'Neill and didn't let the 'Tip' out until after he was in."

"Oh."

"I really think if I were more organized, I'd be a better American."

"Yeah, we'd study the ballot and know what was going on."

"I know we're not stupid.... We just never take the time.... Sissy, what time is it?"

We missed the 11:20 train and had to wait for the 3:15. We called San Bernardino and blamed it all on Amtrak.

"See what I mean? It's everything! We missed the train...our kids have empty baby books...we never frame anything...our towels are stupid...we took the bank's jar...we forgot to get a cab receipt...and we actually have the audacity to teach organization! I've lost my feistiness!"

"Me, too!"

Two

We've Got a Ticket to Ride

As sisters, we had always shared our frustrations and disappointments, turning to each other for encouragement and counsel. We wondered if we were being too hard on ourselves; it hadn't been that long ago that we were stashing pots and pans in the shower stall and drinking out of jelly jars.

With four hours to kill we had time to talk about it. Even in our slob days there was no doubt that we loved our families, but our messy homes didn't reflect our caring. With the best intentions we always failed to see anything through to the finish. We were late to meetings, late for church, and late in paying bills. We were overextended, overweight, and overdrawn. Without meaning to, we wasted time, energy, food, gas, and money. There were continuous apologies, excuses, cover-ups, substitutions, and tears.

Finally, on June 16, 1977, we were both so personally defeated by all the broken promises to ourselves and others that we decided to change. On that day we finally asked, "What is wrong with us?" Until then we had been too busy stamping out fires to stop and figure out how they had started.

We couldn't say we hadn't had a good example, because Mom was immaculate. Jokingly we put the blame on Dad; maybe we had inherited his messy ways. We recalled the confusion in his tackle box. Inside, there was always a dried-up jar of salmon eggs (he'd forget to replace the lid); hooks with dehydrated worm corpses, rusty flies, and sinkers were everywhere. A couple of broken reels he meant to fix were tangled in a nest of their own fishing line. If Dad's tackle box had been a house, it would have looked and smelled just like our homes.

He had a three-horsepower motor that he loved but left out each winter. Every spring when it wouldn't start, he'd have to overhaul it. But since he wasn't one to read instructions, and he always did things at the last moment, the repair work was unpredictable. If we weren't hydroplaning in the boat, we were rowing, and Dad was always promising to get it home and fix it properly. It stalled on us frequently, so we did a lot of drift fishing. What he lacked in organization, Dad made up for in patience. We caught tons of fish every time, except for the time he forgot to pack the fishing poles.

We liked the idea of blaming our problem of disorganization on a genetic defect; it eased our guilt. After all, we didn't hold it against ourselves that we had both inherited Dad's blue eyes, so why should we feel guilty that he had transmitted his messy genes to us? Our simple, unscientific theory that being disorganized was genetic proved to be true. Furthermore, we found that the disorganized gene is dominant at a ratio of ten to one: ten slobs to one immacuholic.

Instead of putting ourselves down for being disorganized, we began to look on the positive side. If it weren't for people like us, we decided, the world wouldn't be enjoying many of the things we have today. If it hadn't been for the pioneer woman who got sidetracked thinking about her old boyfriend while she was whipping cream, we wouldn't have butter. Wine was discovered when some disorganized guy in France took a jug of grape juice down in the cellar and forgot about it for a couple of years. Cheese and yogurt—two more examples. And where would penicillin be if Fleming's bread hadn't gotten away from him? Who knows, today's cottage cheese may be tomorrow's Nobel Prize. Inventions and discoveries, the results of disorganization, have shaped the course of history. Perhaps a sidetracked Columbus missed his mark and yo-ho-hoed himself right into the New World.

Our studies over the last several years have only been done in the laboratory of life. We hope that someday the scientific community will back our findings and lend credibility to our theory. Then perhaps there will be government subsidies and special programs for the disorganized, such as:

- schools with no starting time or attendance records
- preferred parking slots (without meters)
- waiver of all public utility disconnection fees
- automatic income tax extensions (without penalties)
- postage-paid envelopes provided with all account statements
- unlimited cash machine privileges (regardless of balance)
- free maternity care
- coupons that don't expire
- tax deductions for unfinished projects and home remodeling
- automatic driver's license renewals with no picture and no reference to weight gain
- government cleaning crews to mop up after New Year's Eve parties, family celebrations, and weekends.

There is a lucrative market for anyone who can cater to the disorganized. Car manufacturers were the first to recognize it. Newer model cars have bells that go off or a recorded message to remind the driver to turn off his lights, get his keys out of the ignition, fasten his seat belt, and fill up his gas tank. Cruise control keeps the sidetracked motorist within the speed limit.

If contractors were as aware of this as the car manufacturers are, our houses would have buzzers that would go off when we were low on bread and milk, and whistles would blow if the kids forgot to brush their teeth, flush the toilet, or make their beds. Lights would flash to remind us to turn off the stove, feed the dog, and empty the garbage.

We believe that private enterprise should start helping the disorganized public and stop taking advantage of us with 800 numbers, tape and record clubs, and health and fitness spas.

"Have you ever joined a spa?"

"Yeah. I got in on a special lifetime membership. I liked the sound of 'Get a bathing suit body by June.'"

"Did you get one?"

"No, I went for three weeks and found out I was pregnant and then we moved."

"Have you ever gotten sucked into one of those 'order before midnight' deals?"

"Yeah. When the guy said 'not available in store,' it was eleven forty-five...I found my card and made the call."

"What'd you get, the Roger Whitaker album or the Ginsu knives?"

"Neither. I signed up for the Tony Randall Recipe Cards."

"Yikes."

"Yeah."

"I lost my ordering privileges when I got us into that record club."

"Why?"

"We got four cassettes of our choice and then they started sending us their choice...I only had five days to wrap them up again and send them back, so they just kept coming."

"Couldn't you cut them off?"

"I could have if I'd had a stamp.... We've got tapes like the Vienna Choir Boys singing South of the Border hits from the fifties, and a whole bunch of Old Favorites that aren't."

"You can't blame them for that. They told you in the fine print about the five days."

"You should talk.... What about your mock-tooled, fake leather 'Life of the Pioneer' series?"

"Hey, those books are actual accounts of real pioneers."

"So what? You've got the *Pioneer Gamblers*, the *Pioneer*

Escapades, the *Perverts,* and *Paupers and Gold Diggers.* You've got the *Pioneer Everything,* and by the time you finish paying for them, your great-grandkids will be reading about you in the *Great Book of Pioneer Rip-offs.*"

"Maybe I oughta go to some kind of Sucker Control Center!"

"Is there one?"

"Why not? They have a center for everything else. They probably put you in a little room with a TV set and a phone, and every time there's an eight hundred offer, if you start to make the call, they shock your dialing finger."

"I'll go with you."

We smelled popcorn in the station and bought some. Small-talking away the bags, we were still an hour away from train time.

"What did you think it would be like when you got married?"

"Nothing like what it was. . . . When I said 'I do,' I didn't realize how much had to be done."

"Me, either. . . . When I said 'I do,' I was just thinking of the honeymoon stuff."

We both studied home economics in high school and majored in it in college, but we don't think our educational system prepares anyone for the real world of home management. (If it did, nobody would ever get married.)

Equipped only with the knowledge of how to make Rice Krispies squares, white sauce, and biscuit mix from scratch, we had skipped down the aisle into the wonderful world of in-laws, overdrafts, cockroaches, cellulite, income tax returns, teething, hemorrhoids, slugs, stopped-up toilets, jumper cables, map fights, cradle cap, dental floss, ring-around-the-collar, baby blues, Peeping Toms, chimney fires, cramps, obscene phone calls, hamsters, toddlers, teenagers, door-to-door salesmen, and, for one of us, divorce.

Ignorance is not bliss! Ignorance is like sneaking that first bite of Hershey's unsweetened chocolate while your mom's out hanging the clothes. Without all the other ingredients, all you've got is a mouthful of bitterness. In marriage some of those other ingredients are understanding, humor, compromise, faith, love, and maturity. If you are just married for the look of it, then you'll end up with a bitter taste in your mouth.

We blame Hollywood for perpetuating the homemaker myth. We got most of the fuel for our fantasies from the weekly adventures of June Cleaver, Margaret Anderson, Harriet Nelson, and Donna Reed.

At the movies there was Doris Day. She was such a cute homemaker. We helped make her a number-one box-office attraction. In every movie she had a rich and gorgeous husband, two adorable children, a fabulous wardrobe, a maid, and a two-story house with a swimming pool. She made it look so glamorous. She got to do terrible things, and her husband thought she was darling. She could scream and stomp, rant and cry, and even lock him out, and he'd still take her to lunch the next day.

In real life when the wife cries, it makes the husband crazy, and to lock him out is insane. Think of the story of the three little pigs: it was probably written by some homemaker who had a fight with her husband, locked him out, and found he could come down the chimney like a wild animal if he had to. In fact, that's probably how Santa Claus got his start.

When the 3:15 train chugged away from the waving left-behinds, we were on it. We picked out our seats and settled in for the trip, pleased to hear that the dining car was open and only five cars up. Over club sandwiches and ginger ale we continued our conversation.

We both felt frustrated. . . . It could have been the four hours under the clock or too much salt on the popcorn; maybe we just needed a nap . . . but probably it was jealousy over Kac Young and Doris Day because they seemed to have everything.

"Sissy, I thought that after we figured out how to keep our houses clean, we'd never have to think again."

"Me, too . . . but the house was just the fin of the shark."

"I hate to have to say this, but it looks like we need to get organized."

"I know. I'm going to start making a list of what I want to accomplish right now. . . . Hand me a napkin."

"I will, too. . . . The other day I read about a guy who had a hundred things he wanted to do in his life, and just by making the list, he was able to do about thirty things the first year."

"Wow!"

We wrote down our goals all the way to San Bernardino. We wanted to be more educated, more thoughtful, better mothers, interested in public affairs, and more spiritual, genteel, sophisticated, and on and on and on.

The diner strained to a stop in San Bernardino. It occurred to us that the rest of the train was stopping with it, and our luggage was five cars back. We loped through the train, grabbed our stuff, and cleared the tracks.

"Sissy, did you get the goals?"

"Me get the goals? I thought you got 'em!"

"That's just great! We spend an hour and a half planning our future and then you leave our lives on the table."

"Hey, nobody made me a goal keeper!"

"Well, some guy on his way to Barstow's gonna pick up our goals and have a great future."

Gail Dietrich was there to meet us at the station. She was a lovely woman with beautiful red hair. It didn't take us long to see that, like Kac, she also had her life in order.

This time we rode in a spotless Seville, and guest-roomed in an exquisite Spanish hacienda, where we were surrounded by fine art, lovely antiques, delicate china, happy children, and two delightful dogs that were dressed alike.

Gail and her husband, Jack, had wonderful plans. They enjoyed summers at their beach cottage in Mexico and winters at their ski cabin at Big Bear. They asked us when we were taking our vacation and told us that if we would let them know ahead of time, we could use one of their places. We thanked them and, with the intention of following through, wrote their unlisted phone number and address on the back of one of our business cards.

The next day we spoke to seven hundred women, members of the Children's Home Society. As homemakers dedicated to helping underprivileged children, they needed a lot of help to stay organized. As we told our slob stories and shared our 3x5 cardfile system, there was laughter and a warm exchange of understanding. It was good to hear ourselves talk about those slovenly days because they were so far behind us. It made us realize how critical we'd been of our recent muff-ups. If back in those dark times, after devouring our number-three combinations, we'd cracked open a Chinese fortune cookie and read the following prediction:

> "Very soon your homes will be spotless. Traveling across the country, you will speak to thousands of women on the subject of organization. You will write and *finish* two organizational manuals and sell them to one of the top publishing companies in New York, and, collectively, you will lose 104 pounds"

we would have thought we'd gotten someone else's cookie.

That evening in the Dietrichs' guest room we talked to each other about why we had wanted to gain control of our homes in the first place. All of our futile attempts, before 1977, had been motivated by the wrong reason—our desire to impress someone. We both agreed that the only reason to get organized was so that we would have more "free" time to do the things we love to do. Maybe now we were feeling frustrated because that free time had no direction, leaving us like a couple of kids loose at Disney World. If we'd managed to organize our houses, maybe we could use 3x5s again to gain control of things less tangible than laundry and dishes. We wanted to be in charge of our past, our present, and our future, not so that we would impress people, but so that our lives would be more fulfilled. We stayed up most of the night talking about the possibilities.

Three

Early to Bed, Early to Rise...Pays Off

In spite of our sleepless night, Gail Dietrich got us to the San Bernardino Airport in plenty of time for the plane. We felt as if we'd made a new friend when we said good-bye to her. Roaming around the terminal like two old bears who'd skipped hibernation, we realized that Peggy had misplaced her ticket. Checking in for seat assignments at the counter, we learned from the United Airline clerk that tickets are the same as cash, and when you lose one, they don't just give you another. On the plane Peggy was grateful her credit card had worked.

"I feel like such a buffoon. I can't believe I lost my ticket; I only went from Gail to the gate."

"No, you didn't! We stopped in that little airport gift shop and bought the kids 'I Love San Bernardino' T-shirts. How could you forget something we did five minutes ago?"

"So I forgot! Why don't you have me put in a home?"

"My, aren't we recalcitrant this morning?"

"Hey, just because you're dating an attorney, don't flaunt

his vocabulary in my face! And by the way, big brain, where's our bag of shirts? You had them, as I recall."

Our incompetency had reached Lucy Ricardo and Ethel Mertz proportions. The T-shirts were gone, the ticket was gone, and our compatibility was smothered by exhaustion.

As our plane took off we thought we'd spend the flight time working out a comprehensive system to get control of our heads. With paper and pens and tray tables down, we were ready to be creative. We waited for some inspiration. Nothing happened. We waited for the other one to talk. It was quiet. We tried to brainstorm. It was impossible. We even turned to the flight magazine in the seat pocket in front of us for clever ideas. We were blank and cranky. Fatigue had taken charge of our faculties. It had reduced us to a couple of whining witches. We were so tired we couldn't even finish our flight food.

We realized we'd have to catch up on our sleep first and figure out our system later, after our brain cells had recharged and our bodies had rested. We reclined our seats and fell asleep to the hum of the plane's engines.

Passing Crater Lake, the captain startled us out of our doze with a loud history of the lake's formation and informed us that we would land in Portland in forty-five minutes. We couldn't go back to sleep.

"Sissy, I'm sorry I got so testy with you awhile ago."

"Me, too. Everything was bugging me. When this guy in front of me reclined his seat and your air blower blasted his hair into my salisbury steak, it put me over the edge."

"That stewardess set me off, shushing us during her safety demo."

"I think we got kind of loud, bickering over the shirts."

The more we talked we came to the conclusion that if fatigue had caused *us* to be short with each other, it might be the root of a lot of the world's problems today. Take war, for instance. The thought of a red phone in the hands of a sleepless world leader is horrifying. Instead of pacifists carrying BAN THE BOMB placards, they need to get to the bottom line and picket the U.N. with GET MORE SLEEP signs.

The need for a good night's rest goes as far back as history is recorded. Take Napoleon, for example; historians say his basic problems throughout life stemmed from his size, but we don't think that's true. If someone were to find some of Napoleon's old grade school report cards, we're sure it would be our fatigue theory that would be borne out instead.

Eiffel Elementary School   June 6, 1777
7312 Rue des Hors d'Oeuvres
Paris, France 10046

Dear Mr. and Mrs. Bonaparte:
I think you are probably aware of some of the problems we are having with Napoleon at school. I believe they began early in the year when some of the other boys teased him about his size. I have spoken to the other children and their parents about the importance of being kind to those who are different. However, I don't believe that the teasing is the main reason for your son's troubles. I think Napoleon needs more sleep.

During class I often see his head on his desk, and although he stays on task and has no problem understanding the work, he is often listless and irritable. Perhaps you, as his parents, could see to it that your son gets to bed at a reasonable hour so that he will be able to cope better in class and on the playground.

Sincerely,

Morrie Chevalier

Morrie Chevalier
(Third Grade Teacher)

P.S. Napoleon is a good leader and when he gets the other boys on his side he is able to make them do whatever he wants. (Good or bad.) I truly believe that more sleep will help him to blossom into a fine citizen. Perhaps this summer you can establish a routine bedtime for him. Have a good vacation, Leon!

Think of how the course of history might have been altered if the Bonapartes had heeded Mr. Chevalier's advice.

We started talking about our own sleep habits and discussed the fact that, like Napoleon, we didn't have a regular bedtime and we weren't getting enough sleep, either. For the last five years we'd been following the advice we gave in our first book: get up a half hour before everyone else in the family and take a shower, get dressed, combed, and put makeup on.

"Sissy, you know our thing about getting up early?"

"Yeah."

"I hate it! It's just not fair that I have to get up to a cold house and try to wake up in a hot shower while the rest of the family is snuggled under their covers."

"Yeah, but you know it's right."

"Humph."

"Come on, you *know* it's right! The early bird gets the worm."

"Yeah, but what about the early worm and what he gets?"

"There aren't any early worms, only night crawlers that stay out too late."

"Well, I don't care about the early bird, I'm a night owl and I must need at least thirteen hours of sleep a day."

"You sound the way you did back in our slob days when you told me you had to do eight loads of wash every day, remember?"

"Yeah."

"You used to think you had that many loads 'cause you were so far behind, but once you got caught up, you really only had one load a day, and you probably need only eight hours of sleep a day, but you've never been caught up because you don't have a regular bedtime."

"Whoaah."

Before we could make a realistic appraisal of how much sleep we needed, we would have to catch up on the sleep that we had lost at Gail's house. When we landed in Portland, we returned the money jar to the bank and went home to get some sleep.

Beginning a new week, we decided to change our sleeping habits to meet our bodies' daily rest requirements. Some things were obvious. We couldn't get more rest by sleeping later, since in the morning we had to be up in time to get ourselves fixed up, make breakfast, and get our kids off to school, and there was a husband to think about. There is no flexibility in school bus schedules or time clocks.

With our morning responsibilities in mind and our realization that we needed more sleep, we knew we'd have to adjust our bedtime. We had been in the habit of falling asleep in front of the television and waking up, chilled and stiff, to loud TV snow. After crawling to bed with unbrushed teeth and sore necks, we could scarcely be at our best in the morning. Organized people have time to brush their teeth and hair, rinse out dainty things, moisturize, write in their diaries, say their prayers, and set their alarm clocks because they know the difference between getting ready for bed and bedtime. They know that the secret to getting enough rest lies in getting ready for bed at the right time.

We knew what time we should go to sleep, based on our past experiences with the television set. Both of us were always dead when *Dynasty* was over. Since it was over at 10:00 and we wanted to be like organized ladies and floss, rinse, pray, and moisturize, we'd have to start getting ready for bed at 9:30. If you know what your sleep requirements are, you won't have to figure it out as we did. But if you're not sure how much sleep you need, think back to the TV shows you conk out after. Perhaps you're a genius like Edison and you suspect you only need a few hours a night. Still, you owe it to yourself to know for sure. Think back to what time of night you fall asleep over your inventions. If you want to be a more balanced and happy person, shut off the TV or close down the lab a half hour early and get ready for bed.

In the weeks that followed we discovered that, with the right amount of sleep, we didn't feel like martyrs in the morning. In fact, after a while, we actually preferred the morning to the evening hours. It was such prime time that we selfishly chose to claim more of it for ourselves. An hour and a half proved to be ideal for us.

In the early morning there are no interruptions; no favorite TV shows, no phone calls, no requests, no responsibilities and, most important, no spontaneous distractions from our own thinking. (The urge to visit a friend, run to the mall, or call and order something over the phone can't be satisfied at 6:00 A.M.) In those early hours we are forced to be alone with ourselves. It is the only time we can put the world on hold and make contact with our souls. Unlike the rest of the day, with its jobs, car pools, Little League, ballet lessons, spelling drills, doctors' appointments, field trips, report cards, yard work, laundry, and meals, the early morning gives us time to focus on our real purpose in life.

Isn't it funny how the world has a false sense of values? It strives for numbers, not the appreciation of one. It applauds speed, not the art of being still. It perpetuates noise, not silence. It seduces us into fads and lures us away from our own individuality.

Psychologists say that before you set out on any path, you need to know who you are. Taking time first thing in the morning to make contact with the real you, and your purpose, will keep you from wasting a lot of time on someone else's trail. A wise person knows how vital it is to take time each day to be alone.

Even though we'd heard a million times about the early bird and what he gets, we had to prove to ourselves that success begins at dawn. There is power in daybreak. Nature has rested and is fresh and full of energy. In some subtle way, those who have learned the importance of going to bed early and getting up early share in that energy and freshness. Morning turned out to be a gift of time for both of us. Now it is our most valued part of the day.

There is also something very special about witnessing a sunrise. It is such a private experience because it is shared by the elite few who are awake. (A sunset is beautiful, too, but it has to be shared by a million other yahoos stuck in westbound traffic jams.)

Maybe you've been an early riser all your life and you've always enjoyed the benefits of the morning. If you have, then you know why we're making such a big deal out of this.

However, if you've never tried getting up early because you think of yourself as a late-nighter, we think that you'll be shocked at what will happen in your life if you take Ben

Franklin's advice: "Early to bed, early to rise, gives a guy a better shot at success."

With the right amount of sleep and one and a half hours to ourselves in the morning, we had the energy of two young beavers thrown into a pond that needed a dam, and we were ready to do some serious building with a plan for success.

PART TWO

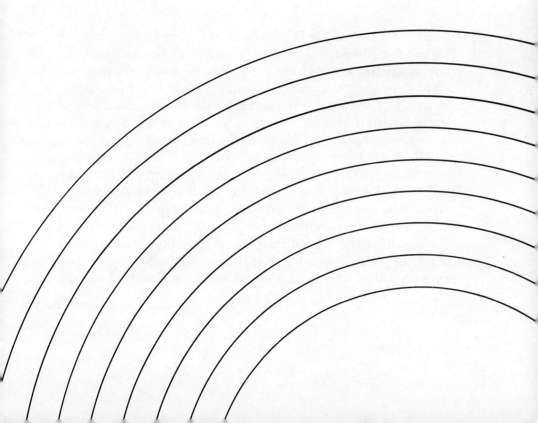

We are at a milestone in our lives. We have been using the Happiness File for more than a year and the changes we have made are remarkable to us. We are eager to share our discoveries with you. They are so simple, yet so profound. We unfold the system for you in Part II, but we want you to proceed with it at your own rate, keeping in mind you have from now until Forest Lawn to become what you want to be. We have organized *The Happiness File* into weeks and months so that it is a clear, step-by-step program. Don't be discouraged if you have less time to devote to the assignments than you would like because there are no real deadlines. To get upset because you can't keep up with our timetable would defeat the whole purpose of this book. Go at your own pace; take only what you think will work for you, and remember that what you are looking for is the *trend* toward improvement.

One

The First Week–
Starting the System

The first week you will be taking Morrie Chevalier's advice
and establishing a regular bedtime (allowing yourself a half
hour to get ready). We also want you to gather the supplies
for the system, set up the cardfile, start collecting inspiration and humor, and make out Daily Routine Cards, which
will be discussed in detail on pages 46–48.

SUPPLIES

We remember how happy we were to get our list of school
supplies at the beginning of a new school year. Gathering
all the things we'd need was so exciting. It took a couple of
special trips to town to get just the right stuff, and we
always got to pick out a special, new lunch pail. Having all
the correct supplies made us feel like we were getting off to
a good start. We think it's really important to get all the
supplies you'll need for the Happiness File before you
begin.

This is a list of what we used to get started. Each item will be fully explained, in order, at the end of the list.

jumbo 3x5 cardfile box
3x5 cards: white, blue, yellow, pink
3x5 scratch pad
dividers:
    January–December
    ABCs
    25 blanks
pen
pencil
pencil sharpener
calendars:
    wall calendar
    small calendar (Year-at-a-Glance)
    pocket-size weekly planner
timer
clock
watch
dictionary
early childhood photos (3x5 size) of:
    yourself
    spouse
    each child
scrapbook
looseleaf notebook
notebook paper
five notebook index tabs

Jumbo 3x5 Cardfile Box

A regular recipe box isn't big enough because your entire life will be on cards. Variety and office supply stores sell jumbo plastic cardfiles in blue, yellow, orange, and green. They are double the size of an average recipe box and will hold the cards necessary for the Happiness File.

Pam's cardfile was a gift. It is an antique oak box, hand-stained to match her kitchen cabinets. It is 3" x 5" wide and four recipe boxes long. It holds her Happiness File Cards, menu cards for a year's worth of wonderful meals, recipes, and her Home Executive Cards, which help to keep her house and yard in perfect order.

Heavy pressboard cardfiles (about the size of a shoebox) are also available, but they're not very pretty. If you do tole painting or enjoy decoupage, you might want to consider buying an unfinished box and decorating it yourself. Spend some time shopping for a container that makes you feel happy just looking at it.

3x5 Cards

For us, 3x5 cards are magic. In our first book our slogan was "We change lives with 3x5s." They work because they're the perfect size: small enough to fit in pockets and purses, but large enough to get your message across without using too many words. They are available in even the smallest grocery store, and as an added bonus they come in colors! We have always used the yellow cards for a daily frequency, blue for weekly, and white ones for monthly or longer. We also use the white cards for addresses, menus, and recipes. Pink cards are used for personal things and inspiration, and we have even gone so far as to have the stationer cut brilliant-colored construction paper into 3x5 cards so we could expand specific topics as we grew with the system. It doesn't matter what colors you use, just so you are consistent. We can tell you that using color in the cardfile will add something to the system that white leaves out.

After you've been initiated into the world of file cards, you'll have to control your appetite for all the other things that come in 3x5 size. Office supply stores are filled with tempting accessories.

3x5 Scratch Pad

We use scratch pads for all the little notes that are temporary and passing; memos that don't require the formality of the thicker 3x5 card.

The beauty of the scratch pad is that it always goes on sale, and when it does you can get at least ten for a dollar! We each keep one in our purse, one by each phone, one by our bed, and one in our desk. It's even nice to keep a pad in the glove compartment of the car, one in the bathroom, and everywhere else you spend any length of time.

Dividers:

January–December These twelve dividers (one for each month) can be purchased at stationery and office supply stores.

ABCs There are twenty-six of these printed dividers (one for every letter of the alphabet). They also can be purchased at stationery and office supply stores.

Blank Dividers Blank dividers are just what they imply. Instead of having information already written on the little part that sticks up, they are blank so that you can write whatever you want.

Label the blank dividers as follows, seven of them with the days of the week:

> Monday
> Tuesday
> Wednesday
> etc.

The days of the week dividers give the cardfile consistency. Each one will have its own cards, which will direct the activity for the day.

Label one blank divider for each member of the family:

> Me
> John
> John Jr.
> etc.

Me This is the place to keep all personal information. In ours we have a progress card with weekly weight and measurements, an exercise log, compliments we want to remember, and cards with ideas for free time, such as:

"10 minutes or less":
Freshen makeup and perfume
Call a friend (even long distance)
Read <u>one</u> magazine article
Fix myself a cup of tea
Play in my cardfile
Write a thank-you note
Read to my kids
Pray or meditate
Pick some flowers
Give myself a BSE (breast self-examination. For a free
     instruction pamphlet, write: American Cancer So-
     ciety, 2120 1st Ave. N., Seattle, WA 98109. Ask for
     the BSE booklet.)

"An hour or two":
Read a book
Visit a friend
Work on a hobby or special project
Watch a favorite TV show
Take a walk
Take a bubble bath
Take a nap
Play the piano
Sunbathe
Play with the kids on their level
Work on my scrapbook

"Half a day":
Go on a picnic
Take a class
Go shopping
Go out to lunch
Go to the zoo
Have an evening out
Go to a matinee
Play tennis
Go swimming
Work on home improvements

Spouse The divider for your spouse contains information about your mate: a gift idea card; a statistics card for union number, insurance group and number, social security number, etc.; receipts; clothing tags; vacation and work schedule cards; serial numbers from his camera, guns, etc.; medical and dental examination records; and any other information you want to keep track of.

Each Child Each of your children will also have his or her own space set off by a divider where you will want to keep the following cards: gift ideas; medical and dental examination records; receipts and clothing tags; sports schedules; lessons with teachers' names and phone numbers; class schedule with teachers' names and phone numbers; names of each of their friends with addresses and phone numbers and their parents' names; I.O.U.'s; allowance record; immunization records; bicycle serial numbers; likes-to-do information; requests; etc.

We will be working with all of the family dividers in depth in Part IV.

Label four additional dividers as follows:

Success
Journal
Inspiration
Humor

Success Nothing breeds success like success, and there is nothing more encouraging than a collection of past achievements. The success divider is the holding tank for all the things (no matter how small) that turned out well because of your efforts. It's evidence of your personal accomplishments: projects you've finished (even if you didn't want to), problems you've solved, loose ends you've tied up, habits you've broken, actions you've taken, and improvements you've made. You never are given trophies for the little accomplishments in life, like forgiving somebody or apologizing when it's hard. There are no awards for potty training a child, waiting up for a teenager, or understanding a husband's busy schedule. By collecting our successes in the

Happiness File we get to commend ourselves privately for achievements that have special meaning to us. The success divider has helped us remember that we are making progress in our personal growth, especially at times when the evidence hoped for isn't in yet.

Journal   This divider keeps our Daily Journal Cards (explained in full detail on pages 49 to 51) in order.

Inspiration   This divider is the place where you will keep all of the things that elevate your thoughts and feelings: words of wisdom, scriptures, and quotes that touch you personally. Don't let anything inspirational get away from you. When you sit down to read a book, or listen to a sermon, have a pen and 3x5 cards with you so that you'll be able to record the things that uplift you. Always date the cards and acknowledge the origin of each inspiration, but don't limit yourself to ordinary sources. Profound truths can come to you from a child, the butcher, a neighbor, nature, or your own spiritual wellspring. What's more, the act of writing them down will enhance their authority over you.

We have found that our collection of inspirational writings never loses its power. It stirs our emotions each time we read from it, but had each piece not been written down, it would be lost in the black hole of insights gone by. Whatever moves you in the first place will move you again, perhaps a little differently each time, but the impact will always be there.

Once a week we pull good thoughts from our inspiration section and disperse a bunch throughout the Monday through Sunday dividers. We also scatter the little mood-boosters around the house, posting them in conspicuous places. There's something nice about blow-drying your hair in the company of Shakespeare, frying bacon to the words of Jesus, or folding clothes with Gandhi. The repetition of reading a card every day for a week will also have an influence on your subconscious mind. Like the effects of subliminal advertising, you will find that truths you have read over and over again will begin to move you toward positive action. We hope you will enjoy our selections of inspiration at the beginning of each chapter in Part IV, and that you will want to copy them down and put them in your own cardfile.

Humor We think that a good sense of humor is probably as important as inspiration. We make each other laugh every day and when something really strikes us as funny, we write it down and file it in our Humor section. We can be in a terrible mood and have it instantly evaporate when one of us reads something funny from her file.

A sense of humor gives you the power to perceive the comedy and absurdity of human life. It's impossible to be bitter, angry, hurt, or depressed when you're laughing. Laughter in your life is as essential as whole grains in your diet.

We have a lot of fun in our organization workshops because we use laughter as a teaching tool. We think that life was meant for enjoyment, but too often people are so serious in their purpose that they forget how good it feels to laugh.

Maybe you haven't been laughing as much as you would like to. When people say, "Use it or lose it," we think they're talking about muscles (and even those can be built back up). A sense of humor is an intangible endowment, and untouchable gifts cannot be lost. Like muscles, your sense of humor might be out of shape, but with regular use it will develop into the life-supporting system it was meant to be.

Everyone was born with a sense of humor. (Babies don't have to be taught how to laugh—they just do it naturally when something delights them.) If you haven't been laughing enough, get really serious about using the humor divider. Use it to hold the cute things your kids say, funny jokes you laughed at, hysterical situations you've been in or heard about, and anything else that tickles you. If something was funny to you once, recalling it will make you laugh all over again. By giving it a place in your cardfile, you will create a hotline to your sense of humor.

Label the remaining dividers with your own personal special interests, such as:

Hospitality
Home Improvement
Vacation Cabin
Books
Politics
Travel
etc.

We will explain more about each divider and how to expand its uses in Part IV.

Pen

The pen was mightier than the sword when used as a writing instrument in the hands of Shakespeare. For the disorganized, the pen is also mightier than the sword when it's sticking up between the cushions of the sofa.

In the olden days pens had holders full of ink. Users were forced to stay close to the pen holder because the instrument had to be dunked after every few words. Pens didn't get lost, stolen by the kids, or chewed up by the dog. Today we have the convenience of taking our self-contained ball points everywhere, but the frustration of leaving them someplace goes with it. Consequently, most of us are without a pen when we need one.

You need to have a pen with your Happiness File so that you can get things in writing before you forget them. An average pen will fit in the cardfile, and we've found it handy to have one on a retractable coil that can be permanently attached to the inside of the box.

Pencil

A pencil is great if it is *sharp* and has an eraser, so you might want to rig up a way to keep it where it belongs. You will see, when we explain the system, how valuable having a sharpened pencil with an eraser can be in formulating a plan for a happy, well-balanced future. A pencil is more forgiving than a pen because it allows adjustments in what has been written, without messing up the paper.

Pencil Sharpener

Thousands of innocent paring knives across the country have been ruined by the ruthless whittling of broken pencil points. . . . Invest in a *real* sharpener and keep it in one place.

Calendars:

Wall Calendar   In our slob days, the only reason we hung a calendar was because we liked pretty pictures. We bought them only to help out the little Girl Scout next door or because we were attracted by the half-price close-out signs in June.

Now we post a wall calendar on our kitchen bulletin boards to log in everyone's comings and goings and keep track of special events. We buy them as soon as they come out in the fall, when there is the greatest variety.

Small Calendar (Year-at-a-Glance)   In our disorganized past we had no plan for the next twelve hours, let alone an entire twelve months. A year at a glance was certainly beyond our vision. Now we depend on our calendars as we do our watches, and we wonder how we could have done without them for so many years.

You will find a year at a glance in the back of your checkbook register. Being able to see the entire year laid out on one page will help you plan farther into the future than just thirty-one days.

Tape the small calendar in the lid of the file box for easy reference. It will save you from running to the kitchen wall when you need a specific date.

Pocket-size Weekly Planner   In those bygone slob years when calendars were objets d'art in our homes, the thought of a pocket-size weekly planner never occurred to us. We didn't even know they existed. Now we depend on them to lead us through the year. (In fact, Pam accidentally picked up a weekly planner identical to hers at the bank and almost started living the life of the loan officer.) We use our weekly planners to schedule activities, appointments, commitments, vacations, deadlines, and any other specific dates that deserve remembering. We keep them in our purses so that when we're out, we have access to our schedule.

Timer

A timer is a wonderful invention. Whether it whistles, dings, buzzes, or beeps when your time is up, it is one of the best tools to keep a genetically disorganized person aware of the time. It can save you from getting too involved with a project, staying on the phone too long, or leaving the neutralizer on your curls beyond the limit. If you're going to be buying a timer, be sure you like the sound it makes when it goes off or you could be driven into rebellion.

Clock

We learned how to tell time in the first grade, and yet we both put aside that knowledge because we didn't have working clocks in our houses. We woke up in the morning to the cat plunking the screen on the bedroom window. We relied for time cues on the regular events of the day, like the honk of an arriving school bus or the beginning of *Ryan's Hope, All My Children,* and *General Hospital.* Hunger pangs told us when it was noon, and the sound of the garage door being raised signaled that it was 5:17—hubby was home and ready to eat. We went to bed when we were tired and woke up again the next morning to the cat's plunk.

If you don't have a good working clock, go clock shopping and see what's available. Today you can find clocks that wake you up and fix the coffee. There are little inexpensive clocks with adhesive backing that can be stuck in all the places you tend to drift. There is really no reason not to be aware of time. (Remember when you buy an alarm clock to be sure to listen to the alarm and think about how it will sound to you in the morning.)

Watch

A watch is a portable clock. For years we didn't wear watches because we'd forget to wind them. Now with battery-operated time pieces we can go a whole year with the correct time on our wrists. We figure that we save about twenty-five minutes a day by owning watches. We don't have to stop people on the street to get the time or wait for it to alternate with the temperature and the Dow-Jones average on the revolving digital outside the bank. We no longer have to run around in stores looking for a clock on the wall, and when we are freeway-bound we don't have to scan the car radio for a disc jockey to tell us how late we are. Watches have definitely made us happier.

Dictionary

Webster defines the dictionary as "my greatest work." (He must have known that his diet and exercise book, volumes of poetry, and his series of "Noah Webster's Fairy Tales" weren't going to survive the centuries.)

We think the dictionary is one of the most illuminating works of English literature. We use it to clarify our thinking in terms of our dreams, goals, strengths, and weaknesses. We each have the unabridged version (which we rarely use because it's too big to carry from the bookcase). The pocket dictionary is too small to go into much depth, but it's just right to carry in your purse or briefcase. Since it doesn't have much room to mess around with deep meanings, it gets right to the point on defining words.

Webster's Collegiate Dictionary is a wonderful book to have in your home. It's not too big and it's not too small; in fact, it's probably a book that Goldilocks would have been caught referring to if the three bears had been literate.

Early Childhood Photos

The baby pictures (that we asked you to find) of yourself, your spouse, and each child should be taped to their respective dividers. Seeing the baby in yourself and in your family members will help you to understand who you are really dealing with. When you look into your own eyes, in your baby picture, you will see the permanent innocence of your own being. Looking at a picture of your husband wearing a sweet grin, a christening gown, and tiny booties can soften even the most bitter argument. When your teenager is being a jerk, a quick glance at his or her baby picture will put things into perspective. These pictures will help you more than you would ever believe. We have included some of the pictures from our Happiness Files in the family album section, at the end of the book.

Scrapbook

We are suggesting you make a scrapbook because it can be fun if you have the time to put things in it. Get an attractive one so that you can leave it out on the coffee table. Make certain it is sturdy; there is nothing more irritating than having a scrapbook fall apart before its time. We will give you ideas in Part IV for using a scrapbook to envision your private dreams.

Looseleaf Notebook

A three-hole binder looseleaf notebook is necessary for working successfully with the Happiness File. We use the 8½" x 11" size because standard notebook paper fits and can be added as needed. We picked out three-hole binders in our favorite color, blue. The right color is important because your notebook has to be attractive to you so that you'll want to use it. (We've even decorated the fronts and backs of ours with pictures that make us laugh.)

Notebook Paper

Always have a supply of it! Hide it if you have kids. Kathy Liden, co-author of *The Compleat Family Book*, says, "Put the pressure on paper, not on you."

Notebook Index Tabs

You can get the kind that you have to lick and stick on a piece of notebook paper or you can get them in a package of five, attached to sheets of heavy paper. Label the tabs as follows:

    To Be
    To Do
    To Have
    Strengths and Weaknesses (S & W)
    Clearing

Put a hunk of notebook paper in each section.

Setting Up the Cardfile

Once you get all your supplies, you will be ready to start your Happiness File.

To set it up put the Monday through Sunday dividers in front, followed by January through December, the family dividers (beginning with "me"), success, journal, inspiration, humor, the special interest dividers, and the ABC's. Keep extra 3x5 cards, leftover blank dividers, and the scratch pad in the back.

Daily Routine Cards

Take seven blank yellow 3x5 cards and write a day of the week on the top of each card (see example below for arrangement of information). Write A.M. on one side and P.M. on the other. After you have established how much

FRONT (yellow)	BACK (yellow)
Monday—A.M.	**Monday—P.M.**
6 Get up—write in journal—be alone—personal study	2 Stop working—half hour free
7 Exercise—shower—dress—hair—makeup—breakfast	3 Children home—snacks and talk Start dinner
8 Be at work	4 Swimming lessons and errands
9	5 Free time Dinner
10	6 Dishes—spelling drill Free time
11	7 Choir practice
12 Lunch	8 Free time
1 Back to work	9 Get ready for bed
	10 Lights out

sleep you need, take that figure and subtract it from twenty-four hours. For example, if you know you need eight hours of sleep, you have sixteen hours of awake time left. Divide that time in half and put half the time on one side of the card and half on the other side.

We both need eight hours of sleep, and with our family responsibilities, we know our life works better if we get up at 6:00 A.M. and go to sleep by 10:00 P.M. We wrote our Daily Routine Cards in pencil one day at a time. It was easier to fill them out as we went, since we couldn't think of a full week's worth of activities all at once.

Within the Monday through Sunday dividers we filed each Daily Routine Card in front of its appropriate divider. These cards became the map that would direct us through each day, and they evolved into a very powerful tool to keep us on the track. At the end of each day, we looked over the card to see what had worked and what needed to be adjusted.

Since everything but the time is penciled in, it is easy to change and we continue to make adjustments even now. During the work week, there isn't as much time for ourselves as there is on the weekend. In fact, if we didn't have our one and a half hours in the morning, we would have hardly any time alone. The days are busy, and especially so on the two or three that have lessons scheduled or sports involving the children and the car. Having an entire day blocked out hour by hour, we are able to trim the time we spend on maintenance (grocery shopping, housekeeping, etc.), and we are also aware of errands that can be dove-tailed or delegated. It is almost easier to organize the difficult days because we are forced to be someplace at a certain time. Those days that aren't as regimented require a self-imposed schedule that keeps our purpose in sight.

We let the Daily Routine Cards reflect our goals of being more, doing more, and having more good and happiness in our lives. Free time is a tricky thing for sidetracked people because we tend to ease up and goof off. Easing up is a positive thing, but goofing off is what gets us.

Our friend Dee Anne is on the system. Her Daily Routine Cards are very brief and divided into bigger blocks of time because she is organized naturally. She doesn't need to be as specific with each hour as we do.

Scheduling tightly is almost a game with us. How much good can be squeezed out of an hour? Hurrying to finish things that aren't that great but have to be done lets us sneak a few bonus minutes for fun.

For instance, one of us used to spend hours paying the bills. First they had to be rounded up from all over the house. Then a checkbook balance had to be pulled out of the tangle in the spotty register. Next came searching for pen, envelopes, stamps, and the pocket calculator (if the kids had played with it and left it on, there was a quick dash to the store for new batteries), and then finally the paying process. With finances in order (see Part IV, Chapter Four, "Prosperity") the bills are a snap. Everything is in one place . . . the *desk*! There is a running balance in the checkbook and a list of bills, their amounts and due dates. When the job is quickly finished and the bills are in the mailbox, there is free time for a special project. What had taken more than an hour before, has been trimmed down to twenty minutes, leaving forty minutes for fun.

With the Daily Routine Cards we are able to block out free time, but we are also aware of spare moments that we can *use* rather than waste. For instance, we use travel time to play inspirational tapes or soothe our busy brains with our favorite songs. Sometimes, while we wait in the car for the kids at their lessons, we write letters to special friends, read the latest home-remodeling magazine, or browse through a travel brochure. Being aware of what we want to accomplish, we can use even the smallest blocks of time to our advantage.

Two

The Second Week– Getting It Together

By the end of the first week you will have made out seven Daily Routine Cards, gathered all the supplies, and set up your cardfile. It will be equivalent to an empty computer, ready to receive your personal program for success and happiness. In this second week you will be starting your journal, setting up your notebook as an information center, and making three separate lists of what you want to be, what you want to do, and what you would like to have.

The Journal
A year ago we realized the value of keeping a journal while we were on tour as spokespersons for American Express. Robbie Vorhaus, a public relations advisor and journalist, traveled with us. We noticed that every day he wrote in a small black book. Early into the tour, when our curiosity was beyond containment, we asked him what he was writing. He showed us the book and said that he had kept a journal for the last six years. He used it primarily for business, as a record of good hotels, special restaurants,

expenses, and conversations with people in the media; but more importantly, it was an editorial account of his life. He said that every day was so important to him that each one deserved to be recorded. He wanted to remember in print every person, place, or thing that had significance in his life. It was incredible, he said, how his daily journal had helped him in his personal growth. He could look back through several years, see how he had felt before, and compare it to now; and he liked being able to thumb through the years to recall specific events.

He read us some of his entries and they were hysterical. He had woven his wonderful sense of humor into the business of each day. He told us that in the months to come he could read his journal and be able to recollect in detail the fun we'd had together. We felt cheated. We would leave the three weeks behind us with a general feeling of joy but without the benefit of detail and continuity.

We were fascinated that, during the three weeks we were together, he never missed a day writing in his book. Robbie said that his journal was an act of discipline and sometimes he had to force himself to sit down and write in it, but the rewards had been unbelievable.

Robbie was naturally organized and was prepared for anything. He always remembered to get receipts; we were never late; and in his briefcase he carried maps, a pocket dictionary, a calculator, a flight schedule book, aspirin, breath mints, gum, sunglasses, cleaner, a camera, film, flash bulbs, bags of airline nuts, and a collapsible umbrella. Though all of that stuff was valuable to him, he told us that the journal was one of his most treasured possessions. By the end of our tour he had us convinced that we wanted one, too.

In the past we had had several diaries and they all ended up the same way. We would get them for Christmas and only write in them until around January 9. We both knew the guilt of an empty diary—guilt that was locked up eternally because we had lost the keys.

Robbie's black book reminded us too much of diaries gone by. We knew we couldn't be held to the dated pages of a leather-bound book. We wanted the freedom to miss a day or two or even a week without feeling as if we had failed.

At first we tried to keep our journal in our notebook, but the size of the paper was intimidating (we felt we should fill up the whole page or it would look as if it had been a skimpy day). Three-by-five cards proved to be just the right size. They were large enough for us to write down how we felt but too small for us to ramble, and we liked keeping them in our cardfile box.

Now with time to ourselves in the morning, we date a white card for the day before and fill it with our recollections of yesterday's happenings. Our memories and feelings are still vivid, but having slept on the events, we are able to be more objective. At the end of the card we rate the day on a scale of one to ten. A score of one we compare with being strapped to the flying blades of a Cuisinart for twenty-four hours. A five-point day is comparable to being the drapes at a Ramada Inn, and a ten is like having Johny Olsen tell you to "come on down" for *"The Price is Right."* (You can see examples of Journal Cards on page 53.) After seven days we average our scores and record that figure on a white Happiness Ratings Card (see example on page 54).

We keep the Happiness Ratings Card in front of the divider labeled "Journal," along with the Daily Journal Cards. If you are writing every day, in a few months you will want to bind the cards with a rubber band and put them away in a small shoe box so that your cardfile won't get too crowded. Annually, we put the Happiness Ratings Card in the shoe box with a year's worth of Journal Cards, and bind them with a ribbon.

Notebook Assignment

Set the timer for forty-five minutes and start three separate lists in your notebook of everything you want to be (virtues), what you would like to do, and what you would like to have. Leave space between each item so that you can give three reasons why you want what you think you want. Give each thing an A, B, or C priority. An "A" will mean that you want to work on it first, "B" as soon as you can, and "C" someday. Here are some examples from one of our notebooks.

You have probably noticed that everything on the list of what "I want to be" had an A priority. That's because most of those qualities are intangible and must be worked on *now* if you are ever to achieve what you want in the tangible realm of "do" and "have."

On the lists of what you want to do and have: if you can't think of three reasons why you included an entry (for example, learning to fly an airplane), cross it off the list because it belongs to someone else. If you find that you have more than three reasons for wanting something (like a new dining room set), make sure it has an A priority.

The lists will grow and change as you do. Be sure to date each entry so that, looking back, you can see a progression. You may laugh at some of the things you thought were important.

Eventually the A priorities will be broken down and fed into the cardfile computer. The Bs and Cs will either move up in importance or they will move out. For now, it is enough to have identified them and written them in the notebook.

Daily Journal Cards

Friday, August 13, 1974
It was 107° in the shade. The air conditioner broke four days ago. The man said he'd come, but he didn't. A swarm of bees came down our chimney, looking for their queen. Paul got laid off. The baby is now three weeks overdue. Paul Jr. came down with chicken pox and Daisy's puppies just learned how to climb out of their box. Paul's mother called to say she's coming (wouldn't say exactly when or for how long). I need groceries but the car has a flat. The phone's out of order (the cable TV guy accidently cut the wrong wire hooking up the neighbors etc.

SCORE 1

March 7, 1975
I wish it would quit raining. We've had the wettest spring in 49 years. I've forgotten what the sun looks like. There wasn't any mail today— maybe no news is good news. We had fish sticks, mashed potatoes and creamed corn for dinner— custard for dessert. Paul is happy about the lug wrench we found at a garage sale. He has Army Reserves this weekend, so I did up his uniform. I called Wards and ordered a couple of vacuum cleaner belts and a mattress pad. I broke my thumb nail prying the lid off the garbage can. The kids are fine.

SCORE 5

October 10, 1975
Hurray! I got on the scale and I'd lost five pounds! Paul surprised me with two tickets to Hawaii! He got a big raise and a nice promotion!! Paul Jr. has been accepted into the gifted youth program, and we found out that the twins are going to be in a Pampers commercial! We put Mother Cennard on the bus. She's gonna spend some time with Paul's sister! I won a ten minute shopping spree at Belky's Food Barn. Our new car came today and we paid off my bridge work. I'm so happy!! Paul sent me a dozen roses for no reason. Reader's Digest bought my Humor in Uniform article and the dress I wanted at the Fashion Tent went on ½ price!!

SCORE 10

Happiness Ratings Card
(front)

JANUARY		APRIL	
Wk 1	6	Wk 1	___
Wk 2	5.3	Wk 2	___
Wk 3	7	Wk 3	___
Wk 4	7.5	Wk 4	___
Wk 5	9.2	Wk 5	___
	7.0		

FEBRUARY		MAY	
Wk 1	10	Wk 1	___
Wk 2	6	Wk 2	___
Wk 3	8.1	Wk 3	___
Wk 4	7.9	Wk 4	___
Wk 5	2.5	Wk 5	___
	6.9		

MARCH		JUNE	
Wk 1	___	Wk 1	___
Wk 2	___	Wk 2	___
Wk 3	___	Wk 3	___
Wk 4	___	Wk 4	___
Wk 5	___	Wk 5	___

Happiness Ratings Card
(back)

JULY		OCTOBER	
Wk 1	___	Wk 1	___
Wk 2	___	Wk 2	___
Wk 3	___	Wk 3	___
Wk 4	___	Wk 4	___
Wk 5	___	Wk 5	___

AUGUST		NOVEMBER	
Wk 1	___	Wk 1	___
Wk 2	___	Wk 2	___
Wk 3	___	Wk 3	___
Wk 4	___	Wk 4	___
Wk 5	___	Wk 5	___

SEPTEMBER		DECEMBER	
Wk 1	___	Wk 1	___
Wk 2	___	Wk 2	___
Wk 3	___	Wk 3	___
Wk 4	___	Wk 4	___

7-17-83   I want to be:

A. More thoughtful
   1. I feel good when I do something nice
   2. I feel good when I'm on the receiving end
   3. I know I'd be happier not missing things

A. A better mother
   1. To help my kids grow positively
   2. To show them a good example
   3. To give them good memories

A. A healthier cook
   1. So we'll live as long as we should
   2. To give the kids good eating habits
   3. To lose weight

A. More well read
   1. So that I can contribute intelligently
   2. For enjoyment
   3. To learn what I don't know

A. More self-disciplined
   1. Because too much indulgence is depressing
   2. I could accomplish more
   3. I admire self-disciplined people

A. More spiritual
   1. I'm sure it's the answer to everything
   2. I want more faith
   3. I want more understanding

7-17-83   I want to do:

C. Go on a cruise
   1. It'd be romantic
   2. It sounds exciting
   3. I envy people who get to go on one

C. Learn to fly an airplane
   1. Zac Young has her license
   2.
   3.

A. Lose ten pounds
   1. I'd like my clothes to fit right
   2. I'd feel better about myself
   3. Exercises would be easier to do

B. Have dinner by 5:30
  1. I don't like going to bed on a full stomach
  2. I'd have more free time in the evening
  3. The kids wouldn't eat so many treats

B. Sell a bunch of junk
  1. I can't get my car in the garage
  2. I need the money
  3. I can't get new till the old's out

A. Pay off my charge accounts
  1. Last year my interest was $372.00
  2. The stuff I charged is worn out
  3. I want to deal more in cash

7-17-83 I want to have:

C. A big diamond ring
  1. Kae Young has one
  2. I want to look rich
  3. I love diamonds

A. A bicycle
  1. I like that exercise
  2. I like being outside
  3. I love to ride hard and then coast

A. New nightgowns
  1. My favorite one is ratty
  2. Doris Day wore cute nightgowns
  3. I don't like to step out of my
   bubble bath and into a flannel disgrace

B. Money in the bank
  1. For a feeling of security
  2. So I'm not embarrassed to go to the bank
  3. For the future

A. New dining room set
  1. Guests snag pantyhose on my chairs
  2. I can't serve enough people
  3. I've always hated the set I have
  4. None of my tablecloths fit
  5. Old set doesn't go with other furniture
  6. I'm embarrassed to have people over

Three

The Third Week–
Working with Your
Assets

Your assignment for the third week will be to compile a personal inventory of your strengths and weaknesses. Leave space for dictionary definitions, because you will be writing the meaning of each characteristic.

Strengths and Weaknesses
Take time to think about yourself and what you perceive your strengths and weaknesses to be. Your strengths will be recognized when you think of things you love to do, things that come easily for you, or talents you might have taken for granted. Your weaknesses will be those things you are ashamed to write down. Keep the lists in your notebook in the section labeled S & W (see the fictitious examples of two completely opposite people: Marguerite White and Katie Diller on pages 61 to 66).

Next define your strengths and weaknesses, using your dictionary. This may not seem to be much of an assignment for a full week, and you might even be tempted to skip it altogether... *Don't.*

Your strengths and weaknesses have a lot to do with your happiness. Looking honestly at both your assets and liabilities, you will be able to see what you have to work *with* and know what you need to work *on*. Defining your strengths and weaknesses will make you aware of what they really mean to you. Becoming aware of the true definitions of the positive and negative words you are using to describe yourself will help you become the person that you want to be.

The dictionary is an inspired work that can cut through our misconceptions and help us see the truth.

This exercise made us see that we have often been victims of false thinking. For one thing, we had always thought that we were lazy, because neither of us likes hard physical labor. When we looked up the word *lazy*, we found out that it means "feeble, akin to becoming weak, droopy, sluggish, lax, or moving slowly." Knowing the definition, we could see that we weren't any of those things. Maybe we got the idea when we were little and didn't want to do our chores. Mom probably told us, "You're both lazy!" because we were disinclined to move as fast on our work as she wanted us to.

Carrying around the idea that we were lazy had a definite effect on us when we became adults, and it definitely was a factor in the condition of our houses. Understanding the meaning of the word, we were able to cross it off our list of liabilities. We think that believing in a false weakness is the same as having it; until you are aware of its untruth, you will not be free of it. Understanding the real meaning of your strengths and weaknesses will give you insight into how they affect your life.

One of our friends, who was involved with testing the Happiness File in her own life, reported back that the definition assignment had been an amazing mind-opener. She had listed as a weakness in her notebook that she often disciplined her children with anger. Looking up the dictionary definitions of the words *anger* and *discipline*, she was amazed to find out that she was "building character with viciousness." Using that knowledge, she saw how inappropriate her method had been and she chose to change it.

Your strengths are a key to your potential for happiness. They are gifts you were given, packed right into your little chromosomes. Your unique use of those God-given talents and attributes will provide you with everything you need to succeed in life.

For example, if you know you are patient because you can wait on hold indefinitely on the telephone, you can be stuck in a traffic jam and not get ruffled, or you can teach your kid to knit, fish, ski, or swim without losing your temper, then patience is one of your virtues and it will be on your list of strengths.

Writing down the dictionary meaning of the word *patient* will make you see the far-reaching effect that virtue has in your life. *Webster's Collegiate Dictionary* defines *patient* as "manifesting forbearance under provocation or strain" and "steadfast despite opposition, difficulty, or adversity." When it's put that way, you can see that it's not just a word, but an active approach to life, which you can call upon more often than you have in the past.

You will also see that with all of its goodness the virtue of patience carries its own potential for misuse. Patience can become a liability if, for instance, you have a grease fire and you patiently wait for it to burn itself out. We say that honesty is a virtue, but Webster says it is "adherence to the facts." That in itself is neither good nor bad. Everybody can adhere to the facts; so we'd have to say that everyone can be honest. The virtue comes in how you choose to use honesty. To use it to tell your six-year-old that the hat he made you and decorated with your prize roses is not only stupid-looking but has ruined the bush would have a crushing effect on his creativity and thoughtfulness.

Don't let your virtues defeat you. Being easily swayed is the negative use of flexibility. Flexibility is being "wishy-washy" in a positive way. We concluded, after looking up all the words on our lists, that ultimately there are no absolute strengths or weaknesses, only a pattern of choices (positive or negative) whose continued use can change the direction of our lives.

Once you have listed and defined your strengths and weaknesses you will be ready to use that information to help you throughout the rest of your life. In Part IV we will give you specific examples of how we spread the things that came easily for us (the things we called our strengths) into the areas we thought were weak.

Katie Diller

June 18, 1983   My Strengths

I have a good sense of humor.

I forgive easily.

I am strong.

I am compassionate.

I am good with my kids.

I am patient.

I am honest.

I have a good personality.

I am loyal.

I have pretty eyes.

I have a good imagination.

Katie Diller

June 18, 1983   My Strengths (Continue

I am a good cook.

I am a good seamstress.

I am healthy.

I am spontaneous.

I am relaxed.

I am generous.

I have an eye for decorating.

I love animals.

I love to entertain.

I am flexible.

I am intelligent.

June 18, 1983   My Weaknesses

I lose things.

I am forgetful.

I am easily swayed.

I go on binges.

I procrastinate.

I am disorganized.

I have no concept of time.

I am a lousy speller.

I don't take care of my body.

I am an impulsive spender.

Marguerite White

June 18, 1983   My Strengths

I always put things in their proper place.

I am decisive.

My weight is perfect.

I am a wise shopper.

I am self-disciplined.

I am kind.

I am a good financial manager.

I am a hard worker.

I take care of my possessions.

I am quiet.

I am punctual.

Marguerite White

June 18, 1983   My Strengths   (continued)

I am well-groomed.

I am careful.

I am conscientious.

I am thoughtful.

I am a faithful wife.

I am immaculate.

I am devoted to my family.

I am intelligent.

I am honest.

I am strong.

I have a green thumb.

Marguerite White

June 18, 1983   My Weaknesses

I am nervous.

I complain too much.

I am not healthy.

I am never satisfied.

I am too rigid.

I have a bad temper.

Four

The Fourth Week–
What's on Your
Mind

In the fourth week we ask you to make a list of the things that are on your mind. Then show you how to take that list, break it down, and feed it into your cardfile, so that you can start taking immediate action to deal with your concerns.

On My Mind
The things that are on your mind need to be written down. Because, as we ourselves do, most people carry their lives around in their heads, and, consequently, their heads are often crammed with confusion. In our seminars we ask the participants to write down, in their notebooks, five things that are on their minds. Invariably a few people will be reluctant to write anything. The simple statement "If you think that nothing is bothering you, then you are probably bothering a lot of people" quickly sets the pens moving. We believe that *all of us* (even Prince Charles and Princess Diana) have things that are bothering us.

Just as we used to try to clean house by tearing up far more than we could put back, let alone clean, we have a tendency to think we can handle more concerns than we can cope with, let alone manage.

The only way we were able to resolve our house cleaning dilemma was to develop a system, starting with a list of everything that had to be cleaned (room by room). Then we could decide how often each job should be done to keep the house from becoming a mess again. We put every job on a 3x5 card so that we could schedule the work within the month. We were able to stay in control of the house (instead of having it control us) because we had direction. All our jobs had been organized into manageable steps, and we never allowed the work to pile up on us again. It was the "pile-ups" that had made the problem of housekeeping overwhelming.

Between the two of us, we can always tell when there is something heavy on the other guy's mind. Usually it's an *accumulation* of bothers that puts the person out of balance. Whenever that happens the following equation is almost always true: $AP \times SD + FM - S \div HITD = MSTOGCH$...
AP (accumulated problems) $\times$ SD (several days) + FM (family members) $-$ S (sleep) $\div$ HITD (hours in the day) = MSTOGCH (more strain than one guy can handle). Usually the strainee has been so buried in concerns that she's not even aware she's acting weird.

"What's the matter, Sissy?"

"I don't know . . . nothing."

"Something's wrong. You don't usually wear your jogging bottoms with a silk blouse."

"Who are you, Gloria Vanderbilt? I couldn't decide what to do this morning."

Don't wait until things get out of perspective. If you handle them regularly, they won't get a chance to stack up on you.

Once a week in the section of your notebook labeled "Clearing," write down as many things as you can think of that are bothering you at this time—the things that are constantly nagging you, like gnats circling a fruit bowl.

Using Katie Diller as an example, we have made up a list of things that might be on her mind in any given week and would have been written in her notebook. Keep referring to her list (see page 71) as we explain further.

If you've never put your concerns in writing before, you might be reluctant to do this. The process might seem to you to be a negative one. If you think about it, though, the only people who don't have *anything* bothering them are either not facing the truth or are bothering a lot of other people. Norman Vincent Peale said that if you want to see people who don't have any problems, go to a cemetery.

Don't be afraid to write things down, even if they are negative. A friend of ours found tolerating his in-laws a long-standing problem. He talked about them negatively every time the conversation touched on the subject of relatives or family get-togethers. His in-laws were obviously bothering him, but what bothered him even more was that he loved his wife and it hurt her that he couldn't stand her parents. When he came to this assignment, he was unable to write down his bitter feelings until it occurred to him that if he felt his anger wasn't worthy of being put on paper, he should try to quit thinking about it and stop talking about it altogether. Writing is only a little slower process than talking, and talking is a little slower than thinking. If the thing that is bothering you would look stupid or petty when other people saw it written down or if you feel it wouldn't be worth the time or effort required to write it down, it might not be worth brooding about, either. On the other hand, writing it all out just once might get it out of your system, and you'd never need to discuss it again.

Getting all the gnats out of your head and onto paper can help you analyze your concerns so that you can handle them in a logical way. When we wrote down what was on our minds, we could see that some of the cares we had regarded as our own really needed to be delegated to someone else. A lot of the stuff we were concerned about either belonged to the past or was too far in the future to be worried about just then. The could've beens, used to bes, how comes, what ifs and suppose he's are naggers that rob us of today's happiness.

If you look at Katie's list, you'll see that each concern

relates to the past, present, or future and that she has classified them accordingly. Take your own list and in the margin classify each item as Katie has: past, present, or future. This will make it easier for you to sort things out.

First you can deal with anything on your mind that stems from the past. You'll probably have only a few of such things listed because your life is already filled up with present and future concerns.

You may have regrets like Katie Diller's: "I missed the Johnny Mathis concert," or "I didn't go to my class reunion because I felt fat."

Transfer your list of past-related concerns to a white 3x5 card. File it in front of January and forget about it until then. In that month your job will be to clear everything up and focus on starting over with a feeling of freedom. We hope, after everything's been taken care of, you'll *never* drag the past around with you again.

In January when Katie Diller looks at her cards from the past, she may laugh about feeling hurt when Robert complained about her dinner. Or she may realize that Robert has a pattern of being constantly critical. If that's true she'll make some decisions about how she wants to change their patterns of behavior in the New Year. She'll also be alert to any announcements that Johnny Mathis is coming to town, and she'll have done something about her body by the next reunion.

For now she has enough to deal with in the present to worry about the past. She'll cross those items off her list and move on to the things to do in the future, projects that can wait for at least a month.

Look over your "to do" list for the future. Estimate how soon you think you can take care of each item and write the month in the margin as Katie has. There may be two or three things to work on next month, a couple the month after, and so on. Some may even be scheduled for six months to a year ahead. Put each month's list on a separate 3x5 card or scratch paper. The cards can be filed in front of their respective dividers to be handled in calendar order. A Tickler Card (see example on page 72) kept in front of the Sunday divider will remind you to check what's coming up

June 22, 1982   On My Mind   Katie Diller

Present - Pray	My brother's surgery
Present - To do	I can't find my glasses
Future - July	I think I might be pregnant
Present - ?	I'm 20 pounds overweight
Present - Routine	I need to balance checkbook but I'm scared
Present - Call	The washer is broken
Present - Call	I need to make dental appointments
Future - Sept.	I need to clean out the pantry
Present - Routine	I need to pluck my eyebrows, can't find tweezers
Future - July	I need to have the cat spayed
Present - Bob Jr.	I need to clean the garage from garage sale
Present - Routine	I need groceries
Present - Do	I need to get stuff from the cleaners
Present - Call	I need to sign Toni up for swimming lessons
Present - ?	I suspect Robert is fooling around
Present - ?	The house is a mess
Future - Nov.	I'd like us to have a family portrait
Future - Sept.	I need to clean closets, cupboards, & drawers
Present - Buy	We all need summer clothes
Future - May	I want a piano
Future - Oct.	I want to make some Christmas presents
Present - Routine	I need more exercise
Present - Pray	I'm afraid my neighbor's daughter's on drugs
Past - Jan.	I didn't go to my class reunion because I felt fat
Past - Jan.	I missed the Johnny Mathis concert
Past - Jan.	Robert criticized dinner

in the approaching month; and at that time you will be able to decide how much you can actually handle. Those items you can act upon will become part of the present and will join others you are currently working on (as you will soon see).

When you're faced with taking action, some of the future cards may still have to be moved farther ahead. That's all right. Just date them and move them forward.

Don't feel guilty at not being able to handle everything you listed. You are not neglecting anything; you are merely facing the fact that some things have a lower priority than others and *have* to be rescheduled.

TICKLER CARD

MONTHLY	SUNDAY
Check next month's divider for things to do and dates to remember.	

When past-related concerns have been crossed off the list, filed in front of January, and forgotten for now, and those classified for future handling have been assigned to a later month, you'll be glad to see that you can probably cope with what's left within the next week. The items in the present are the only ones you should be tackling. As you read over your list decide which items have priority and what actions you will need to take. Some will require establishing a routine, such as balancing the checkbook, dieting, exercising, grooming, and grocery shopping. These should be transferred directly to the appropriate Daily Routine Card. The remaining items might include places to go, things to buy, people to pray for, calls to make, or things to do.

Using Katie's list as an example, make notations in the margin of your own notebook of the actions you plan, such as routine—go—buy—pray—call—do. (If you can't decide what actions to take, the problem is probably more serious or deeply rooted. Put a question mark beside any of those items; we'll show you how to handle them separately in a minute.) If you have things on *your* mind that really should be the responsibility of your spouse or kids, put those things on cards (one for each person) and stand them on end in front of each guy's divider. They will remind you to delegate those burdens to other family members, and crossing them off of your list will relieve some of your tension. Sharing concerns and things that have to be done gives the *whole* family free time to have fun. When one person is under the pressure of too many things on her mind, she can't be free to enjoy relaxation. Having things already written down and set aside to delegate (not merely bearing them "in mind") will make it simpler for you to get cooperation from everyone involved.

When you're finished marking your list, you'll be ready to transfer everything (belonging to the present) to 3x5 cards. As we said before, things that require a routine go on the Daily Routine Cards and everything but the question marks goes on an Immediate Action Card. (You might want to organize the items into little groups as the example on page 74 shows.) Throughout the week we cross things off the Action Card as they are taken care of, but we also add a few new things as they come up.

We keep the Immediate Action Card in front of the current day for easy reference and to make sure we remember to give it our attention. Every evening we move the card to the next day. Usually by the end of the week everything on it has been taken care of, and the 3x5 can be filed in front of the success divider. Any leftovers are put on a new card, and carried over to the next week's things to handle.

If anything lingers longer than you think is reasonable and it's really pulling you down, you probably need help in handling it. Help can come from a professional, a close friend, your mate, a family member, a book, a seminar, a lecture—any person, place, or thing that can give you the boost you need in solving a more serious, stubborn problem.

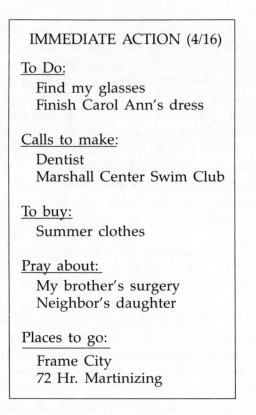

IMMEDIATE ACTION (4/16)

To Do:
  Find my glasses
  Finish Carol Ann's dress

Calls to make:
  Dentist
  Marshall Center Swim Club

To buy:
  Summer clothes

Pray about:
  My brother's surgery
  Neighbor's daughter

Places to go:
  Frame City
  72 Hr. Martinizing

When you're trying to work through some of those difficult perplexities on your own (the ones you marked with a
question mark), you have to break them down into manageable segments.

Take the devastating suspicion our fictitious Katie has
that Robert is fooling around. She doesn't know what to do
with her mistrust, even though she has been haunted by it
for some time. It's likely that a marriage counselor will have
to intercede, but not before Katie has given the problem
some thought.

On a dated 3x5 Problem Card, she stated her concern in
simple terms, "I suspect Robert is fooling around," and she
decided on a deadline. By a certain date she must either
resolve her suspicions or seek outside help. Then she wrote
down as many possible action steps as she could think of
(see example on page 75). Some of her first ideas weren't
wise actions at all; they were a product of panic, such as,

"tail him" or "go through his pants, wallet, car, desk, Rolodex." She recognized how unsatisfactory they were when she saw them in writing. After she'd thought of some real solutions, she realized that taking action before she'd had time to think things through would not be a good idea. Asking Robert, "Is there someone else?" would probably not work either. If she had to *ask*, chances are there was another woman and even if there was, Robert would probably deny it. Besides, if her suspicions were only a figment of her imagination, based on her own insecurity and lack of self-esteem, her accusations could drive him away. What she has to deal with is the *underlying cause*, not the *overwhelming symptoms*. There is nothing she can do to *make* Robert love her; she can only change the way she feels about herself. As she brainstorms for ideas about what she'd like to change, her attention is off Robert and *his* problem and now focused on herself. What she has to keep in mind are her own strengths (from the list she made in her notebook) and the reality that even if she were perfect, Robert might still have his problems.

PROBLEM CARD

6/16—I suspect Robert is fooling around. Deadline: Sept. 1st
Tail him. Go through his pants, wallet, car, desk, Rolodex. Ask him. Pray about it. Lose weight. Quit biting fingernails. Tone down laugh. Be on time. Clean the house. Regain my self-respect and remember my strengths. Talk less and listen more.

Each of the action steps will have to be worked into the cardfile. Since they all demand attention now, they'll be put in the section of the days of the week. Some will require a routine like taking care of her nails or praying. They will be transferred to her Daily Routine Cards. Others will go on her Immediate Action Card and rotate throughout the week until each thing is taken care of, and the leftover question marks will have to be broken down even further on a separate Problem Card.

It's interesting that many of the elements that Katie decided to work on to help her solve her problem were already concerning her because they showed up on the list of what was on her mind. She just didn't realize that they affected her relationship with Robert. A lot of worrisome things turn out to be interrelated. Goals of what you want to be, do, and have will show up in your weekly concerns, because they will be on your mind. Brainstorming over a problem will return you to your strengths and weaknesses, and everything will go back to your goals again.

What's great about this cause-and-effect interlocking is that solutions dovetail, too. In solving one problem by cleaning up her house, Katie will probably find her glasses and her tweezers. Exercising, she will lose weight; and by balancing the checkbook and organizing the finances, she will be able to set aside money for summer clothes and, in a few months, even the piano.

Concerning Katie's problems with Robert: some things that are on the Problem Card will need special handling. Things like "be on time" can go on their own card with ideas about...*how* (see example on page 77).

The card can then be put in her cardfile and rotated and read daily until following its suggestion becomes a habit, or it can be posted in the main place where she is most likely to get sidetracked—by the telephone, near the TV set, or in her sewing room.

> Be on Time
>
> How??
>
> 1. Wear my watch and set it a few minutes ahead.
> 2. Use the timer to keep myself on the track.
> 3. Set out my stuff the night before.
> 4. Double the time I think it'll take to get ready.
> 5. Overestimate travel time.
> 6. Think departure time—not arrival time.

Other Think Cards can list just key words such as: listen, remember strengths, self-respect, thin thighs. When they are conspicuously posted, they serve as reminders of what she's working on without being an exposé of her private thoughts. The bottom line of working effectively on herself is the truth that with or without Robert, Katie will have become a happier person by virtue of her own self-improvement.

Remember that in order to keep your concerns from piling up to the point where they equal more strain than one person can handle, you'll probably need to make a list in your notebook of what's on your mind once a week. Let a blue card serve as your reminder and file it in front of whichever day of the week you choose to clear your mind. The more often you do this, the easier it will be and the fewer concerns you'll have. As you read over your notebook list you'll realize that a lot of the things have taken care of themselves without your doing anything more than just being aware of them. You'll need only a few minutes a week to get yourself organized enough to do this and to find peace of mind.

PART THREE

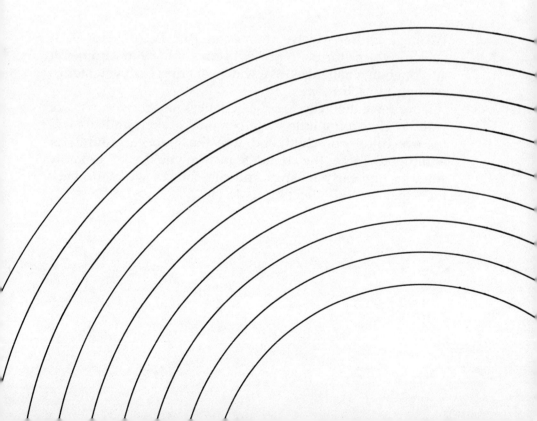

We have chosen twelve themes in Part IV (one for each month) which, for us, represent some of life's most difficult and ongoing challenges. We will be sharing with you stories relating to each theme.

Before we tell you our experiences as grown-ups, we want to give you a little more personal background. As it is for everyone, our childhood was the practice ground for adulthood. To get the complete picture you'll need to know some of our early feelings and the choices we made back then that are still affecting us today.

One

The Witch
and the Rosebud

From Pam—October 29, 1947

Halloween was fast approaching and I was going to be a witch. This would be my first year to trick-or-treat. Even though I could scarcely wait for that big night, I was even more excited about this day because of what my mom and dad were about to bring home . . . my new baby sister.

Mom was organized, so she had decorated the house and made my costume early. Even though she was nine months pregnant, she was still a stickler for detail and a master at follow-through. She made my costume from an old knee-length black taffeta skirt of hers. She put a black ribbon drawstring in the waistband and pulled it to fit around my neck. Instantly the skirt became a full-length witch dress. She cut slits in the sides for my arms. She smoothed her long black gloves all the way to my armpits, and into the leftover fingertip space she stuffed cotton so that I had long scary fingers. I wore real witch shoes: high-buttoned ones like the Wicked Witch of the West had.

Inside the front coat closet Mom hung a cardboard skeleton as tall as Dad. Guests laughed when she opened the door to reveal a skeleton in our closet. I was only four and a half so I didn't get the joke, but it tickled me that he was in there. Mom put orange pumpkins and black cats everywhere, and she filled a big glass candy bowl with licorice and orange jelly beans. I loved to plunge my hand into the candies and stir. I never liked either flavor, but it was fun to play in them and feed them to Ella Mae, the family dog, who was more like a close relative.

From the living room window I watched and waited for Mom and Dad. Ella Mae sat in the big overstuffed chair with me. She was a generic dog with white wiry hair and a black spot over each eye.

Time seemed to move as slowly as Heinz catsup, uninterested in my wanting it to go fast.

The weather couldn't decide what it wanted to do. One minute it was wet and dreary and the next, crisp and sunny. I'd popped in and out of the house like one of those people on a Swiss clock. Sick of putting my boots on and taking them off so many times, I had ended up just sitting and squirming. As the sun bowed in and out of the clouds, the living room went from light to dark as if God were testing some new dimmer switch.

Ella Mae's ears perked up as our 19-something-or-other Pontiac pulled into the driveway. Granny, who had been taking care of me, chirped, "They're home!" I could hardly stand it. I watched Dad jump out of the car and dash around to the passenger side. He opened the door and carefully helped Mom out of the car. She held a huge parcel of pink blankets. I had never seen a new baby, but I was shocked to think it could be that big. I could have easily fitted inside those covers myself. Mom's arms could scarcely reach around the bundle. Excitement began the instant they walked through the door. Granny rushed to help Mom with her coat, and Dad gently took the bundle out of Mom's arms. Ella Mae did her customary welcome-home dance, but my attention centered on Dad as he placed the plump package on the couch.

As layer after layer of pink was peeled off, like pulling petals from a huge rosebud, I was pleased to see the bundle get smaller. Finally he came to my baby sister, Peggy, sleeping in the middle. I looked at her tiny hands and feet, and Mom and Dad let me touch her. She wore a pink knit bonnet, and when Granny took it off, her fine blond hair, full of electricity, stood up like pile on a cheap throw rug that's been dried too long without Downy. She slept through all the unwrapping.

My parents put the baby in the crib in their bedroom. As I peered through the bars I was eye-level with her sleeping face. I kept a prison-guard watch, waiting for her to make a move. She kept sleeping. I didn't know a lot about real babies, but Ella Mae had had two batches of puppies since we'd gotten her at the dog pound. I knew a puppy's eyes didn't open until it could almost walk. (Once I had gotten in trouble for trying to pry them open.) I assumed this baby wouldn't open her eyes for a long time, either. I thought she looked like a new puppy, or maybe more like an old man. She was making faces in her sleep, and I wondered what she was dreaming about.

Without a warning she opened her eyes. We looked right at each other! I was flabbergasted. I probably thought, *At this rate she'll get to go trick-or-treating with me this year!* I ran into the kitchen with the news. "The baby's eyes are open and they're blue, just like mine!"

In the next several weeks all Peggy did was sleep. In rare moments when she was awake all she did was eat. I loved it when she cried. Her voice had the same startling effect as a smoke alarm going off. Dad would fly for the formula. Mom would snatch her out of the crib. Ella Mae would howl. I found the commotion a welcome relief from the monotony.

When the tiny alarm went off I was entertained. I began experimenting with it. I discovered that it had an extraordinarily long fuse and that I could have a lot of fun with it before it would detonate. I could straighten it out, roll it over, prop it up, comb its hair, blow in its face—and it would keep on sleeping. It had an impressively high pain threshold, but I found that its feet were extremely ticklish; as if I were striking a match, I could tickle them and they would ignite.

Mom and Dad moved the alarm in with me a few days before Christmas. Although I loved the wonderful smell of baby powder and Ivory soap (Mom was immaculate, so I never experienced the smell of dirty diapers until I had babies of my own), sharing my room was like sharing a Popsicle. Popsicles never split down the middle. When you pulled the sticks apart one guy always got seventy-five percent, while the other guy got what was left. I felt as if I were expected to give the baby the bigger part of the Popsicle.

My room turned into a nursery. Her crib, her dresser, her Bathinette (a big thing that held rubber hoses and a bathtub that, after the bath, turned into a changing table), her walker, her jumper, her diaper pail, and her buggy pushed my furniture into the corner and crammed my toys into the closet. My dresses got smashed to make room for hers (the prettiest little dresses I'd ever seen).

As Peggy grew she got cuter and cuter. When she was at that darling toddler stage, my first permanent teeth came in (the front ones that are always too big for your face when you first get them). I felt ugly. I also realized I had to share much more than just my room: my mom, my dad, cookies, M&M's, and Ella Mae. I'm sure Mom and Dad tried to make me feel good about myself, but I was smart enough to realize I was no match for "the baby." No matter how equitably divided things probably were, I felt they weren't. For all the joy this new baby brought, the problems that went along with her were more noticeable to me. I got in a lot more trouble after the arrival of Miss Peggy. I was scolded and she wasn't.

"Don't touch that; it's the baby's!" *How much will a harmless suck off her bottle hurt?*

"Shh, the baby is sleeping." *I can't laugh anymore?*

"You know better than that!" *What's wrong with sharing my candy cane with the baby?*

"You're a big girl now; that's for babies." *Gerber vanilla pudding is just for babies?*

"Don't talk like a baby!" *When she does it, it's darling.*

I remember wishing I were little again. I also remember wishing my adorable little sister would finally grow up and join me in the life of crime I had begun since her arrival. I wanted to see her get in trouble for a change, so I worked out an intricate plan. I discovered that "the baby" could hold three crayons in each of her chubby little hands at one time. (That realization came when she got into my crayons and started sogging the papers off them.)

I also knew the strict rules in our house, and she didn't. I put red, blue, and yellow colors in one of her hands and black, brown, and green in the other. I showed her, with a gesture, how to color our bedroom wall. When she was well into the project, I went into the living room and pretended to be looking out the window. Our house was small, and I could hear Mom in the kitchen.

"Mom."

"What?"

"Where's Peggy?"

"Isn't she with you?"

"No, do you want me to find her?"

"Yeah."

I let a reasonable amount of time pass and then I went tearing through the house into our kitchen.

"Mom, the baby is coloring the walls!" (I have to admit she had colored much more than I had ever imagined she could. She not only swirled the six colors like sparklers, but she had started at one corner and run the entire length of the room, leaving a tricolored streak on two walls.)

The one thing I hadn't counted on was that Peggy was starting to talk, and when Mom said, "Why did you color on the wall?" Peggy answered, "Sissy tell me to." We both got a spanking.

Sometimes I got in trouble when I was only trying to help . . . with Peggy's hair, for instance. Almost from the first time I saw it I wanted to work with it. It was different from doll hair. Doll hair was easier to put rubber bands on, and I could cut it. I tried brushing Peggy's hair (that usually worked on Ella Mae), but it was too fine. It wouldn't stay where I wanted it to. It needed body.

Since we were supposed to be napping, I couldn't leave the room; the supplies for my experiment were restricted to the products on the Bathinette. The baby oil cut the static, but the original problem remained ... no body. I discovered the answer in a twelve-ounce jar of petroleum jelly. After I shampooed it into the six-inch strands, they instantly did what the comb said. As the baby drifted off to sleep I was pleased with what I'd done.

I didn't regard the experiment as a disaster until Mom tried to get the goop out. Shampoo wouldn't touch it. Granny said she'd heard that cornstarch takes grease out of fur. They tried the starch, and Peggy's head became encased in a plasterlike cast. Her hair looked dirty for weeks.

There were four and a half years between us, and I started school when she was one. I remember feeling proud that I got to climb on the bus all by myself. Peggy and Mom were always in the overstuffed chair, waving to me as I walked to the end of the block to catch the bus.

One day Miss Capron, my kindergarten teacher, announced to our class that there was going to be Guest Day. We could bring our brothers and sisters. I couldn't wait to get home and tell Mom. If Peggy could go, I would be able to show her my new world of paints, scissors, crayons, and playhouses. She would ride the bus with me; I'd help her climb the steps!

They wouldn't let her go. They said she was too young. I was so disappointed. On Guest Day as I walked to the bus stop, I saw Joyce Davidson, a two-year-old who lived two houses down from us, playing in her front yard. *Since Peggy can't go to school with me*, I thought, *I'll take Joyce.*

I took her by the hand and asked if she'd like to come to my school. She was too young to know what I meant but thrilled to be going somewhere. As I helped Joyce onto the bus I felt lucky to have found a surrogate sister on such short notice, and it was an unexpected adventure for Joyce. For months she had watched as I climbed on the kindergarten bus, and I'd always suspected she would like to go along. We were both delighted with the trip to school.

The bus picked up all the regulars, and by the last stop it was crammed with Guest Day enthusiasts and their siblings. We were caught up in a party atmosphere, like a busload of Elks on their way to Reno.

We arrived at school and went to my room. Miss Capron

led the flag salute and welcomed the visitors. She read us a story and then we had free time to play house and color. The room was noisier and more crowded than usual, but we were having fun. We sang and Miss Capron played the piano. Instead of the usual graham crackers and warm pineapple juice for snacktime, we were served Dixie Cups and homemade chocolate chip cookies. Joyce and I were unaware of what was going on back in the neighborhood.

The sheriff had been summoned when Joyce's mother discovered she was missing. The surrounding woods had been searched and the nearby lake dragged. Mrs. Davidson was being consoled, and my mother had joined all the neighborhood mothers in a frantic search to locate the missing child.

Meanwhile, we were winding up one of the greatest days of my life. In fact, it was perfect until rest time. While relaxing on my rug Joyce did something I hadn't counted on. The room was subtly permeated with the effects of Joyce's efforts. My classmates and I were all potty trained and disgusted.

In a whisper Miss Capron asked, "Did you bring an extra diaper for your sister?" "She's not my sister." "Who is she?" "She's my neighbor." "A neighbor? Did her mother say you could bring her?" "No, she just wanted to come." The next thing I knew, Joyce and I were in the office. The principal was asking me questions I couldn't answer, and I sensed trouble was on the way. I felt accused but didn't know the crime until Mom and a tranquilized Mrs. Davidson came to pick us up.

For the next three years I gave up waiting for Peggy to grow up. I joined the Brownies (Mom was our leader). I was proud of my uniform, my beanie, and my pin. Peggy attended all the meetings, but she took part only in the treats. Mary Ann became my closest friend, and we enjoyed the privilege of staying overnight at each other's houses. I learned to skip, roller skate, and ride a bike. I could read and order food from a menu. I was given new boundaries and more responsibilities.

In the spring of my third-grade year, my family began considering moving to the country. We needed a bigger house and more room for Mom to plant a garden. I remember the day we rode out to look at the farm. The drive took more time than I thought it would, but when we got there, it was worth it. The house and the land were beyond any of my dreams. I couldn't wait to move.

From Peggy—???
I can't remember the first time I consciously realized that I had a sister. I wish I could think of some specific moment when I discovered her so that my recollection would be as interesting as Pam's. She seemed to have been there always (like Ella Mae and Mom and Dad).

My early memories are vague, recollected through my senses rather than my mind. For instance, when I hear a lawn mower before dinner, I get thirsty, but I don't know why. When I walk in a street with loose gravel, it takes me back to a good feeling, but that's all. I've never cared for the taste of asparagus, but the smell of it cooking makes me feel happy, for no apparent reason. I don't remember Pam shampooing my hair with petroleum jelly, but maybe that explains why seeing an open jar of Vaseline makes me very nervous. And to this day I never allow anyone or anything to touch the bottoms of my feet.

The one incident I do clearly remember was the first time I got separated from Pam. I was in my late twos. Mom and Dad took us to Sunday school, kissed us both on the cheek, and left us inside the door. Always before, they had kept me with them; I was confused about why, all of a sudden, I was going "in" with Sissy. She held my hand and I held my quarter. Dad had given it to me while we were in the car, and I was concentrating on not letting it get away from me. Maybe we would buy some candy in there, I thought.

We were all dressed up. Mom had fussed over us a lot that morning, and Dad kept telling us how pretty we looked. Our dresses were alike, and Sissy had a purse. We both wore black patent leather Mary Janes. I liked the sound they made as we walked on the wooden floor. Inside there was a long hallway with lots of white doors on both sides. We walked up to the first one and Sissy knocked. My quarter hand was getting sweaty. I peeked at my coin while we waited for an answer.

Suddenly the door swung open and an old lady with white wavy hair and a big smile stood at the threshold. She was too happy and too friendly for a first meeting. I stared at her teeth while she exclaimed over our matching sister dresses. Quickly she moved in on us and took my hand (the one with the quarter in it), making me drop my money. I let go of Sissy's hand for a second to grab the falling coin, but it hit the floor and rolled. I went after it while my captor held on to me. Then I heard her say, "You go on, Pam. She'll be just fine with me." Terrified, I turned around and saw my sister going out the door. I screamed and pried the lady's fingers away from mine and ran after Pam. The lady came down the hall after me. She tried to coax me back to the little room. "Don't you want to go find your money?" I didn't care anymore about the candy I had hoped it would buy. "No!" I sobbed. "I want my Sissy!"

It was agreed that for the good of the church I should attend my sister's first grade class, at least until I could handle the separation.

By the time I was three years old I was clearly aware that there were two of us, and one got to do lots more than the other. I watched Pam play outside with her friends while I was stuck in the house. (Once she was allowed to take me out in the backyard, but I ate some primroses and had to go back in.) I watched her ride her bike out of sight like the Lone Ranger, while Ella Mae and I sat in a big chair by the window. I wanted to go too but I was "too little." She got to go to school and take money with her. Mom tied it up in a hanky and pinned it on her, and she got to ride the bus.

It didn't seem fair. She could cross the street, walk the dog, push the grocery cart, dry the dishes, make her own peanut butter sandwich, and reach the cookie jar, but I couldn't. Probably the thing I hated most was having to take a nap while she was running, skipping, skating, riding, or playing. Usually I could hear her outside laughing and having fun, and I felt left out.

There was only one advantage to being left alone in our

room: I could get into all my sister's stuff. Her crayons were better than mine and she had a lot of them. They were pointed, and they all had their wrappers. Even the short ones had points. (I didn't know it was possible to sharpen crayons until I had my tonsils out when I was in the fourth grade and Verna Doyle brought me the Crayola box of sixty-four with the secret sharpener in the side.) My color collection was kept in a small tin Band-Aid box. Paperless, they were sticky, stubby, nicked little victims of child abuse. I'd leave them in the hot sun, and they'd pour out of the tin in a marbled mass of multicolored wax. (Little did I know it was a danger signal of things to come. Later in life I would leave my makeup in the car and let the sun bake my foundation and melt my lipstick. I would leave wet laundry in the washer until it could climb out on its own, and I would ruin garden hoses, roasts, paints, and hand tools...all because they were left out.) I would break the crayon block into chunks and happily scribble on any paper I could find.

In Pam's absence I often felt moved to add my own creative touches to her finished pictures. Any time I'd come to an uncolored page, I'd fill it in a little for her. Quickly tiring of one theme, I'd move on to a new page. I could easily finish off a whole coloring book while Sissy was helping to set the table.

I loved Pam's dolls, especially Gretchen. She was a lady-doll (bigger than a Barbie doll, but with the same things going for her) and she had nice hair, too. I always wanted to see Gretchen take a bath or go for a little swim, but she couldn't; she had the nonsubmersible feature that electric frying pans had then. She was a tough doll to get to. Pam kept her sealed inside a big doll trunk that had a semichild-proof latch on it. When I did get it opened, it was a shock to see how full it was. I had no idea Gretchen had so many clothes. There were crumpled shorts and tops, dresses, coats, hats, purses, belts, underpants, socks, shoes, high heels, and a wadded-up bride dress with a delicate wadded-up lace veil. Nothing was hung on the tiny hangers (they littered the trunk floor along with her ice skates and jewelry). The little drawers inside the trunk were crammed too full to open and the whole case was too full to close. It was a real mess, but worth getting in trouble for. (Little did Pam know that someday her closet would look just like Gretchen's trunk.)

Chucky was another of her dolls. His rubber body could take getting wet, but his head couldn't. Once he accidentally took a dive and it left him permanently impaired. His eyes sank back and squeaked when he was laid down, and you could look into his sockets and see the inside of his head. He'd been left out in the sun too long and was seriously jaundiced because of it. Quite frankly, I was a little scared of him so I left him alone, but Sissy loved him in spite of his problems.

Pam's dollhouse kept me the busiest. I loved to change it around. I'd put the little baby in my pocket and make the big kids all go to bed in there. While they were sleeping, I washed the furniture and the roof. My sister went wild.

When I was four I had accumulated quite a few toys of my own. I got a trike, and once in a while on a nice day, Mom would let me ride it up and down the cement walk. Our little room was overcrowded with our belongings. There was talk of a bigger house.

We moved to the farm at the beginning of summer. I would soon be five. With warmer days and no more worries about busy streets, Mom let me out of the house to join my sister.

Two

EEE I EEE I OH

We moved from that overcrowded little house with its tiny patch of grass to a forty-acre farm in a thicket of evergreens, surrounded by purple mountains, fruited plains, and amber waves of grain. The special beauty of it all was that we got to experience all the joys of farm life without having to do any of the work. Ours hadn't been a real farm in twenty years; and since Dad was busy as a partner in an oil distributing firm, he intended to keep it that way.

In contrast, the four other families on our road made farming their livelihood. The Bettses' place was the biggest. They had so much livestock that they had to lease our property to grow enough feed. A farmer with one hundred head of hungry heifers considers a field serious business. To us it was just a playground. When the soil was freshly plowed we played in the dirt, and when it rained we played in the mud, but once he had it planted, we stayed away until the growth was tall.

Nothing stimulates a little girl's homemaking instincts

more than five acres of waist-high alfalfa. When the field in front of our house was ready, we moved in. Like housing developers, we trampled out an entire neighborhood, picked two of the choicest lots, and crushed our four-bedroom ramblers next door to each other. We dragged out blankets, pillows, sleeping bags, throw rugs, old sheets and towels, Kool-Aid, crackers, apples, oranges, dolls, tea sets, teddy bears, and anything else we could sneak past Mom.

When our homes were completely furnished, we spent the next week playing house. We were out there every day from breakfast to dinner, until late one afternoon, as we were smearing peanut butter on crackers with one of Mom's knives, we saw Mr. Betts coming down the driveway in his flatbed truck. It stopped and Mr. Betts got out to inspect his crop. We dove onto our green kitchen floor and hid, pretending he was a burglar. We heard him coming closer and closer to our property. He walked through the walls of the house next door. We shuddered to think he might break into our house next. We didn't breathe as we listened to the alfalfa crunching under his feet. He came closer and closer; then the crunching stopped, and the silence was broken by some words we can't repeat. Mr. Betts was mad! He charged back to his truck and tore off down the driveway toward our house, throwing gravel into the air. He went inside...Dad was home...we were in trouble. We hadn't thought of the alfalfa as somebody's garden; to us it was like a gigantic lawn that had grown out of control. It reminded us of the grass when Dad would let it go for weeks. Besides, with so many acres of it, what harm could a little crushing do? we thought.

Mr. Betts estimated the harm done at one-third of his crop lost. Mom explained to us that it would be like a couple of moths making their home in Gretchen's trunk of clothes and destroying one out of every three of her outfits. We were sorry.

We brought our stuff in and put most of it away, and we stayed out of the field until the harvest. When that time came a huge riding lawn mower cut the alfalfa and left it to dry in continuing rows about five feet apart. In our bathing suits and tennis shoes, we played "ocean" in the hay waves until men came with a strange machine to bale it.

We made up for the grief we caused Mr. Betts over the crop damage in the time we saved him by stacking bales into a high-rise. During the construction of our snazzy split-level we were surprised to discover several items we'd missed since the crushing episode. We were able to retrieve, baled with the hay but sticking out enough to grab, a pillow case, some doll clothes, a dish towel, and a set of measuring spoons. We wondered what else might be inside the bales that we couldn't see. We worried about Mr. Betts's cows because still missing was a flashlight, the umbrella, some Tupperware lids, and the Scotch tape.

Of all the farms on our road, the Hathaways' was our favorite. Visiting their barnyard was like going to the state fair. They had every animal Old MacDonald had, plus Kenny (their eight-year-old son and our only playmate).

The baby animals were the most fun, and there was always something newborn. Mrs. Hathaway let us pet the calves and hold the chicks. The piglets were squealing little bundles, awful to cuddle but great to chase and sometimes catch. We loved the goats, especially Bonnie. Her horns were warm, and she had a long beard that made her look masculine. We cut it off with Mom's sewing scissors and she looked better, but Mom was mad because we left the scissors somewhere over at Kenny's, and she had to buy new ones.

The most exciting, yet fearsome, thing about the Hathaways' farm was Ferdinand, the bull. He was pastured in a large sloping meadow with a tree at the bottom. Restrained only by an electric fence, he always seemed tense and irritable as he grazed and watched our every move. When he was preoccupied by his water trough and feed bin at the top corner of the pasture, we dared to enter his domain with a large piece of plywood, a stepladder, and Mr. Hathaway's carpenter apron. We were going to make a treehouse.

The plywood fit perfectly into the branches of the tree. Kenny nailed it into place, while we held the stepladder and watched for Ferdinand. When the plywood was secure we nailed Dad's stepladder to the tree, and the project was complete.

We played matador, draped in Mrs. Hathaway's red bathrobe, Mom's red-checkered tablecloth, and Kenny's devil costume. We could tempt Ferdinand into a raging chase every time.

We would climb the ladder according to age, with the youngest always feeling the heat of Ferdinand's breath on her heels. Safe in the tree, we had to wait until Ferdinand got either hungry or thirsty, but, fortunately, we had provisions up there to hold us for hours.

One day we went over to Kenny's, wrapped in red, anxious for a confrontation, and were disappointed to learn that Ferdinand, the steer, was in the freezer, cut and wrapped.

As much as we loved to go to Kenny's, we spent most of our time on our own property. Our farm had lots of vacant outbuildings. The barn was full of old tools, rusty buggy parts, broken furniture, and things we were told to stay away from. It had a dirt floor and enough stanchions (those cow-holder deals) to secure a dozen milkers. Mice families with batches of little pink babies lived in the wooden feed boxes. Because it was so full of stuff, the barn made a wonderful hideout when we played "outlaw." In "outlaw" the bank was the laurel hedge. Riding up to it on imaginary horses with Mom's silk scarves tied bandit-style around our faces, we'd strip the hedge of its shiny green currency and gallop off to the barn to hide.

There was a loft in there, but no stairway. We rigged up a secret lift. Using some of Dad's rope and the pulley at the top of the barn, we tried to pull ourselves up in a bucket....It didn't work. Still, we vowed never to tell anyone about the secret. We robbed our own house to fix up our hideout. Sneaking food, blankets, and other household goods out there, we made ourselves at home. The barn leaked, ruining several library books and one of our bedspreads, but Mom never knew. She was so happy we were getting along with each other and enjoying our new home that she rarely interrupted us. Once in a while she'd give us the signal (two blasts on the horn of our family's 1953 Buick) to come in.

As infrequent as it was, we hated that sound because it always meant we had to do some housework or get cleaned up. The only other interruption was lunch. Mom was strict about having meals on time. Every day at noon we'd come in, gulp our lunch down as fast as we could, and head out again. We were never very hungry because our farm had so many cherries, plums, apples, pears, and berries, and we were constantly robbing the trees or raiding the garden and taking the grub back to our hideout in the barn.

Connected to the barn was a little pigless shed with an attached pen. It had a regular door for the farmer to go in and a courtesy door to allow the pigs to move freely from their house out into the fresh air and mud.

We pilfered the garage for paint and remodeling tools and turned the pighouse into a clubhouse. We boarded up the courtesy door with a piece of plywood and installed a padlock on the farmer's entrance for security. We took an ironed tablecloth from the linen closet, dishes from the cupboard, and the cardtable and folding chairs from the utility room and set up housekeeping. We found an old can of tar in the barn and smeared it on the roof with a toilet brush to fill up the cracks. It oozed through, damaging Mom's tablecloth and a couple of turquoise scatter rugs we'd borrowed from the bathroom on our trip in to get the brush.

From inside the clubhouse we cut an opening into the barn with Dad's hacksaw. Once inside the barn, we covered the hole with an old backless phonograph cabinet that had a Victrola on top and a place for records below. The mahogany doors on the cabinet concealed our secret passage. Unlike the unsuccessful pulley rope and bucket affair, this idea really worked.

We loved it when people came to visit and brought their kids. We'd play hide-and-seek with them, making sure we were seen going into the barn. With a thirty-second lead time, we could enter the padlocked clubhouse through the record player and ditch even the cleverest visitor. Once inside our club, we'd replace the sawed-off board and bask in our ingenuity. When we lost the key to the padlock, the record player was our only doorway. Unfortunately, the table and chairs were too large to fit through the Victrola and remained entombed in the pighouse forever. It was just as well; the roof-patching job failed to stop the rain, and the set was permanently warped and rusted.

We did more in the clubhouse than hide; we dabbled in private enterprise. We thought up ways to make money and planned how we'd spend it. We allowed Kenny Hathaway to join the club for a sizable initiation fee and weekly dues. We caught crawdads and sold them; cut flowers from Mom's garden and made corsages and sold them; picked berries, baked cookies, brownies, and cup cakes and sold them; wrote, produced, and directed three-person extravaganzas and sold tickets to them; put out a weekly newspaper about the Hathaways and Mom and Dad and sold subscriptions to it; and promoted an insect fair complete with thirty-four different varieties of bugs, worms, and snakes and charged admission to it. The consumers consisted of the four farm families on our rural road.

Summers were wonderful, but winters had their own special delights. When the snow came, the fields became our ski resort. We strapped Mom's turkey roaster to Dad's old wooden skis and took turns racing down the hill like beginning skiers who hadn't learned how to snowplow. We built igloos (and furnished them), made snowmen (and dressed them), and spent part of our time in the house.

Our two-story house was more than a century old. It was one of those "don't judge a book by its cover" houses. On the outside it looked like every other two-story farmhouse with a porch, but on the inside it was like something out of *House Beautiful*.

The main floor had been renovated by the previous owner. A massive rock fireplace dominated the thirty-foot living room, where floor-to-ceiling windows overlooked a sweeping view of the steep canyon below. The large country kitchen had been redesigned by a home economist who had considered every aspect of efficiency without altering any of its original charm. There was a pass-through counter into the formal dining room, where French doors opened onto a shady veranda. During the remodeling the door to the upstairs was removed, and a new L-shaped oak staircase was put in. The wall separating it from the hallway was opened up with handcrafted shelves of rich woods and glass.

At the landing a generous opening was cut out of the narrow wall and a leaded glass window was set in. The beveled window, finished with a fine oak casing, allowed a glimpse of the formal dining room beyond. The remaining wall leading up the stairs was paneled in oak. Visitors were impressed with what they could see, but with no light in the stairwell, no one knew that the elegance ended at the top of the stairs, where a piece of plywood and an old sleeping bag covered the opening.

The upstairs had never been finished. There were no ceilings or walls, only exposed rafters and studs. There was no heat and no plumbing, but it was a perfect place to make a nest. We begged to move up there.

After a lengthy winter discussion, Mom and Dad agreed to let us move on a trial basis, as soon as the weather got warmer. We made our plans, and when spring came, we packed our things and made the move.

There were three roughed-in rooms on the second floor, and we had the whole place to ourselves. Mom never came up there to check, because it was too hard to crawl through the sleeping-bagged doorway. Besides, she spent too much of her time scrubbing, polishing, and vacuuming the main floor to have any concern for the unfinished upstairs. She left it to us and assumed we had the same natural desire for order she had.

"How does your room look?"

"Fine!"

"Great!"

We were free to move from one creative project to another, never putting anything away. We made a hammock out of a sheet and some of Mom's clothesline. We tied the line to the sheet at two corners and hitched it to the rafters. It was unruly but challenging. We strung up a captain's chair, too. It made a great swing but threatened to snap a rafter when we swung double.

We spent a lot of our time in our room. We avoided having to go downstairs, because when Mom would see us, she'd think of things for us to do...like housework. We invented ways to stay self-contained upstairs. Having no bathroom up there posed a problem. The thought of using a chamber pot disgusted us. We opted for the windowsill above the dining room, facing the secluded canyon. Sitting on the edge with our feet outside the window, we watched the trickle as it flowed down the mossy sloping roof, out of sight. Our parents never knew. We were always careful never to use the sill facilities during a dinner party.

Years later, when Dad installed a TV antenna on the roof, he was puzzled by the two distinct paths carved out of the green moss. He told Mom that it was strange that the moss was only dead in two strips. He said it looked like somebody had poured a couple of bottles of weed-killer out the window and let it run off the roof. He never figured it out.

To avoid having Mom come up to our room, we told Kenny never to come to the front door when he wanted us to play. It was too risky. She might come to get us and discover the rat's nest we called home. (She had no idea how many of her dishes were up there, how much laundry was under the bed, or how much paper and garbage littered the floor.)

Our invention to get around Mom and talk to Kenny required the use of the garden hose. We sneaked it upstairs and it dripped, leaving a trail from the garage to our room. We ran the hose down the side of the house from a hole we made in the siding. We taped Mom's funnel to the end upstairs and instructed Kenny to speak into the end on the grass when he wanted us to come out and play.

We had seven wonderful years to revel in our disorganized natures. In our messy domain we developed housekeeping standards that would follow us throughout much of our adult life. The farm was a great place to grow up and will always be the source of our fondest childhood memories. The summer before we started junior high and high school we moved to a stylish three-bedroom brick house, less than a mile away.

When moving day arrived, Mom went upstairs to our room to help us organize our packing, and the clutter hit the fan. Confronted by the evidence, she had to admit that she was the mother of two deeply rooted slobs. There was about to be a domestic revolution. For one thing, the new floor plan put us in separate bedrooms, with Mom and Dad's room in between. Under our mother's constant surveillance we would feel the pressure of involuntary reform.

Three

The Jerk and the Graduate–From Pam

The tension that developed from the new floor plan was not the only problem. My relationship with Peggy was beginning to deteriorate. I've seen the same sort of thing happen with my own children as one passed from childhood to adolescence, leaving the other one behind. I was sixteen and Peggy was only eleven when we moved to the brick house. The age difference between us was the same as it had been when she was an infant and I was five; but the gap was now too wide for us to be playmates, and our friendship dissolved. We had turned into two people with absolutely nothing in common. I was wearing a bra and nylons, while she wore an undershirt and knee-highs. I was driving a car; she was Schwinn-bound. I was cheerleading; Peggy was jumping rope. I was dressing up for dates, while she was dressing up the cats in doll clothes. We fought about everything: whose turn it was to do the dishes, who had left the milk out, whose fault it was that we were late, and on and on and on.

It seemed to me that overnight Peggy had become a jerk.

She stared at people, asked stupid questions, and wiped her nose on her sleeve. She embarrassed me constantly. One time she sat in the middle of the waiting room at ballet school and cleaned the junk out from between her toes, in front of all the parents and some of my ballerina friends. Once she came out of Mom and Dad's bedroom, wearing Dad's athletic supporter like a halter top. She asked how the thing was supposed to fit. I was humiliated because Dennis Rady, one of my classmates, had come over to visit me and witnessed the whole thing.

She got into all my private stuff. She played with my makeup, drenched herself in my Evening in Paris, blasted her braids with my Spray Net, and read my personal notes. She followed me and copied everything I did; and if she wasn't tattling on me, she was mocking me. She was always too loud and she could never sit still. In church she would sing off-key on purpose, and when she'd whistle, spit flew everywhere. She could make herself look so pathetic that my dates would invite her to go with us. When I got my driver's license, Mom and Dad made me take her with me almost everywhere I went. (They felt sorry for her, moping around when I went someplace without her.)

I was so grateful to be in school. I had six blissful hours each day, free of my obnoxious little sibling. I loved high school. It was like one continuous social gathering. I gossiped, giggled, flirted, and procrastinated. My grades were okay but could have been much better if I had been organized. I never turned anything in when it was due. I was always tardy, and I didn't allow time for homework.

I still have term-paper dreams where my classmates pass forward thick volumes of research in colored folders, while I try to recall the assignment. Then there's the recurring nightmare where I plead with Mr. Furno for a book-report extension.

I took advantage of the fact that my last name was Young. Oral reports were usually presented alphabetically, allowing me an additional three days to write mine. When the presentation order was reversed, however, Vicki Zoller was the only person who stood between me and fate.

My weekends were taken up by dances, parties, sports

events, hamburgers, french fries, Cokes, and cleaning up my room, which was one of the battlegrounds for Mom and me. Every Saturday I was forced to clean it up or stay there all weekend.

My sewing created the same kind of chaos that the hammock, hose, and captain's-chair chaos had at the farmhouse. The machine was always out; the ironing board was always up; the iron was always on; and pins, threads, scraps and patterns were everywhere. I made all of my own clothes. (If our Singer had had a mileage meter, I know that by the time I got married I'd have stitched myself around the world.)

I fashioned my garments with the skill of a tailor, but nothing was ever finished. My motto was, "If it doesn't show . . . don't sew." It was a wise axiom, I reasoned. Why hem a blouse when it would be tucked into a skirt? Why sew a button on a waistband when you could wear a belt? Why put a hook and eye anywhere when a safety pin would work? I didn't stay-stitch, baste, preshrink, mark, or interface unless it was to earn an A in Home Ec.

I was a marathon seamstress. I could start sewing early in the morning and almost sew myself to sleep. On those red-eye sew-a-thons, I'd never come out to eat. My room was littered with chicken bones, apple cores, pop bottles, and candy wrappers. The only thing that would make me quit once I was on a "sew" would be a stupid mistake like stitching a collar into an armhole or putting a zipper in upside down. Then I'd realize I was too tired to rip it out and do it right, so I'd go to bed.

My senior year flew by, but academically I crawled my way through college prep courses to a cap and gown. Mom made sure that I had earned credits in all the right classes. I was anxious to go away with my friends to a university, but it didn't happen. After graduation I realized that, unlike my friends, I hadn't saved any money for college.

I tried to get a job when school was out, but I'd waited too long. My college-bound friends had been working every summer for four years, and they had sizable amounts put away to help with their tuition. I ended up in a small junior college that was still in its infancy.

I graduated two years later with a thousand other students who were there only because they couldn't go anyplace else. With an A.A. degree, I was once again faced with the fact that I still didn't have enough money to go away to school. I should have tried for a grant or a student loan, but I waited too long to fill out the papers.

Disappointed again, I got married in the fall, after a turbulent yet passionate courtship. When I met my husband-to-be, the first thing I thought was that he looked like Wally Cleaver. I loved Wally; I thought he was darling, and I figured anyone who looked like him would be a perfect date.

Our dates were anything but perfect. We fought about everything. We embarrassed each other. He was harsh with me; I sulked and cried. He was insulting and tactless; I was retaliatory and stubborn. For every negative trait I displayed, he showed me one of his own. We brought out the worst in each other on every date.

If we went to dances, we fought over where to park the car, what door to go in, and who had the tickets, when it was time to leave, and how to get to the place to eat afterward.

If we double-dated, we inevitably caused the other couple to end up picking their fingernails as they tried to ignore our confrontations. Spiritually, emotionally, and intellectually we were incompatible.

At the expense of sounding as love-crazed as the cartoon skunk Pepe Le Pew, who is so desperate for romance that he courts a black cat with a bit of white on its back, I have to admit that I wanted romance.

At eighteen I hadn't learned the difference between passion and love. In my optimism I thought the turbulence would dissolve with time. Time only threw us deeper into the backseat of his 1949 Ford. By the time I was twenty none of the problems between us had changed, but he still looked like Wally Cleaver.

In *Sidetracked Home Executives* (the first book I wrote with my sister), I told about my fifteen-year marriage and eventual divorce. Rather than dredge up the details of a stormy decade, I'll summarize the entire affair by saying the marriage was doomed from the courtship.

As Peggy grew up and the gap closed again, I thought about how things might have been different if I had been patient enough to wait for her to join me in adulthood. Maybe we could have rented some kind of an apartment and explored the grown-up world together as we had explored the farm.

But by the time she graduated from high school, I was expecting my first child. The messes I had made throughout my youth were nothing compared to the pigpen I created as a homemaker with three babies.

Four

The Snit and the Courtship–From Peggy

Since the information has already been given by my *older* sister that she was sixteen and I was eleven when we moved to the brick house, I won't make a fool of myself by repeating it. I actually enjoyed reading her version of our time together as children, even if it was a bit slanderous. As usual, the younger sister has had to wait for her turn to speak; however, I rather enjoy having the last word.

Pam had become an arrogant snit. Impressed with her pompoms, perfume, and petticoats, she thought she was "it." For every weird person I may have looked at on the street, she spent equal time staring at herself in the mirror. When she practiced cheerleading she watched her reflection in the big living room window. She adjusted the rearview mirror so that she could see her face. She looked at herself in spoons, hubcaps, pie plates, store windows, and china washed in Joy. She was constantly primping, plucking, posing, and pampering herself.

In my own defense I'd like to say that I may have gotten into her makeup from time to time, but I used her Evening in Paris only once (when I spilled it on my pajamas and tossed all night with an upset stomach). The Spray Net I confess to using frequently. (My hair never has had much body and the lacquer made it behave.)

The deal about wiping my nose on my sleeves, I admit. Cleaning between my toes in public, I deny. The athletic supporter was unfortunate for both of us and remains an embarrassment even now.

The trouble wasn't so much that I wanted to get into her teenage stuff as it was that I wanted to play with the toys she had outgrown. They remained in an abandoned pile in the back of her closet, waiting for her to decide to give them up. She never did. (In fact, Gretchen is probably stashed somewhere in the back of one of her closets to this day.)

Pam always took advantage of her seniority and my gullibility. Once she told me that if I made her bed for two weeks, she would take me to Fairyland. (She had been there numerous times and always returned to tell of the great Root Beer Ocean, lollipop trees, cotton candy clouds, and, of course, the wise and powerful Genie.) I wasn't quite sure how long two weeks was, but I knew I had been making her bed for a long time with no trip. She gave me some phony story that it was taking extra time for the Genie to approve my visit. I threatened to tell. She was forced into making the arrangements.

We went into the bathroom. Instructing me to kneel down on the throw rug in front of the tub, she sprinkled me and the rug with Mom's talcum powder, which had some magic ingredient that would give us the power to fly. She told me to inchworm my way, with the rug, out of the bathroom and down the hall on the hardwood floor as fast as I could. If I did it right, she said, I would gain enough speed to take off on the magic carpet and fly through the patio doors toward Fairyland. Somehow I couldn't get up enough speed.

I was ten years old when I discovered that M&M's came in different colors. We bought a color television set, and during a commercial, I watched a little chocolate M&M walk out on a diving board, jackknife into a pool, and pull himself out at the other end . . . green! Until that time I had only seen the dark brown ones. Just as she was in charge of our clubhouse dues, Pam also always handled the disbursement of candy. I was told to open my hands and close my eyes and I would get a nice surprise. I was always thrilled to open my eyes and find my treat. I never questioned the honesty of my benefactor. I gratefully accepted whatever she gave me, without paying attention to what she kept for herself. (Someday I'm going to buy a little bag of M&M's and count how many brown ones there are compared to the number of colored ones. I have a feeling it was another Genie deal.)

I was eleven years old when I started junior high school. Those of us who lived out in the country had to ride the bus to school in town. It was hard for me. In grade school I had always walked, adjusting my pace so that I could get to the flagpole when the bell rang. Although some mornings I had to run, I was rarely counted tardy. Catching the bus was a concept I couldn't quite absorb. For the first few weeks I missed the bus every morning and had to ride into town with Dad. He drove me to school in his big Standard Oil truck. The brakes were loud, and I didn't like it when we'd pull up in front of the school and screech to a stop in front of my peers. I felt self-conscious parachuting out of the truck in my billowy skirts and starched petticoats. There was no dainty way to exit that vehicle.

One day in the third week of school, as I leaped out of the truck, I caught the safety-pinned hem of my full skirt on Dad's fire extinguisher and ripped the gathers away from the waistband, exposing my underwear to a gawking group of classmates. I made the decision that day never to miss the bus again. I figured out a pace that would get me to my stop at the same time the bus got there. Although on many mornings I loped alongside it like a car-chasing dog, I was never left behind.

The junior high school was so much bigger than Salmon Creek Elementary. I was confused for weeks. (I still have locker dreams where I can't tell which one is mine, and when I do find it, I can't remember the combination.) It was hard for me to get used to calling recess P.E., and I kept referring to the sports field as the playground. There were so many things to remember: schedules, teachers' names, and where my classes were.

Having an older sister lay the path for me was great. My teachers all liked Pam and linked us through our blue eyes and our last name. . . . I was "in."

I can remember looking over the city boys and singling out Danny Jones and his friend Mike Tesdahl. I thought they were both very cute. Their homeroom was next to mine, so we passed in the halls a lot. My locker was near theirs, and we had the same lunch period. I flirted whenever I saw them, and they seemed to respond.

Pam was in high school by the time I started junior high. I'd watched her go to dances for four years, and when it was announced that there would be a Get-Acquainted Dance the next Friday at 7:00 P.M., I was more than ready. I went home and told Mom, who said I should figure out what to wear and get it all ready early. I thought that sounded like a great idea; but procrastination had already become a very strong force in my life, and I didn't follow through.

At 5:00 P.M. on Friday I was frantically pawing through my closet, trying to find something wonderful to wear. I'd tried on five or six clown combinations and was almost in tears when Mom came in and suggested that we ask Pam if we could look in her closet for something. We found a dress on the floor in there that looked lovely after Mom pressed it and put it on a hanger. (Behind Mom's back, I was forced to relinquish two weeks allowance to my sister for the use of her property.) The dress was navy blue taffeta with a scooped neckline and a nice wide cummerbund. With a few cleverly hidden pieces of masking tape and a couple of quick passes through the sewing machine, it was perfect.

I shed my undershirt for the first time and wore a tiny bra, especially for the dance. I was a vision; I whirled around the bedroom like Cinderella. The taffeta rustled provocatively, but something about the look was off.

"You're too flat," Pam said.

"Even with my bra?"

"Yeah. You look like Grandpa McLaughlin."

"Thanks a lot!"

"Here. Stuff these in there." She handed me some wadded-up stockings. They were just what the dress needed. I felt like a real woman.

At the dance I stood with my girlfriends and chatted as if I were merely there to hear the music and visit, but really I was scouring the gym in search of Danny and Mike. I spotted them in a group of boys using the same chatting technique that I was.

Halfway through the evening, just as I was about all gossiped out, Danny came up and asked me to dance. We were the same height. It was the first time either of us had danced with a member of the opposite sex. My heart was flying and I forgot to breathe as we took one step forward, two steps back, and Frankensteined our way past the first basketball hoop. Finally I took a shaky breath, and the pungent smell of rancid Old Spice cleared my sinuses. We were at the second hoop when he spoke.

"Mike wants to know if you'll go with him."

"Where?"

"Steady."

"Oh . . . steady . . . right . . . sure." I was thrilled.

The dance ended and Danny returned me to my friends and rejoined Mike. I told Kathy Nevin I was going steady and she loved the idea.

"You and Danny make a darling couple," she said.

"No, I'm going with Mike!" I was about to explain when Mike came over and asked me to dance. That familiar piercing scent of Old Spice made my eyes water. Again we one-stepped forward and two-stepped back in the same style that had taken me backward around the gym the song before; only this time, because of a faster tempo, we were able to make four times as many revolutions.

I found out later that Mike had gone home with Danny after school that day so they could get ready for the dance together. Mike's mom had bought him a sport coat a couple of sizes too big so he could wear it for more than just one year. Danny's coat was too big too. Like my dress, it was a hand-me-down. Mrs. Jones had given the boys a quick dance lesson before dinner. She told them to concentrate on the basic "two-step" and go for style later, since they were doing well not to trip over the pattern in the carpet. When they were all ready for the dance, they were both victims of an overdose of Mr. Jones's decanted after-shave.

At the end of the song Mike and I were winded. While walking me back to my side of the gym, he said, "What's that on your dress?" I jerked my neck to my chest to see what he was looking at and with horror I realized I'd danced a stocking right out of my bra! "Darn lining!" I said as I stuffed it back in place.

Mike and I went steady for the next six years. In high school we double-dated all the time with Danny and his various girlfriends. I was never ready when the boys would come to pick me up. They'd have to visit with Mom and Dad while I dressed and put my makeup on. By the time we were seniors, my parents had enjoyed many hours of conversation with them; and although they liked both boys, I learned later that they hoped somehow Danny and I would get together.

When we were in the seventh grade Danny and I were eye to eye, but by graduation he had grown into a handsome 6'2" string bean. He had a beautiful singing voice (he still does), and at the commencement exercises he stood alone on the stage before a huge audience and sang "The Impossible Dream." As I watched and listened to him, I felt a strong attachment that transcended friendship. I remember thinking that I should look away before someone saw how I was looking at him, but my eyes refused to move.

I was glad when the song was over and the loud clapping ended my trance. I told myself silently, *Of course your heart is pounding . . . he's your friend . . . your brother almost, and you're nervous for him.* I reasoned with myself that it was only natural that there would be some attraction there; he had appealed to me from the very beginning. I refused to admit that what I felt was anything more than deep admiration for a dear friend, enhanced by a moving rendition of a popular song. But the feeling was different and I knew it. I put it aside.

Mike went away to West Point. I enrolled at the junior college in our town (the same one Pam had to go to . . . for the same reasons). Danny wasn't sure what he wanted to do. He had won a music scholarship to a state college in eastern Washington but had turned it down. He didn't feel right about taking it. (He told me he thought it would be wrong to accept a scholarship for his voice when he didn't want a career in music.) He was also being influenced by the six o'clock news. The Vietnam War was escalating, and he was entertaining some heavy John Wayne fantasies. Aside from the movies, he felt a strong patriotic responsibility to help end the war. He decided to enroll for one quarter in the same local college I was going to attend. It would give him some time to think and decide what to do next.

It was fun having a guy as my best friend. I enjoyed hearing about the way he saw things differently from me. He could give me the male viewpoint, and I could give him advice about his girlfriends.

We talked between classes in his car. (We couldn't sit in my car because it was too full of junk, and it smelled as if something had crawled under the seat and passed away.) Danny's car was immaculate. It was a silver 1960 Comet. He washed and waxed it every Saturday and kept the inside showroom-clean. It was a joy to ride in. The little evergreen tree hanging from the rearview mirror emitted the gentle aroma of pine needles. (I didn't have a rearview mirror. . . . It fell off one summer, so I used my makeup mirror whenever I needed to back up.)

His ashtrays were clean enough to eat from, and he had a tasteful litter bag, which he kept empty. There were mushrooms growing in my car, not edible ones, but the orange kind that hook on to tree trunks. My trunk leaked (Dad had the best intentions, but he never got around to sealing it), and the moisture seeped into the car's interior, providing optimum conditions for fungus growth on the backseat. Trash was everywhere. I didn't have a litter bag. In fact, my whole car was like one big litterbox on wheels.

I found myself eager for classes to let out so that I could meet Danny and we could talk. Our values in life were the same. When we discussed marriage (not ours, of course), he told me that when he married it would have to be for life. I agreed. We talked about how we'd raise children. Mine would be nurtured with a combination of love and discipline. His would be, too. We shared our deepest thoughts and confidences. Although we attended different churches, we both had the same faith. Sometimes we would talk ourselves right through the next class.

In October I got an "I want to date other girls" letter from Mike. I was heartbroken and felt as if I'd been dumped. I cried in Danny's car until his windows fogged up from all the humidity. He stopped me from wiping his windshield with my hand. Taking a cloth and spray cleaner from the glove compartment, he did the windows while we discussed my dilemma. He told me I should start going out myself.

"I've been out of circulation for six years. . . . Who'd ask me out?" I wailed.

"I'll take you out. Guys will see you dating, and they'll know you're available," he said.

We decided to go to the game together that night. He said he'd pick me up at 6:30. I skipped my next class and went straight to the mall for a new outfit. When I got home I took a bubble bath, did my nails, and rolled my hair up with Dippity Doo. Mom asked me where I was going. I told her Danny was taking me to the football game. She saw the new clothes, smelled my perfume, noticed my painted nails, and accused me of going to a lot of trouble for a brother. I denied it.

At 6:29 the doorbell rang. Danny visited with Mom and Dad while I redid my nails. (I had wrecked the new polish attaching my garters.)

We had a wonderful time at the game. The next day we skipped classes and played golf. Every day I looked forward to going to school. When we were apart, I thought of things I wanted to tell him. I loved Danny's sense of humor and I respected his opinion about everything.

In the next few weeks there were car picnics, long walks, movies, and lots of laughs. As genuine friends, we were able to be ourselves. We were free from playing any of the ego games dating couples often play.

The holidays were approaching. Danny took me Christmas shopping. It was magic. Helping me through the crowd of people, he took my hand, but when we got out of the tangle of shoppers, he didn't let go. When we said good night at my front door, Danny kissed me. I felt that old junior high, first-dance feeling, except that we weren't kids anymore.

"I think I'm falling in love with you," he said.

"When do you think you'll know?" I asked.

"I've loved you since the seventh grade, if you want to know the truth."

"I love you, too."

It was the first time we'd admitted that we were in love, but there were a few problems.

The quarter was over, and Danny had to decide what he was going to do. The army recruiter was tempting him with a full-color leaflet showing the glamorous life of a private. The busy week of the pamphlet's strong, handsome enlistee included pictures of him stretched out on a beach towel in Honolulu next to a bikinied native, later enjoying champagne and T-bones at a candlelit table for two, and laughing after hours with his buddies at a disco. There were shots of him seated at the helm of a shiny new tank (riding in a parade) and in the lab, sharing a microscope with an intelligent-looking brunette technician. On the last page of the brochure Private Doe was seen standing at attention, in full dress uniform, proudly saluting the American flag.

Based on the color snapshots, it appeared that the private's life was one of toasting, tasting, touching, testing, tanning, and traveling; and to an eighteen-year-old it looked great.

Mike added more glory to the military setting when he came home on Christmas leave from West Point and urged Danny to join the Army team. He also told him that he was still in love with me and intended to pick up where he'd left off and patch things up. Danny had thought that because of the breakup letter Mike didn't care anymore; suddenly our romance looked like a betrayal of friendship.

There was no denying that I had been in love with Mike. Danny knew it, Mike knew it, and I knew it. I was flattered that he wanted me back, and I still felt a twinge when I saw him; but I also loved Danny. It was an awful time of confusion and mingled emotions. One day I went out with Mike in the afternoon and had a date with Danny that evening. They passed each other coming and going.

When I thought about the two of them, I had to admit that they were both really special men; but when I thought about which one I couldn't bear to lose, it was clearly Danny.

On January 3 I got a phone call. It was Danny. "I just wanted to say good-bye," he said.

"Where are you?"

"Over at the airport. . . . I enlisted last week and I leave in an hour."

"Wait . . . Don't go. I'll be right there!"

In tears, I told my dad, and he said he and Mom would drive me in their car (mine was out of gas). On the way I told them that I was in love with Danny and that I felt I was losing him because of Mike. Dad said Danny probably wanted to give things a little time and distance.

It seemed unfair. Just when I'd made up my mind that I wanted him, Danny went for the brochure and joined the Army. I guess he thought Mike and I would get back together if he left us alone. I tried to persuade him that it was over between Mike and me, but it hadn't been that long since I had fogged up his windows over Mike, and he thought it was one of those rebound deals.

I saw him standing by the gate. People were already starting to board the plane. We ran into each other's arms as if we were doing a commercial for Wind Song cologne.

"I love you!" I said.

"You need to be sure."

"I am."

"I've gotta go."

"Can't you say you enlisted by mistake and you want to take it back?"

"I'll write to you. . . ."

He was gone. I couldn't do anything to stop him or change his mind. The proof that I loved him would have to come with time.

I told Mike that I was in love with Danny. It shouldn't have been hard for him to see why . . . he loved Danny, too; but he was stunned.

For months Danny and I wrote to each other and Mike wrote to me, but I didn't answer his letters.

When Danny came home on leave in February the next year, he looked more wonderful to me than ever. He had a maturity that I hadn't seen before.

Evidently the reality of boot camp, drill sergeants, and airborne school had aged him. There had been no steaks and champagne. Instead, he'd washed tanks, slept in dirt, eaten C rations, folded parachutes, and said "Yes, sir!" for the last year, and he knew the worst part was yet to come.

For the first time he seemed to know exactly what he wanted. He asked me to marry him. . . . I said yes, and even though we knew he would be going to Vietnam soon, we became engaged.

I called Kathy Nevin to ask her to be in the wedding. "Guess what, Kathy. . . . I'm getting married!"

She loved the idea. "You and Mike make a great couple."

"No, I'm marrying Danny!" (It took some explaining.)

We were only nineteen and our parents had to go to the courthouse and sign so that we could get a marriage license. (I still don't understand why Danny could join the Army without his parents' consent but couldn't get married on his own.)

On May 13 we were married. Danny went to Vietnam two weeks later with the 173rd Airborne Division as a paratrooper. We spent those first thirteen months of marriage in awful separation and the next four years in terrible arguments over the one wedge between us: my disorganization.

PART FOUR

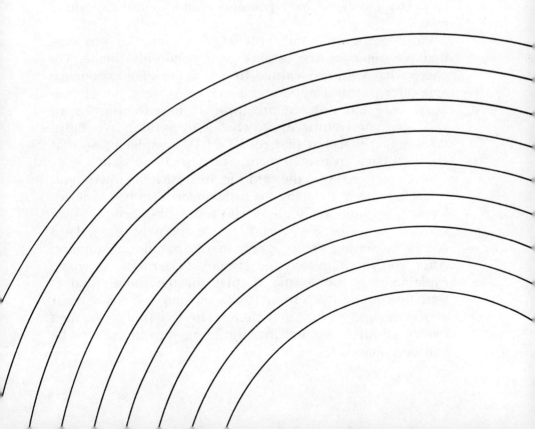

In Part IV we have divided the twelve months of the year between us and will take turns sharing a story that illustrates the monthly theme—an aspect of life that we consider vital to happiness.

Of course, like everyone, we have both had meaningful experiences in all these twelve areas. Unfortunately, if each of us spilled her stories, this book would be too thick. As it is, some of the chapters are longer than others because of the depth of the subject.

Many of our experiences have been almost too painful, private, or difficult to relate. Writing about them brought back tears we thought had long since dried. Others were really funny, and recalling them made us laugh all over again. All of our stories come from the depths of our hearts; and we hope that by exposing our vulnerability we will help you face your own personal challenges in a positive way.

We begin each month with special quotes or proverbs that we think are the essence of the monthly theme. We share what we have learned from our personal experience and offer practical applications for you, using the Happiness File. A month-by-month approach to self-improvement will keep you from trying to change everything overnight. We suggest that you first read Part IV completely, so that you will have an overall picture of what lies ahead.

After you've set up the card file, turn back to January and begin the system by doing the assignments Pam has outlined. January is traditionally the month for starting over, and we wanted you to have a second chance at a new year even if you're beginning the program in the middle of summer. After you've completed the January "clearing" (as we've explained), go on to the chapter for the month that is actually coming up. Proceed with our suggestions at your own pace, and be sure to remember to have fun! In the next twelve months we trust that the improvements you make will be remarkable.

One

January–Starting Over
–From Pam

"Regret for time wasted can become a power for good in the time that remains. And the time that remains is time enough, if we will only stop the waste and the idle, useless regretting."

—ARTHUR BRISBANE

January is traditionally a month of fresh starts. It's supposed to be the time to make New Year's resolutions, but before Peggy and I developed the Happiness File, I always found myself thinking about resolutions when it was 11:55 P.M. and I was "Auld Lang Syning" my way into the new year, pumping my face with fattening party food, and faithfully clinging to my wish to lose weight.

I always used to think that the great moment when the new year started was such a big deal. I liked to call the "time lady" so that I could get the clock in the kitchen set exactly right. Invariably some time hog would tie up her line and I'd get a busy signal.

As the final countdown proceeded I'd feel, for just a

second, a oneness with everyone who had that starting-over feeling. It was nice to think that men and women everywhere were celebrating New Year's Eve and another chance to do better.

But New Year's Day was *never* a good day for me to start over. I always slept in; and when I got up, I'd polish off the rest of the mixed nuts, smoked oysters, cocktail rye, and California dip. Spending most of the afternoon in my bathrobe, I'd mentally take down the Christmas tree (which threatened to become a holiday torch) and watch the Rose Parade on television. With the bowl games as background noise for my good intentions, I'd piddle away the rest of the day, chipping at the horrendous party mess in the kitchen. By nighttime I'd have thought a lot about making some resolutions, but usually I would feel that it was too late, because I was supposed to have had them ready the night before.

If I'd only taken the time to look up the word *resolution* in the dictionary, I would have seen why I was never successful with it. Aside from "good intent" (I've always had great intentions), resolution, according to Webster, is "the act or process of reducing to simpler form; as the act of analyzing a complex notion into simpler ones." When it's put that way it's obvious why I shied away from that New Year's Eve tradition.

Genetically disorganized people don't own brains that can automatically break large jobs into smaller ones, much less convert notions of self-improvement into steps of action. The Happiness File is the tool that took all of my projects, problems, dreams, and plans and reduced them to manageable parts. If you follow this plan, you will be making resolutions all year long. Your growth will be gradual as you break down problems and build on your desires, step-by-step.

Take a moment and look at the subjects we will be focusing on throughout the next year: February—Love and Romance; March—Dreams; April—Prosperity; May—Health and Beauty; June—Parents and Kids; July—Freedom; August—Appreciation; September—Work; October—Laughter; November—Hospitality, Friendship, and Giving; December—

Faith. Make out a white 3x5 card with the monthly themes (see example below), and tape it in the lid of your card-file along with the Year-at-a-Glance calendar. We have chosen the subjects that have meant the most to us, and chances are you will be interested in several of those areas, too.

We've permanently put away the old idea of making a bunch of resolutions in January. Instead, we use this month to reflect on last year and clear up any unfinished business, so that we are free to move forward, unencumbered by the past. You'll be able to take your brand-new calendar with its 365 blank squares and start this new year with a feeling of freedom.

To make the greatest progress in the months and years ahead, you will probably have some clearing up to do. Maybe you'll need to apologize to someone, write a letter that's long overdue, mend a broken friendship, send a baby gift before the kid graduates from high school, forgive an enemy; return library books, borrowed dishes, a lawn mower, or tools; keep a promise, clear up a misunderstanding, or straighten out your finances.

MONTHLY THEME CARD

January—Starting Over
February—Love and Romance
March—Dreams
April—Prosperity
May—Health and Beauty
June—Parents and Kids
July—Freedom
August—Appreciation
September—Work
October—Laughter
November—Hospitality,
    Friendship, and Giving
December—Faith

This is the perfect time to take advantage of hindsight. Look honestly at last year's dirty, dog-eared, and tattered calendar, and think about how you would have liked things to be different. Do you wish you had taken more free time? Could you have been more organized? More patient? More loving? Is there more you wish you had said to someone you loved who has passed away? How did you feel physically during this last year? Did you feel fat? Did you talk about anyone behind his or her back? Did you laugh a lot? Did you spend much time worrying? How often did you get angry? How much fresh air did you get? How many new friends did you make? How much TV did you watch? How many books did you read? Ask your own questions. Write them in your notebook in the "Clearing" section and answer them. (Be sure to date your thoughts.)

If you feel that there is a lot you would like to have changed last year, don't get discouraged. Mary Pickford said, "If you have made mistakes, even serious ones, there is always another chance for you. What we call failure is not the falling down but the staying down." Let last year's calendar remind you of the unfinished business you want to attend to. Make a list in your notebook (be sure to date it), and then assign a priority to each item. Once something has a priority, you can decide whether you will take action now or later.

In Part II we had you write down everything that was on your mind. We told you to put all the future naggers in the months section of the Happiness File, and all the past gnats in January. Take them out of the January divider and decide, right now, what to do about them. (See an example of a list of past gnats on page 123). You will notice that each item has an A, B, or C priority, according to its urgency. The As would be the gnats that are flying around your head daily. Take them off the list and put them on the Immediate Action Card that you rotate daily among the Monday through Sunday dividers in the cardfile. This will delegate action within the next week.

The Bs are things to take care of within the next six months. Put them on 3x5 scratch paper and file them in whatever month you decide you will be taking action. The

```
September 17, 1982
Return Dee Anne's broiler ------A Immediate Action Card

Send a thank-you to Gail
   Dietrich --------------------------A Immediate Action Card

Find Gail's address on back
   of business card ---------------A Immediate Action Card

Write letters to:*
   Grandma Dot--------------------A Immediate Action Card
   Aunt Vi ----------------------------B March
   Bernice ----------------------------B April
   Al--------------------------------------C August
   Judy—Piano---------------------A Immediate Action Card

Call:
   Carole------------------------------A Immediate Action Card
   Mr. Tanner-------------------------C June
   Dianna ------------------------------B February

Return library books ------------A Immediate Action Card

Return Ruth's punch bowl --------C June

Talk to Dave-------------------------B May
```

Cs have a low priority for action, but you do intend to do something with them before the end of the year.

Remember, we didn't say you had to do everything all at once. Clearing up your past may take months or even years. The important thing is that you've gotten all that unfinished business out of your head and into your cardfile,

---

*Chapter Eleven, November—Hospitality, Friendship, and Giving, will help you get the people you care about into the Happiness File so that you can write or call on a regular basis.

where you will take action on it, if not now, then eventually.

You might wonder about Ruth not getting her punch bowl back until June, or Al not getting a letter until August. In our book on how to organize your housework, we wrote about jobs piling up. To avoid that, we took the cards for any jobs we couldn't get to on any particular day and filed them into the future, according to their frequency. A weekly task was filed a week away, as if we'd done the job. We did the same thing for a monthly job. Our credo, "File it and forget it," did not allow us to neglect a task, but to table the work appropriately. Justifying that postponement, we admitted that if we hadn't done the job in eight years, what harm would waiting another week or month do? Ruth hadn't seen her punch bowl in four years, so what was another six months going to matter? I thought. (She probably had forgotten who had it, anyway.) Al hadn't had a letter in seventeen years! Eight more months wouldn't alter the course of his life. On the other hand, Judy and the piano had become an A priority, a loose end that needed my immediate attention. Judy, my neighbor, had a piano for sale. I had told her I'd buy it in October, as soon as I had the money. When October came and the money didn't, I was embarrassed. I avoided her scrupulously. As the months passed she was one of those gnats in my mind. Every time I saw or heard a piano, I thought about her. That kind of past gnat needs to be cleared up. I never did buy the piano, but I did write to Judy with the truth and an apology. The minute the note was written and mailed, I was free of the guilt.

It's very important to take action on leftover business, even if you must delegate it to the future. You will have a wonderful feeling as each thing from the past is taken care of and you move forward into a happy new year. With the past off your mind, you will be ready for a fresh start.

When we wrote *Sidetracked Home Executives* one of the main questions readers asked was, "Where do I begin?" Anyone who is disorganized has a very hard time figuring out where to start. In the case of a messy home, when everything is torn up and pleading for immediate attention, the natural reaction of a disorganized person is to scatter and panic. Back when we were confused, we arbitrarily chose to start at the front door and clean clockwise. It turned out to be the perfect place to begin.

On the subject of being happier and more self-fulfilled, the same question comes up. "Where do I start?" In the introduction to this book we said that your home was the key to becoming the fulfilled person you want to be and that the doorknob to happiness was right under your nose. That's because we were referring to the knob on the front door of your house.

Interestingly enough, the answer to "Where do I start?" is the same. You start your journey to more happiness at your own front door.

Remember Dorothy's ruby slippers in *The Wizard of Oz*? She had to run all over the place, searching for the way home and, in the end, found that she'd had the answer with her all the time. William Shakespeare said, "What you are speaks so loudly I can't hear what you say." What are you?

Turn the knob on your front door and take a good honest look at yourself. Shakespeare also said, "Of all knowledge the wise and good seek to know themselves." Your home and possessions will tell it all. It wouldn't take a mind reader to scan your home and its contents and come up with pages of information about you. A quick look in the refrigerator would reveal how you eat. Your bookshelves would tell what you read and, consequently, what your interests are. Everything in your home has a reason for being there.

If a stranger could drag data from your house, think what *you* will be able to see. Start at the front door with your notebook open to the section marked "Clearing" (set the timer for thirty minutes to one hour) and, moving clockwise, look at everything as if you were panning with a movie camera. Look at each wall and what is hanging on it (if anything). Look at the windows, the light switches, the furniture, and take notes. Try to be just an observer. Don't get into desk drawers, start cleaning out closets, or moving things around. Just observe and write it all down. Let your possessions call up past experiences. You may discover that these clearing sessions will take more time than you expected.

When I did this exercise for the first time, I thought I'd get all the way around the house and back to the front door in an hour. Five minutes into the exercise, I was facing my china cabinet. I looked at the three plates and two cups and saucers I'd received as wedding gifts twenty years before. In my notebook I noted: "I do not like china pattern." I thought about that for a second. Why did I pick it in the first place? I never did like it. The thought came to me, *Mom and Peggy liked it.* I had chosen it because it was their favorite. I had never added any pieces; I had never fed anybody on it, I just kept it. For two decades I had lived with, and carefully dusted, seven pieces of china I didn't like.

The clearing exercise is a timed examination. In that period all you do is look, ask yourself questions, and take notes. The action will come later.

The action I subsequently took was fun. I called our local department store and found that that particular pattern had been discontinued ten years ago. (I guess a lot of other people didn't like it, either.) I gave the china pieces to Peggy and Mom and I picked out a china pattern that *I* love! I told Mom that I never did like the pattern, and that I was going to start over by picking a new one. Getting the china out of my life was wonderful.

One of my problems in the past (I still have a residue of it today) was wanting approval, to the point of doing what others wanted me to do, regardless of my own feelings. I avoided offering opinions of my own because they might not be what other people would approve of; consequently, I spent a great deal of time acting according to other people's opinions. Bumping into the china was a shock. The plates were evidence of a past fault.

When you do this clearing exercise, pretend you are at your own estate sale. Let your belongings tell you about yourself. Besides exhuming things like the china, a rather extensive list of home improvements will emerge. Take the time to write down *everything* that comes into your mind.

You will find that this exercise will stir up more deeply rooted thoughts—subjects that you weren't consciously concerned about but still affect you in a subtle way.

We all have subconscious fears that are as energy-draining and happiness-sapping as our conscious thoughts. The trouble with subconscious negative thoughts is that they are sneaky. They are insidious in how they affect us. They can surface as sickness, poverty, and inharmonious relationships.

I have had a fear of men almost all of my life. I was never scared they'd hurt me physically; I was just afraid I could never please them. Yet I have always attracted men I couldn't please; actually, men who couldn't be pleased by anyone.

The men in my life, before 1983, were negative, domineering, and critical. When I finally began to see the pattern emerge, I couldn't understand why I attracted such unpleasant people. Freud said, or maybe it was my Home Ec teacher, that sometimes a child who has had negative experiences with the parent of the opposite sex will attract similar experiences as an adult. But that couldn't possibly have been the case with me, especially since my dad is the kindest, gentlest, most unselfish person I know. (That fact can be verified by *anyone* who knows Dad.)

It remained a mystery until one day, when I was continuing my psychological trek through my house, I came to a jar of paintbrushes that had belonged to my Grandpa McLaughlin. I thought about him for a minute, and suddenly I recalled an experience I'd had with him.

I was four years old. Mom had gone shopping or out to lunch and had left me for the afternoon with my grandparents. That day Grandpa and I were down in the basement. He was busy at his worktable, while I rode my tricycle in circles on the cement.

Grandpa was a frustrated artist. He was extremely creative and very intelligent, but he hadn't developed either gift to the degree that he knew he was capable of doing. He was the most negative person I've ever known, and we all called him Grandpa Don't.

I liked to be around him when he was puttering because he would get engrossed in a creative project, and, for that time, he'd be happy. That afternoon he was putting the finishing touches on a hobby horse. I had watched the piece of wood turn into a toy for me, and I was excited for the project to be completed. Circling his workplace, I spied a piece of rope under his table, and when I went under there to pick it up, I got the bright idea to tie Grandpa's leg to one of the legs of the table. He was so consumed by his creation that he was unaware that his leg was lashed in place, and when he went to walk away, he fell on his face. He was furious and probably hurt. I ran. He untied himself and caught me before I made it to the top of the stairs. He picked me up, under my arms, and took me to Granny and said, "Keep her out of my hair!"

Thinking back over the incident, I started to cry. I thought, how stupid to cry over that little incident. Grandpa never ever spanked me, and that was the *only* time he ever physically hurt me. The answer came quickly. He never *physically* hurt me, but he did hurt my *feelings* a lot.

I was always in his hair. Suddenly I realized something else I'd never thought of before. When I was eight months old my dad joined the Navy and didn't return until the end of World War II. My mom and I moved into her parents' home for the duration of the war. I was three when Dad came home. For more than two years Grandpa Don't was the male in my life, and although I have no recollection of that time, I know he had a great influence on me. It occurred to me that the men I have attracted, especially my ex-husband, bear a resemblance to my grandfather, not only in looks but in temperament.

I'm not a psychologist and I don't know exactly why finding out events from the past has helped me, but dredging up that information has changed my relationships with men in a positive way. For one thing, I no longer attract men who cannot be pleased, and that has made a big difference.

You may have similar experiences when you do this clearing exercise. Whenever I have a realization, a breakthrough from unawareness into understanding, I write it on a Realization Card, date it, and file it in the success divider.

The wonderful thing about self-awareness is that when

REALIZATION CARD

Realization 7-19-82

Grandpa was hard to please because he didn't get to do the things in life that he knew he could.

Being artistic myself, I know how my kids can "get in my hair," but I love them dearly.

Grandpa loved me dearly, but as a child, I was always in his way.

I no longer need to try to please people, especially men.

AFFIRMATION CARD

Affirmation 7-19-82

I deserve a man in my life who is happy with his own life and therefore capable of appreciating my love.

you have a breakthrough into understanding, it improves your life!

Besides making a note of the realization, I wrote an affirmation on a 3x5 to keep me reminded of my new awareness until it was well established in my mind (see example above).

Since I'm single, I did the clearing exercise alone. Peggy asked Danny to go around the house with her, and I have to say I never saw so much activity. For months after their initial clearing every time I'd go over there, something had changed.

Peggy realized that most of the things "to do" that came out of their clearing exercise went on Danny's list with an A priority. Until he figured out what was happening, he was working like a dog. If you are married, you could have some great fun doing this together, but be careful not to put too much on the other guy!

This clearing process will take time. It took me about ten hours to go completely around my house, using some of my quiet time in the morning, and free time on the weekends. Peggy and Danny went from their entryway, around the living room, and three feet into the kitchen (which took them about two hours), and they both had enough to work on for the next year.

Another person in our test group went entirely around her house in one hour. (She also had enough to think about, repair, and work on for the next year.)

A bachelor who agreed to do this clearing exercise did it in jest, because he considered his house to be somewhat of a joke. Three years earlier he had entirely gutted it, intending to remodel. (He'd never remodeled anything in his life, and when he realized the scope of the work ahead, he was overwhelmed.) He told us that our clearing exercise would not apply in his situation. We agreed that maybe, in this case, the exercise wouldn't work. It seemed that the bare rafters, subflooring, and exposed electrical wiring in the drapeless, counterless, and applianceless place that he had called home for three years wouldn't reveal anything about the intelligent, handsome, and successful man.

We were wrong. He stood at the front door and for the first time realized that he didn't want to live there. Not only did he not want to live in that house, he didn't even want to live in that city. The work he had to do for himself in the following year was to figure out where he wanted to be.

You don't have to confine this clearing exercise to January. You might want to make out a weekly or monthly card that says "Clear for an Hour" and do just a little at a time. You'll know what will be right for you once you get started. The point of the clearing exercise is not to see how far you can get in an hour or to clear the whole house in a month. The main reason for this exercise is to use your house as a counselor. It can help you let go of the past, by putting it into perspective, because you will be looking back with new understanding. You are an adult now; you are wiser; you have experience between yourself and the past, and that growth can be used to put anything behind you. Be sure to do this whole clearing process in the spirit of happy self-evaluation. If you don't make it fun, you will defeat the whole purpose.

Now you are probably wondering what to do with all the information you extract from looking thoughtfully at your home. Just getting it down in your notebook is a great step; but to improve the quality of your life, you'll need to take action. Your list from the clearing will be no different from the one you made of things that were on your mind, except that this list is the result of being "reminded" of things.

Handle it the same way you did the problems in Part II. Categorize each item by giving it an A, B, or C priority. Put the A priorities on your Immediate Action Card or on your Daily Routine Cards. Put the B priorities in the January through December section to be dealt with in the next six months, and put the C priorities beyond six months. (See an example of a page from the clearing session below.)

Some things needed to become routine maintenance. (In the September chapter on work, I have recapped our original 3x5 cardfile system for organizing and maintaining a home.)

Example from a Clearing Session

5-11-82

Front Door:

Maintenance	A	Door needs to be dusted weekly/blue
Maintenance	A	Door needs to be waxed monthly/white

June (Michael)	B	Fix hole in wall from doorknob crashing into it
Immediate Action	A	Get a doorstop 95¢
Maintenance	A	Take better care of entryway plants weekly/blue
Things to buy	B	Get a picture for left side of French doors $25
Family room	C	Need a lounge chair for family room $150
Grocery list	A	Get batteries for TV remote control $2.50
Daily Routine Card	A	Spend more time with kids (one on one)
Immediate Action (Peggy)	A	Wet towel on chair gets kids' attention
?	B	Want a piano?
Immediate Action	A	Call or write to Judy
Realization	A	Do not like china—20 years—Why? Mom and Peggy liked it, I never did
Immediate Action	A	Give china to Mom and Peggy
Things to buy	A	Pick a new pattern
September (Joanna)	B	Organize bookshelf
Things to buy	A	Need good pair of scissors $10
Success	A	I love my barstools and countertop
September	B	Clean carpet
June	B	Put TV schedule on 3x5 weekly/blue
June	B	Return Ruth's punchbowl
April	A	Clean out desk
June	B	Call Bernice
Immediate Action	A	Establish a place for newspapers

Example of something that will take more than a few steps:

5-11-82

I want a piano

June—Call American Music
(they owe you $300)

June—Call all the piano stores
for prices

A—Look in classified ads

A—Start a savings fund

A—Sell Oldsmobile—write ad

July—Look at pianos and decide the kind you want

You may want to read our first book, *Sidetracked Home Executives,* if very many things from your clearing involve clutter, disorder, or maintenance.

Some things on the clearing list are things to buy. Beside each item I put an approximate price. Start a 3x5 card of the things you need to buy. You could make out two cards, one for things under $10 and one for those items over $10.

People will show up on your clearing list. If they are people you will want to write to, send something to, apologize to, for example, put them on a card and file it in November. (Chapter Eleven is devoted to thoughtfulness, friendship, and hospitality. We will show you how you can stay in regular contact with the people you care about.)

Any big thing, such as the piano, gets a question mark because it should go on a separate card with room on it for brainstorming (see example above). Brainstorming will produce a list of action steps to help you start moving toward your goal. Just as Katie used the system when she was afraid that Robert was fooling around, you can use it for arriving at steps that you can take now and in the near future to reach your goal.

Be sure to consider delegating as much as you can to other members of your family. I'm a single parent and my children's father lives about thirty miles away. With that distance separating him from them, it's so easy for me to feel the entire weight of raising "our" family. If I feel a burden, it's my own fault, not his. I have to remind myself frequently that raising the kids is half his responsibility too. A Reminder Card with current events about the children moves throughout the days of the week with a notation to "call their father" at least every other day and tell him what's going on.

Use the family dividers to hold information that comes up in the clearing process that involves the other members of the family; things they would like to have, as well as chores and projects you think they should do, will surface. In *Sidetracked Home Executives* we recommended having family council meetings. It is good to have a divider for each member of the family, because after the clearing there will be volumes of new business.

All this self-appraisal makes you aware that every part of your life indirectly affects every other part. If you are disorganized, it will show up when you write down what's on your mind. It will also appear in the clearing exercise and it will surface again on your list of what you want to be, do, and have. Changing just *one* thing changes other things as well.

Keep in mind when you do this starting-over clearing process that it should always be an adventure. Learning about yourself takes time, and when you've looked at your home with new eyes, you'll have enough to do for the entire year. Self-improvement is an ongoing quest, and when next January comes around, you'll be ready to evaluate your surroundings again.

You will be so pleased with your progress in the next twelve months that at 11:55 on December 31, you will really have something to celebrate.

Happy New Year!

Two

February–Love and Romance–From Peggy

"Love is patient; love is kind and envies no one. Love is never boastful, nor conceited, nor rude; never selfish, not quick to take offense. Love keeps no score of wrongs; does not gloat over other men's sins, but delights in the truth. There is nothing love cannot face; there is no limit to its faith, its hope, and its endurance."

—ST. PAUL I CORINTHIANS 13:4-7
The New English Bible

February makes me think of Lincoln...and love. It's the month that gives us Valentine's Day and, along with it, cupids, red construction paper hearts, frilly white doilies, and $3 greeting cards. On the 14th, florist trucks, with the darting flower guy silhouetted on the side, speed happy bouquets all over town. Sweethearts send secret messages to each other through the personal column of the newspaper, and helium balloons, kisses, and huge heart-shaped candy boxes are exchanged by lovers across the country all in the name of romance. But what happens the rest of the year, after the balloons lose their oomph and the chocolates are down to the jelly-centered rejects? Since February is traditionally the month for sweethearts, it's a perfect time to put a little romance into the file.

I decided to dedicate one hour of my free time each week to being more romantic and being a better wife. I'll explain how I used that time to program my husband into my cardfile so that, with a little planning, every day of the year could be a celebration of our mutual respect, friendship, and love, but first let me tell you a little more about our relationship.

Danny and I have been married for twenty years, and even though our first five years were seriously threatened by my disorganization and his moodiness, we were able to work things out. Like two feuding schoolchildren who fight over the rules of a game but still want to play together, we wavered in our feelings for each other in those early years. Danny would get very frustrated with me and my inability to organize, set priorities, and follow through; and I'd get my feelings hurt easily by his quietness, indifference, and irritability.

I had intended to make our home cozy and clean from the start, but the process eluded me. I could picture the house organized, but when I'd go into action to make the visualization a reality, I'd only make a bigger mess. I can remember wishing that I could twitch my nose like Samantha on *Bewitched* and clean the place up just once ... make it perfect ... start with total order ... and then I'd keep it that way. I also used to wish I could turn the room upside down and live on the junk-free ceiling.

When Danny came home once and found me in the garage, stripping the finish off the coffee table, he couldn't understand why such a project had taken me away from making the beds, doing the dishes, vacuuming, and getting dressed. When I explained that I had intended just to dust the table but then realized I'd been putting off refinishing it, he did not appreciate my logic or efforts. Simple basics that meant so much to him (like toilet paper in the bathroom

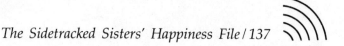

and dinner on the table) were things Danny had to fight for. One time, a month before he left me, he told me how hard it was for him to care so much about me and watch me defeat myself day after day. My enthusiasm began to fade.

Danny had known about my disorganization from our school days. Back then he had laughed at my last-minute maneuvers, creative substitutions, and laxity. He thought it was cute... until it affected him. Our bedroom was a cave (like my old car). Our tangled finances were testimony to my disorganized record-keeping and addiction to clearance sales. Our communication consisted mostly of accusations, arguments, and intimidation.

When we were in school I was aware of Danny's moodiness. Back then I had seen his flares of temper as a fiery show of righteousness and strength (he was baby-sitting for his little sister). I appreciated his silence as an inward, almost spiritual quietness. I did not disturb him or question his thoughts. I left him to himself, and shortly he would return to my company, seeming more refreshed and almost enlightened. I was so secure as his friend that I could allow him his privacy; and since his temper wasn't directed toward me, it had no bearing.

When we were married the quietness drove me nuts! In my insecurity, I thought we should have no areas of singleness. I invaded his seclusion with relentless interrogation: "What are you thinking? Are you mad at me? Why are you quiet? What's wrong? Do you still love me? Is there someone else?" until I wore him down.

I was his clinging, demanding helpmate, ready to assist him in any way I could toward becoming a better husband. He became indifferent (something I hadn't seen before in our courtship), more quiet, and highly temperamental. A nasty-looking black growth appeared on the palm of his hand, and he continuously dug at it, irritating it, and making it larger. He had trouble with his digestion and took antacid tablets hourly, and he developed a prescription case of dandruff. I pounded at him with my message of togetherness and communication until I finally drove him away. He wanted a divorce. In our five years we had thrown that word at each other like a sharp spear, and finally we had done more injury to our relationship than we thought we could repair.

When Danny left, I sat alone (I was seven months pregnant with our first child) and cried. I cried until my head ached and my ribs hurt. I tried to figure out what had gone wrong—why I'd lost him. Neither of us had intended to hurt the other when we married. We had only thought about loving each other, but love wasn't enough. We had both been scared by the absence of love in the heat of a quarrel; and since we were quarreling every day, love seemed very far away. I needed a good friend, someone I could talk to and cry with; but Danny was my best friend and he was gone. I thought how nice it would be to sit in his car as we used to and just *like* each other again. We hadn't had a good talk in years because both of us were always yelling.

Those days of separation were the worst of my life. I felt betrayed, abandoned, and desperately empty. I sat for hours in my rocking chair with my arms around my huge stomach, rocking, crying, and wondering what the baby and I were going to do. I thought about our marriage vows and how they had crumbled under the strain of everyday problems. I thought about security and affection and wondered what I'd done to deserve being hurt so deeply at a time when I needed to be loved. I wondered, "Why a baby now after five years of trying . . . why now when I don't even have a husband anymore?" I thought about dying.

I'll never forget the phone call I made to my parents. They had no idea that Danny and I were having trouble. They loved him as much as if he were their own son; and when I told Dad that Danny had left and wanted a divorce, he was speechless and heartbroken. They wanted me to come home, but I couldn't make any decisions. I drove over to Pam's house. As I sobbed out my story she hugged me with nonjudgmental understanding and compassion. Danny's parents wanted to help, too, but there was nothing anyone could say or do. We had to figure things out on our own.

In my emotional upheaval I began to develop some serious problems with my pregnancy. My doctor saw me immediately and said, "Okay, what's going on!?" I told him, through tears, that my husband had left me, and instead of saying "Oh, you poor little dear" or something comforting, he said, "Quite frankly, I don't care what's going on in your romance. I do care about your health and the birth of this baby. Now, you've got exactly seven days to get your life in order. When I see you next week I want to see a mature, composed woman who's about to be a mother." He scolded me and left the room.

I cried and talked out loud to myself about his insensitivity and lousy bedside manner. I argued with him behind his back, saying I needed more than seven days to heal my broken heart; and, reassuring myself that I was already mature and composed, I left the examining room.

In the car on the way home I turned on the radio in search of comfort. A minister was giving a talk on problems. *Ha,* I thought. *What does he know of* real *problems? Nobody knows how much I hurt.*

I was only half listening to him when one clear sentence leaped out of the dashboard at me and held my attention. "Calamities are opportunities," the man said. It was the sentence that gave me rest, then strength, and, finally, understanding. The calamity I experienced proved to be my greatest opportunity in life: to see that I am never alone, that there is a power within me that is greater than my feeble thinking. I can call upon it and it will respond with direction when I am ready to listen. It taught me that I am capable, strong, and forgiving. I stopped looking for security and love outside myself. I stopped trying to hold on to Danny and stopped my demands. Ironically, freeing him was the one thing that brought him back.

While we were apart Danny was doing his own soul-search. The day of his appointment with an attorney he sat in the car in the parking lot, unable to go in. Something told him it was wrong. (Call it God or the Lord, a Voice, the Creator, or the Force, it doesn't matter; but it was with him, guiding and directing him to the right action.) When he told me that he had changed his mind and didn't want the divorce, I have to say that I had some fears. If he didn't mean it or things hadn't changed, we would have to go through another separation, and I was scared.

Danny said that if I couldn't take him back, he would understand, but that everything was different now; and he would still spend the rest of his life making it up to me, taking care of me and providing for the baby, even if we lived apart.

We both came to the self-realization that we could not look to each other for happiness, that we had to be happy in our own right, and then we could share that inner happiness with each other. Danny realized that he loved me and that his love would have to be unconditional if our marriage were to work. He accepted my faults and gave me time and the freedom either to continue with them or change them. (It was another six years and two more babies before I got organized.) He learned to be more mellow; and, once again secure as my friend, he was open with his feelings and his moodiness was rare. I knew that I loved him, too, but it was a greater realization to know that I would be all right without him. It was that knowledge that freed me to leave him alone.

With the healing of our relationship there was instantaneous healing of Danny's hand. The growth truly disappeared overnight with no evidence of its ever having been there. The dandruff and the upset stomach also became history.

I have wondered how much our being friends helped us get through those terrible times that defied our love. I don't think our marriage would have endured the hardships if it had not been for the depth and longevity of our friendship. I have a plaque in the kitchen that says, "A Friend Loveth at All Times" (Proverbs 17:17). Kathy Nevin gave it to me when I got married. I know she was referring to the friendship between the two of us, which began when we were in first grade, but it has been the key to my successful marriage. As friends Danny and I have been kinder to each other than we might have been as mere lovers. Too often lovers let pride keep them apart, but true friendship has a way of dissolving pride. As companions we have comforted each other in life-threatening illnesses and shared each other's sadness at the loss of people we both loved. We have forgiven each other for falling short of our original vows; and because of our wonderful longtime friendship, we have been able to love again...more deeply and with more dedication to each other's joy than ever.

In writing about love and romance, I felt I should say something about positive fighting. Danny and I have learned the right way for us to fight without wrecking our romance, and, because of that, we have been happier. Today when we disagree we have a few rules that we adhere to strictly. No yelling and no crying. (I hate to be hollered at, and Danny loathes tears.) We fight with facts, and try to leave emotions out of it. When one of us has been wronged or hurt by the other, he or she says so. We speak the truth in love, not as a reprimand, but as a way of keeping our relationship open and honest.

We also don't play around with the thought or threat of divorce as we used to. The dare "Why don't you just leave?" "Well, maybe I will," is dangerously tempting when two people are angry, and, if it's said enough times, it soon becomes an option and then a reality. Marriage, for us, is togetherness, not separation; so when we have a problem, neither of us gets to walk out or hang up on the other.

We don't take literally the admonishment in the Bible "Don't let the sun set on your anger." If we're mad at each other and it happens to be getting dark out, we don't spout an insincere apology just for the sake of getting it over with and going to bed. If it's important enough to fight about at 8:00 P.M., it deserves some time for deliberation (but not more than twenty-four hours). If we are wrong, we apologize. If there is a stalemate, we call a truce and disarm. Whether the outcome of the disagreement will be an apology or a truce, the rule is that both parties must put away their ammunition and get a good night's sleep. (Danny accepts this rule more easily than I do. Once his head is horizontal, he's asleep.)

All of our rules are based on the fact that we are reasonable partners who love each other and want to keep our marriage happy and alive. There have been times, though, when we have both been uncooperative, irritable, defensive, and stubborn, so we have a rule that there can only be one jerk at a time. It is wise. Whenever one of us is being a jerk, the other guy must be the observer (not the judge). While the jerk rants, the observer simply observes. In his observations he must not record, ponder, or take personally any of the jerk's irrational statements or behavior. Since we are both jerks once in a while, we both know that nothing is meant by what is said when one is in the process of being absurd. With that in mind, it has always been best if the observer leaves the jerk alone until the jerk has had a nap or time to work out his (or her) problems on his/her own.

I really think that differences of opinion can bring growth and closeness as long as they are expressed with love. Believing that, I'm not afraid to fight anymore. Conservatively liberated, I am also no longer obsessed with teaching Danny how to be a "total husband." Danny will never "rap" on command, "share" in a group, "role-play," or go on an "encounter." He will never put his arm around me at a party like the guy in the Geritol commercial and boast, "This is my little woman and I'm darn proud of her!" But he *is* proud and I know it. That's just not his style; and if all of a sudden one day he started doing those things, *I* would be the one who was embarrassed. I'd think he was going through some sort of mid-life crisis or something.

Don't make the mistake of looking at someone else's romance and wishing it were yours. I did that once with a couple I knew who had a yacht. I thought about how romantic it must be. I pictured them sipping champagne and whispering sweetnesses to each other while drifting into the evening sunset in their floating luxury. They're divorced now. The boat was partly what did it. The wife was afraid of it and scared of the water; yacht fuel costs as much as the average house payment; the husband really wanted a speed boat; repairs came up; and every time they took it out, there was a big fight!

I don't think there's much romance in a relationship that's all messed up on the inside. From my own early marriage experience, I know that we couldn't fight all day, then all of a sudden flip a romantic switch at sunset. Danny and I went to a marriage counselor, and that may be the answer in situations like ours and my boating friends'. If you are in similar circumstances, don't be ashamed to get help.... Go alone if you have to, but get help.

I read a book recently by a well-known psychologist who said everything is either growing, stabilizing, or diminishing. Applying that truth to my marriage, I wasn't about to be content with a romance that fell into the "stable" category. I don't want to be complacent just because I know our relationship isn't diminishing. I want it to grow! I want it to continue to be more fun, more friendly, and more romantic.

If your relationship with your mate falls into the stable area, as mine did, you're probably very comfortable. But if you'd like it to be always growing, it'll take your continual attention; and that's what the Happiness File can help you plan.

Focusing my time and energy on Danny for the month of February was a positive step in itself. Giving him my attention was like watering the fern.

I like to read good books about marriage. In my notebook, in the section about what I want "to be," I wrote that I'd like to be a more frequent reader, and I decided that I'd try to go to the library every two weeks. (I have a blue card in Monday's divider to remind me of it.) I also want "to be" a better wife, so while I'm at the library I kill two birds with one book.

The last book I read about how to keep the romance alive in a relationship was called something like *Lifetime Romance*. The title caught my attention, but the book nauseated me. The couple reminded me of a ninth-grade twosome from my junior high days who couldn't stop handling each other and spent every lunch hour in the bushes outside the band room. Furthermore, the author of the book wasn't married and didn't have children, so her advice didn't take into consideration the lack of privacy most couples with kids must deal with. "Fill the tub with champagne and take a seductive bath with your mate." My sixth-grader had just completed a drug and alcohol abuse unit in school and would have been very concerned about the empty bottles in the garbage can. But in nearly every book I read I can find at least *something* I can use. After reading one book I decided that Danny and I needed a lock on our bedroom door. I can highly recommend installing one just for romantic peace of mind.

From other books I learned to sprinkle talcum powder (I like baby powder better) in between the sheets when I change them for a delightfully fresh feeling when we climb in at night. (If you try this idea and like it, you might need a blue weekly Reminder Card: "Powder the Sheets.") I also realized that my nightwear was *stupid.* Most of it was old and flannel and unromantic. My one robe had originally been hot pink pile but it had shed over the years, leaving my elbows exposed through the nylon backing. It had to be pinned shut each morning because eight years earlier when I'd had Allyson I'd left the belt at the hospital. Purchased with warmth and comfort in mind, it had served me well, and I had become as attached to it as Allyson had to her blanket. Pale pink and ragged with hundreds of washings, it had to *go* (for the sake of romance). When I first showed up in my snazzy new nightgown, Danny said, "What are you wearing that for? It's not our anniversary." Now every three months I buy a new nightgown and I've made dust rags out of all my old ones except one. (I save it for snow storms or when I feel sorry for myself and need hot cocoa and flannel to make me happy.) I don't pay much for the nighties (the cheaper the better, I believe), but I do spend more for new underwear (I buy something new every three months and throw something away that's old). I put a Reminder Card in the month section so I'll know when it's "time to buy new lingerie." From books, I discovered how important good grooming is to romance. I always suspected it had a bearing, but I've found that soft hands, shiny hair, clipped toenails, fresh breath, perfume (lots of different smells for different moods), bubble baths, and plenty of rest are absolute essentials to romance. Besides the fact that my husband appreciates those things, I feel much more provocative and feminine when I take care of myself.

I used to be ashamed of my hands and never wanted Danny to look at them. Pam suggested I get a professional manicure once a week until they looked good. At first I was too embarrassed to go in and I thought it extravagant, but she persuaded me to make the call. Just knowing I had the appointment, I began wearing rubber gloves to do the dishes, and I started using hand lotion. My hands improved quickly, and from the beauty parlor lady I learned the whole weekly manicure regime. I went four times at $6.50 a visit and now I do my nails myself. I have a blue Reminder Card to "Manicure My Nails," and I keep a small container of lotion and a file in my purse. Next I'm going to tackle my toes.

I used to worry that the bookstore clerk or the librarian would think my marriage was on the rocks if I checked out a title like *What Happened to the Honeymoon?* but then I realized that the employee's life doesn't revolve around my marriage and what books I read. Dare to see what's going on and what you can learn by reading information about romance and love.

I have to say that even with so many good books on the subject of the physical marriage relationship, I have received more positive help from those with a spiritual slant. I like to be inspired to listen instead of talk, or to be more patient and kind. I like to discover one of those breakthrough paragraphs that gives me a new insight on a problem that has bothered or bewildered me.

One of the breakthroughs I want to share is what I learned about being appreciative. Early in February I had made a list of everything I could think of that would make our marriage more romantic. It was a Hollywood-inspired list that included flowers, surprises, midday phone calls, little wrapped gifts, sweet notes, and other things I'd seen Blake Carrington do. Among all those other things, I had also decided that Danny should give me at least one compliment a day. Reading the selfish list back, a voice inside me asked, *"How many compliments do you give him?"* Since my inner voice never argues with me (it only advises and then lets me choose), I chose not to think about how often I praise him. *Maybe,* I thought, *I should keep a log of how many days Danny went* without *giving me a compliment.* Instead, something told me to keep track of how much appreciation I gave him. I was ashamed to find out that although Danny did so much that deserved commendation, I seldom told him so.

That evening I watched him with renewed awareness of kindnesses I had come to take for granted. He'd fixed me a nice hot cup of tea because I was chilly. He'd built me a wonderful fire in the family room fireplace (he had to go outside to get the wood, so I know his slippers got wet), and he'd seen to it that the kids did the dinner dishes without fighting. Later that night I watched him check all the doors to make sure they were locked and tuck an extra blanket around one of his sleeping sons. When I took time to think about it, there were lots of things he'd done just within the last week, all without any words of appreciation from me. He'd fixed the clasp on my pearl necklace, tightened Ally's skates, gotten the squeak out of the oven door, pumped up a bike tire, and worked on the yard. And that was only part of the list.

It gave me a lot to think about, and I decided it might be a good idea to write down the things Danny did that I had come to expect rather than appreciate. Anytime I start feeling overburdened or martyrlike, I look at the list and know I don't have anything to complain about. I made a pledge to myself that I would consistently be aware of what Danny already did for me, and I would compliment him at least once a day. It's a little embarrassing to admit that I had to have a daily reminder, "Have you shown your appreciation today?" on a yellow card. But that's what it took for three weeks. (After twenty-one days it was a habit, but until it became a habit, I needed the nudge.)

With my focus off what he should be telling me, and on what I wanted to tell him, things started to happen. Danny noticed my attentiveness, naturally, and began seeing things about me that *he* had taken for granted. The compliments were flying back and forth, tenfold, as we became the Romeo and Juliet of Clark County.

I should have known enough about the law of "just returns" to realize that whatever I wanted, I had to be willing to *give*. If I wanted romance, I had to be romantic; if

I wanted to be appreciated, I had to show my appreciation; if I wanted to be showered with gifts, I had to be a showerer.

Once again I went over the Hollywood list in my notebook, but this time I tried the "back to you" approach with each thing I wanted Danny to do for me. I was quickly aware that I had been as unromantic as he was. Besides taking him for granted, I never surprised him with little gifts, lunches, dates, phone calls, or notes, either.

You probably know your mate better than anyone else in the world. Use what you know to create more love and romance in your life. Use your notebook to write down all the things you know he loves. Then read it to him and watch him smile. Ask him what he'd like to add to the list, and I'll bet you'll be surprised. I had no idea that Danny loves gummy bears and artichoke hearts, or how important it is to him to have a clean car and lights turned out when the room is empty.

There were foods on the list that I knew he loved and that I hadn't cooked in years, and there were simple things he wanted to have: magazines in the bathroom and the chance to read the newspaper before I'd cut it up for coupons. Since I shopped once a week, I went through his list and added items from it to my standard grocery list. (In our second book, *The Sidetracked Sisters Catch-Up on the Kitchen,* we suggested making a large grocery list containing anything you ever buy, duplicating it enough times so that you'd have one for each week, and then posting the list on the kitchen bulletin board every week to be marked off as supplies run out.) My grocery cart took on a new personality when I'd added the things to it that Danny loved.

Unlike foods, some of the items on his list were expensive and I would have to save for them; but, looking at the calendar, I realized that there were at least five occasions on which I buy him gifts: Christmas, his birthday, Father's Day, our anniversary, and Valentine's Day. For the first time I was in tune with what *he* would like as a gift rather than what I would like him to have. (There's a big difference between a new pair of slacks and a pair of binoculars.)

My first opportunity to give him what he yearned for

came with Valentine's Day. I had always bought Danny a nice bottle of my favorite after-shave and a mushy card. Turning to his list, I decided to buy him three bundles of split kindling at $1.59 each and bake him a German chocolate cake. (I skipped the card altogether.) I tied up the bundles with a big red ribbon and made the cake in the shape of a heart. Danny was delighted!

Then in May when our anniversary came, I took out the money I had stashed away to buy him something very special...a new wedding band (his original one was broken). Remembering the list, I decided (against my will) not to buy the ring but to get him a drill press instead. I knew exactly which one he wanted, because every time we went to the mall, Danny dragged me through the tool section at Sears. To satisfy myself, I had his old wedding ring repaired. His response to the drill press was overwhelming, and I felt so happy seeing him happy. Now I choose something from his list for each gift occasion and plan ahead so that I either have the money or am able to order the item in time for the celebration.

Throughout the year, whenever Danny mentions something he'd like to have, I write it on a piece of scratch paper and file it in his section of my cardfile. The ideas help me later when I'm trying to think of some little extra surprise packages to give him at Christmas. For surprises throughout the year, I use the list and transfer to a white card one special treat for each month (see example on page 149).

Danny thinks of work as "love made visible," so anytime I do something nice for him that takes time rather than money, he is especially touched.

With his favorite things in black and white, I can see new ways to show him my appreciation of him as a good husband. Reading Danny's list of things he loves, I note with interest that the absence of some of those things had been the source of many of our disputes: no soap in the shower, no cap on the toothpaste, no ice in the ice trays, and every light in the house left on. It is also interesting to find that most of the things Danny loves I do, too. (It is a nice reminder of how much we have in common.)

SPECIAL TREATS

Jan.	Gummy Bears
Feb.	A lb. of unsalted nuts
Mar.	A bag of hard candies
Apr.	A Hickory Farms beef stick
May	A cherry pie
June	A carwash
July	Homemade ice cream
Aug.	A John Denver tape
Sep.	Some Presto Logs
Oct.	A German chocolate cake
Nov.	A ski magazine
Dec.	Divinity

In February I buy twelve Valentines and mail him one a month. I send them to the police department (he's a policeman) and mark the envelope "Personal." Of course, I don't tell him that a card filed in front of the February divider reminds me to do this every year.

We have a weekend alone together once every three months. (I write the dates in my pocket planner as well as on the calendar.) For the last one, I did the inviting. I sent him a progressive invitation (five days in a row), saving the date, time, and place until the last letter. It was fun to keep him in suspense and not to give him any other clues. The weekend was a great success.

Once a week on Friday night we go on a date (I have a Reminder Card with the baby-sitter's phone number on it, which stays in front of Wednesday's divider); and once a month I fix a romantic candlelight dinner at home (the kids go to their aunt Sissy's).

The best thing I've ever done for our romance was get practical. I let the cards remind me to be thoughtful, and it's made a remarkable difference. On Danny's divider I have a picture of him as a baby on one side and a photo of us as a couple on the other. (I love to look at us together because I can see the closeness from another side and it is a nice feeling.)

Focusing my energy and attention on Danny for the whole month of February, I was inspired to make up a list of what qualities I would attribute to "the perfect wife." By looking over my list, I could see that by developing those qualities, I would not only be a better wife, but a much nicer person.

Pam and I learned so much while we were working on the Happiness File, and one of the things that was really enlightening to me was looking up our strengths and weaknesses in my dictionary. I decided that the list I'd made in my notebook about the perfect wife's traits was just a list of meaningless words unless I understood exactly what they meant and how they applied to my life. After looking up every attribute, I worked out for each a statement that helped me understand what I was striving for.

1. Patience—I must be calm and steadfast despite any opposition to *my* beliefs, opinions, and attitudes. Schwoooo!
2. Wisdom—I must have the ability to judge fairly and equitably the behavior and actions of my husband.
3. Virtue—I must show moral excellence, not only in what I say but in my everyday actions.

4. Empathy—I must learn to accept and understand my husband's feelings even if they are not as fully communicated as I would have them be. I must be able to see myself in his sneakers.
5. Kindness—I must be affectionate, gentle, and helpful in all my dealings with him.
6. Trust—I must have confidence in my husband, not just respect him, but believe in him and allow him to achieve his personal goals.
7. Humor—I must keep laughing when something is not really funny.
8. Knowledge—I must constantly try to learn more about relationships, myself, and my husband.
9. Enthusiasm—I must be excited and absorbed with interest in my husband.
10. Love—I must have strong affection arising out of personal ties based on admiration, benevolence, common interests, warm attachment, passion, and devotion, and I must have unselfish loyalty and concern for my husband.
11. Flexibility—I must be willing to give in sometimes and bend my thinking so that I don't become stubborn or closed-minded to my husband's ideas.

Since I was feeling a little like the man of La Mancha after making the list, I had to remind myself that Danny had loved me since I was eleven and he was twelve; and if he loved me just the way I was, any improvements I'd make toward being *my* idea of a perfect wife would only enhance his love. I also neutralized my feelings of inadequacy by rereading my strengths in my notebook and by thinking about the things I was already doing that were nice. For instance, I always bring Danny a hot cup of coffee in the morning, and I walk him to the door and kiss him good-bye when he leaves for work. In the evening I have one of the kids get the newspaper and I put out his slippers. I take a few minutes before he gets home to fix my hair, touch up my makeup, and put on some perfume, and then I meet him with a kiss when he comes in the door. All those actions of love are simple little things that I feel good about doing. They don't take much time and they mean an awful lot to Danny.

It's amazing, but just knowing what I want to be has helped me stretch my character and make some very positive improvements. I put all eleven of the virtues on a 3x5 yellow card and filed it in front of the divider labeled "me." It's a nice reminder of what I want to be as a wife. Danny's noticed that my frustration tolerance is higher, and I know I've been a real encouragement to him by my efforts.

Just before I finished writing this chapter, I thought it would be right to ask Danny, "What does love and romance mean to you?"

He looked at me the same way the mynah bird in the pet shop at the mall does when I try to get something out of him.

"Let me put it another way," I said. "What do you do that you think is romantic?"

...Same look.

"Okay, what do *I* do?"

"You're a *great* cook...you really amaze me with how you do tacos...and that meal you made Sunday..."

"Danny, I'm talking about love and romance."

"Yeah, so am I."

Maybe we who have practical husbands shouldn't limit our mates to the traditional expressions of romance (like poetry and candlelight dinners where *he* makes the reservations). Maybe they have an entirely different idea of what's romantic. When my good friend told me that her husband wasn't romantically spontaneous because he didn't like spur-of-the-moment dates, I reminded her of the day that he decided to build her a cabin at the beach and how, six months later, they were hammocking in front of their lovely new cedar A-frame. Spontaneity, like romance, is in the eye of the beholder. If your husband thinks you'll be thrilled that he changed the oil in the car...be thrilled. Love can be expressed in more ways than you may be accepting, and it'd be a real shame to turn it away because you didn't recognize it by its cover.

Three

March–Dreams
–From Pam

"From Socrates to Edison, every forward step taken by mankind through revolving centuries, every advance by humanity towards the ultimate goal, has been led by some valiant dreamer whose eyes were fixed upon the dawn."

—G. E. DINGER

March makes me think of shamrocks, lucky charms, and leprechauns. Kelly-green dye gets into the hands of playful party people who tint everything from dips and drinks to underwear. Without the St. Patrick's Day enthusiasts, March seems like a rather unexciting month. The trees are still winterized, the tulip and daffodil bulbs are reluctant to pop up, and even the grass is not yet in the mood to tempt the Toro into its first mowing. The drizzly days and nights make me thankful to have a warm, cozy home. I love to sit by a crackling fire, watch the storms come and go, and daydream.

One of *Webster's* definitions of the verb *to dream* is, "to consider as a possibility." What would life be like without the promise of possibility?

We all have the power to dream, to use our imaginations to conjure up wonderful things.

I've always enjoyed dreams of grandeur. I love to drive in fancy neighborhoods and wonder what it would be like to live in a mansion behind an iron gate. I like to read those magazines for rich people and mull over travel brochures. I'm curious about famous people. I've tried to picture what it would be like to be famous; to have somebody come up to me and say, "Didn't I see you on the cover of *Time* magazine?" and I'd get to say, "Yes."

My dreams have been so much fun because they have taken my life out of the rut that we ordinary people can get into. I have been accused of living in a dreamworld and I suppose I do to some extent, but I recommend it. Everything I get involved in gets a full shot at my power to dream.

I love to make things with my hands, so tailoring has been a wonderful avenue for my imagination and creativity. There was a time in my married life that everything my family wore was handsome and I was proud of it. I couldn't wait for someone to say, "Where did you get that dress?" and I could answer, "I made it." It wasn't exactly *Time* magazine, but I enjoyed the recognition.

Word got out that I could make truly unique things. I was flattered to hear that my handiwork had attracted the attention of a public relations manager at a Portland radio station. He asked me if I could make a dog costume.

The station had an artist draw up a picture of what was envisioned. It was a rather avant-garde dog, sort of a Huckleberry Hound in a Mighty Mouse cape. "Duke, the Wonder Dog" would glitter across the back of his uniform. He was to be covered in shocking pink fur and dressed in bright green satin trousers and vest, wearing square-framed purple sunglasses.

The staff of the station explained to me that they wanted the head of the dog to be big enough to make the entire animal about eight feet tall. (They said they could supply a six-foot guy to wear the costume.) They were extremely concerned about what the huge head would be made out of, since they'd had a hard time with a papier-mâché cow they'd previously used as a mascot. It rains a lot here, and they said the cow didn't hold up very well marching in the last two Rose Parades because of the rain. In fact, at the last Multnomah County Fair, the cow leaked on the guy inside, during a guest appearance in a cloudburst.

They left it up to me to figure out what materials to use for Duke's head, and for $400 I agreed to go for it. This was the first job I'd ever had outside of my home, and I was impressed that it was connected with show business. They told me Duke, the Wonder Dog, would become famous, appearing on billboards, marching in parades, and showing up at ribbon cuttings and anything else that was a big deal in Portland. I loved the thought that something I was to make would become a household word, and I had dreams of developing this new sideline into a lucrative business, even though I hadn't the slightest idea about how I would make the dog.

I thought a lot about the material to use for the head, and the idea of Styrofoam popped into my mind. When I asked around I was told to see if a place called Plastic Time had what I needed. Twenty minutes later I was thrown into the world of resins (a world I wasn't quite ready for). The man said that what I should get was what they used for the heads at Disneyland. I agreed. Neither one of us knew what that was, so I went home with a gallon each of two chemicals that, when mixed together, would make Styrofoam. I was excited.

In the next few days I tried to figure out how to make a mold, because the stuff I bought had to be mixed together and immediately poured into the waiting shape of a dog head. The answer came: the beach. The ocean is eighty miles away, so I opted for a spot on the Willamette River. At that time I just had two children; Mike was five and Peggy Ann was not quite two. They were excited to get to go play in the sand. We packed the car with the usual: playpen, diapers, diaper bag, blankets, favorite toys, food, bottles, and, this time, a shovel, a large roasting pan for mixing, and two gallons of soon-to-be Styrofoam. We were on the river by 9:00 A.M.

I planned to dig, out of the sand, a perfect hole shaped like a dog's head; then I'd mix the two ingredients together and pour it into the sand. It was hard to dig a hole four feet deep. For one thing, I wasn't in good physical condition and the river sand was full of rocks (more like boulders), beer cans, and driftwood. It did not have the consistency I'd expected. As I got further into the project I thought perhaps an eighty-mile ride would have been a better alternative; at least the sand at the beach is sand all the way to Singapore. Four hours into the hole the kids got cranky. My spirits weren't especially high either. I was getting fed up with nosy folks asking me why I was digging the huge hole. Also, the deeper down I dug, the harder it became to keep an eye on the kids, and then I hit clay. We took a break and had a wonderful picnic. I cautioned the children to stay away from the hole (if either one had fallen in, they would surely have broken bones).

When I resumed my project, I found it very hard to tell, by the hole, how cute the dog was going to be. When I'd dug what I'd guessed would be a mold that at least resembled a dog head, I proceeded with the next leg of my project. The container I had just barely held the two gallons of chemicals, but I thought it would be all right if a little of it spilled over while I stirred. I imagined that I'd pour the stuff into the hole and that the chemicals would start their work and foam *after* it was poured. I was shocked.

The concoction instantly swelled up and foamed over the turkey roaster, leaving barely enough to fill up the hole in the sand. The gooey lava bubbled and stank as it cooled. I eagerly tried to unearth my creation, but it wouldn't come out of the ground. It was as hard to pull up as a stump. I had to stop a jogger and get him to help me. Together we yanked, and out came the most disgusting-looking object I'd ever seen in my life.

"What is it?"

"Oh, just an experiment."

"Interesting...What are you going to do with it?"

"Oh, nothing."

I went back to Plastic Time. This time the man told me about fiberglass. He said that I'd need to make a form to put the material on but that it would certainly make a sturdy head. I agreed.

What kept me going was my vision of Duke cavorting with happy children at parades and grand openings and the recognition I would receive when Duke made his début in front of the station manager.

Fiberglass is a very serious substance. It looks like angel hair (that white Christmas hair) in fabric form. It is dipped into chemicals and then placed on a form where it gets very hot and then dries as hard as a Corvette. I made my head form out of papier-mâché and then covered the entire thing with the fiberglass.

For six weeks my house smelled like some kind of a manufacturing plant. Since I was disorganized, fiberglass was everywhere and the whole family was itchy. (The filaments had a way of working themselves up pant legs and sleeves, underneath elastic bands, and in between the sheets on the beds.)

When I was finished, the head weighed about eighty-five pounds. I had to rent a portable Skil saw and saw two scallops out of the base of the head so that it could rest on the shoulder of the person who would be wearing it. I also had to rig up a harness that would hold the head securely to the victim. The harness was made of leather and it crossed under the arms and buckled at the waist.

By the time I'd finished with Duke I was sure I didn't want to make costuming a business.

It wasn't because of the money (I broke even), it was because I had new ideas; and I was sick of sewing fake fur.

By coincidence, about a year after I sold the dog, I ran into a longshoreman who boasted having a part-time job being Duke, the Wonder Dog. I came forward to receive credit, but it wasn't pleasant when he found out that I was the dog's creator.

"Why did you make him so (beep-beep) heavy? The (beep-beep) head must weigh a hundred pounds." I tried to explain, but the man was wild.

"You know, last week I was over at The Enchanted Mountain for Kiddy Day and some little snot got me off-balance and the weight of that son of a (beep) head pinned me to the ground like a damn turtle." I apologized.

"Did you hear that I fainted in the Fairytale Parade?"

"No."

"Yeah, it was on the six o'clock news."

"What happened?"

"Well, it was so blasted hot in that head because it was a hundred degrees that day that I couldn't get any air. But I figured out what to do."

"What?"

"I installed a battery-operated fan up in the top of the head. I built a little shelf up there and it works great!"

"A fan. What a great idea!"

"Yeah, I figured, what's another ten pounds? I just wish the fan didn't make so much (beep-beep) noise. The kids are always tryin' to get me down to find out where the buzzing's coming from."

In spite of the negative weight factor, Duke was darling. (There's a picture of him in the Family Album section.) The recognition and praise I got for the way he turned out wasn't enough to make me aim for a career in costuming.

Dreams aren't etched in stone. You can drop them, change them, pick them up again, and you can hang on to some when you know you'll never do anything about them.

When Peggy and I were little, Granny used to take us shopping in downtown Portland. We'd catch the Greyhound bus out on the highway (Granny didn't drive) and have an all-day outing. On the way home the bus route always took us past an incredible grand old theater, a building like the Historical Society fights to restore. Its huge marquee in millions of brilliant lights flashed out the words, "THE BLUE MOUSE." It left us spellbound, but we were always tired and on our way home, so we couldn't stop to go inside. Granny would say, "Next time we come to Portland we're gonna go straight to The Blue Mouse!" The three of us pictured a nonstop medley of Walt Disney features: Pinocchio, Snow White, and Bambi, one right after the other. It would be an animated film festival, interrupted only briefly by Sylvester and Tweety. We dreamed about it. We told Mom we were going. We saved for it. We waited . . . and waited . . . and . . . waited.

Eventually, "next time" turned to "someday." We still thought about it, but not as often. And every once in a while Granny would say, "We've got to go to The Blue Mouse!"

Years passed and Granny's feet were bothering her, so just Peggy and I went shopping in Portland by ourselves; I was a licensed driver by then.

"Wanna go to The Blue Mouse?"

"No, I've got a date tonight."

"You wanna just drive by it?"

"Sure. What street's it on?"

"It's right after the bus depot and just past Manning's."

We saw the flashing lights in the distance. Maybe we could spare the time. As we got closer the lights caught our attention less than the people lying on the sidewalk.

"Sissy, lock your door!"

The Blue Mouse had become an X-rated adult theater. Next door was a topless bar and a tattoo parlor. Across the street was a bookstore with blackened windows and a pawn shop boasting, "Diamonds—Tackle—Guns." We were devastated. At what point had Pollyanna given way to Linda Lovelace? We didn't tell Granny. We couldn't spoil it for her.

It had been a beautiful dream, and years later we heard her tell our children, "Someday I'll have your mom take us all over to The Blue Mouse." Granny is gone now. She never knew what had become of the theater, but the fantasy was worth every minute we spent imagining it.

Maybe there's a Blue Mouse in your life . . . something you've always wanted to do, or be, or have, and it hasn't materialized.

Jiminy Cricket said, "When you wish upon a star your dreams will come true," and Snow White sang, "Have faith in your dreams and someday your rainbow will come smiling through." I'm more inclined to agree with Ms. White than the cricket. Not all of my dreams have come true, but they have been worth every bit of my time and, like a rainbow, they have added the color that has made my life a joy.

Dare to dream. Risk using your marvelous imagination. Einstein said, "Imagination is more important than intellect." Don't be scared to let your imagination soar.

A multimillion-dollar industry devotes its entire bankroll to fantasy. If Hollywood can do it, if Disneyland/World is rolling in it, if *Dynasty* can be picked up for another season, then you can indulge yourself by conjuring up a few wild and crazy notions.

If you have forgotten how to dream because somebody told you to knock it off, it's a snap to get back up in the clouds. Take at least an hour (get a sitter for your kids—you need time to yourself) and go to the biggest newsstand you can find. It might be at your bookstore or in your combination grocery and variety store. Spend the entire hour looking at magazines. Whether your interest is underwater stump blasting or southern Caribbean yodeling, there is a magazine on the subject. Browse through the magazines and let them pull you right off your Nikes. Buy a couple of them and consider subscribing to at least one.

The monthly or weekly arrival of a periodical that satisfies your interests will keep you from losing sight of your dreams. I subscribe to several magazines, and the day they arrive I attach a few white 3x5 cards to the cover with a paper clip. Whenever I sit down to read I take a pen with me. If something strikes me as funny or inspirational, I write it down. I write any information I want to remember on cards. My spelling and vocabulary have improved through my practice of writing down words that are new to me. I also remember more about who is running the country because I record names and titles in writing when I come across them.

Another great thing about magazines is that they are loaded with pictures you can paste in your scrapbook. Confucius said a picture is worth a thousand words. Cut out pictures of your dreams for your scrapbook. Gather a collection of possibilities in full color. What better way to develop your imagination than with pictures that help you dream?

To take off with a dream, you need to have a flight plan. Recently Peggy and I were stuck in Houston because there was no place to land in Denver, where we were to catch a flight home. The captain said he was adhering to the fuel conservation plan, and so, to prevent having to burn gas circling over Denver, we had to wait in Houston for a gate.

Circling burns fuel. If you take off too soon with a dream, you'll burn up unnecessary energy and maybe even crash. I'm thankful that I had only been asked to make one dog and that I wasn't commissioned to make costumes for the Ice Capades. I could have been responsible for some nasty accidents on the ice, not to mention increasing the noise pollution with all the fans whirring away inside the costume heads.

Pick a specific dream (from among those in your notebook in the "be," "do," and "have" sections) and decide to start right now making it a reality. Before you start, though, promise yourself that you will keep it a secret. If you tell a friend that you are going to write a play or run for mayor, you might get a discouraging response. Telling your dreams defuses the energy in the idea. Maintaining your solemn vow of silence, proceed as you did when you broke down the things that were on your mind into manageable segments in Part II.

You start taking action to realize your dreams by recording the dream on a 3x5 card and as many steps as you can think of to make it come true. The magazines you've started reading will help you to brainstorm. The library is a great place to locate information you may need. What's most important is to start taking action now. Some actions can be scheduled on the Daily Routine Card; some others will go on the Immediate Action Card, and some will go in the monthly section to be worked on later.

Take some of your quiet morning time to work on your scrapbook. Get excited about your dreams. You deserve to take time to dream, to consider the possibility of reaching your highest goal. Not so very long ago we thought the earth was shaped like a plate, and now we've set foot on the moon.

Who's to say we can't realize our fantasies? And besides, if a dream is never dreamed, it can never become a reality.

Sweet Dreams

Four

April–Prosperity
–From Peggy

"Man was born to be rich, or inevitably to grow rich, through the use of his faculties."

—EMERSON

Life's financial challenges are sometimes hard to deal with and prosperity can be elusive, but spring provides fresh starts and flourishing new growth. April is a good month for spring-cleaning the closets of your mind, throwing out old, negative ideas that are keeping you from achieving the prosperity you were meant to enjoy. April is also a good time for cleaning out the drawers of your desk and organizing your bills and file cabinet. Disorganization, like negativity, may be standing in the way of your financial success.

April is a perfect time to concentrate on prosperity. I like the fact that the month opens on a lighthearted note with the whole country laughing on April Fool's Day. I think the director of Internal Revenue made up that holiday, but he should have had it fall on April 15 so we could send little tricks along with our returns. "I didn't earn anything this year... April Fool!"

In my disorganized days tax preparation consisted of an annual, one-day frenzied compilation of receipts, canceled checks, interest payments, and expenses. I would start the hunt on the morning of the 15th, chasing down deductions in violent pursuit of enough for a refund. At 5:00 P.M. (still in my nightgown), I would call Danny at work and tell him to bring home a bucket of chicken if he wanted dinner. I wouldn't stop to eat with him. I'd just grab a chicken leg and keep working. (There's nothing more distasteful-looking than animal fat on a 1040... unless maybe it's grape juice stains on a loan application.) By 8:00 P.M. Danny would have fed the kids, bathed them and put them to bed, and be ready to sit down with me and go over what we'd done for the last year.

Perusing a year's worth of canceled checks can be like a stroll down memory lane, unless you've only got a few hours left till postmark. Without the pressure of time, reading old checks together could be as pleasant as looking through the family photo albums. "Oh, look sweetheart, here's a check to Carl's Costumes on October 31st." "Yeah... great party, huh!" "Here's one to Shorty's Nursery in December." "Oh, honey, that'd be the Christmas tree." "Who's Kevin Cammerano for ten?" "Hmmm... Cammerano... I don't know." But when the clock is ticking toward a penalty, tempers are short. "Connie's Clothes Closet, $75! What'd you buy there?" "How do I know? It was seven months ago... don't start hounding *me... you* wrote one here for $80 to Tools R Us.... What was that for?"

I read once that how you feel about money is greatly determined by the sum of your past experiences with it (good or bad). Danny and I have lived on both sides of the prosperity fence, and I know what it's like to face financial desperation. I have had to cash in bottles, roll pennies, baby-sit, clean houses, and sell things just to cover an insurance premium or pay the phone bill. During those difficult times it wasn't easy to think positively about money.

Early in our marriage Danny and I struggled financially

every month. After his discharge from the Army, he went to the University of Portland, and I got a job at our local newspaper. I scarcely made enough money to pay the rent and help with his college expenses. We fought constantly over our financial affairs.

In my disorganization I'd lose bills, bank statements, forget to log in checks, shop for groceries without a list, and, in general, waste money. Payday came once a month. (I think one of the special compensation programs for the disorganized should be an every-other-day payroll system.) By the end of the month about the only things left in our pantry were noodles, peanut butter, and popcorn. I used to do a lot of things with noodles... noodles and tuna, noodles and hamburger, noodles and cheese, and Pasta Surprise (that's noodles and noodles... surprise!).

Even after Danny took a full-time job as a policeman, times continued to be hard for us financially. We had three babies in three years, and the economy seemed to be against us. I had quit my job to be home with the kids, but I was always trying to earn a little extra money on the side. I sold cosmetics door-to-door.

Walking in the rain with my huge demo case, I told myself to celebrate the fact that the position was only temporary, but that was hard to do. It rains a lot where we live, and I really had to *force* myself to put on my fake fur coat and hit the streets. I don't know what it was about that coat, but in the rain it gave off a peculiar odor of wet chemical fur. Although the scent was offensive to me, I was disgusted to find that it aroused desires in the male canine community. (I had every dog in my territory after me, and on many a stormy day the only thing between me and a Great Dane was a stout shot of Here's My Heart.)

During my stint as a solicitor I was aware that the selling job wasn't precisely what I wanted, but it was flexible... too flexible for the undisciplined person I was. In six months I made $83. (I had spent too much time visiting with each customer while taking her order, and then when the stuff came in I wasn't in the mood to put my coat on and deliver.)

Decanters, pomanders, spoon rings, brochures, and lipstick samples littered the living room rug for days while I unpacked my order and tried to organize it into little white bags. Danny begged me to give it up. Finally, when my little boy told his Sunday school teacher that his mom worked on the street just about everywhere, I agreed to quit.

Webster defines the word *prosperity* as "the condition of being successful or thriving, especially economic well-being." I think that prosperity is a process. It starts with a recognition of untapped abundance, not in terms of cash on hand, perhaps, but in terms of abundant talents, ideas, and abilities within that are just waiting to be used. Letting them out, developing and sharing them with others, is what brings compensation in the form of cash.

At a lecture on prosperity several years ago, I was inspired by the statement "Prosperity is all around you!" I left the auditorium and began looking for cash. I thought I'd find the green stuff in the parking lot, but I didn't. I looked for hidden bills I might have forgotten in old purses and coat pockets; there weren't any. I watched the mail for an anonymous windfall; nothing came...except a sweepstakes entry. *Aha!* I thought. *This must be it! I'm going to win a bundle of money.* But it didn't happen.

I had gone to the lecture in the first place because I was experiencing borderline poverty. Searching for some kind of magic way to gain prosperity, I had taken careful notes as the wise man spoke, but in my urgency and blind desire for financial security I had missed his point. It was true he had said that prosperity was all around me, but he also said it was within. As I listened I wrote, "You cannot get something for nothing. . . . It is thought plus action which equals success."

For several years I continued to think positively about our finances, but I kept looking for prosperity outside myself. I looked to the City of Vancouver (my husband's employer) for more money in our paycheck, and I still entered every contest that came along, until one day, as I was filling out an entry blank, the clearest little sentence came into my head: *"Give it up."* At that moment I was sure I was never going to stumble onto cash or clean up on a contest. What I didn't know then was that cleaning up the house would lead to the prosperity I was looking for.

The other day I heard a comedian tell of a similar experience. David Brenner said that his dad always told him, "Someday our ship will come in!" The father said it over and over while he was growing up, and finally David really believed it. It wasn't until after he was a successful comedian that he realized their ship had come in and *he* was it! If someone had told me back in the days when I was a rotten house-keeper that I would be earning the equivalent of several sweepstakes winnings by helping people get organized, I would have thought it was a cruel joke.

For the first workshop that Pam and I taught, I didn't have anything to wear (and I mean that literally). We had cleaned out our closets, and I had dumped most of my clothes because they were all too big. (Getting organized had helped me lose a lot of weight.) In the cleaning process Pam had persuaded me not to be afraid of giving things up. She said that the only way we'd have room for new and nicer things would be to let go of the old. I'd let everything go, I guess, because I had to borrow a jacket from Mom, and a blouse and skirt from Pam, just to face the class. Even though I didn't have anything nice of my own, I was still able to make myself feel good by fixing my hair, doing my nails, polishing my shoes, and having everything clean and pressed. None of those actions cost any money, but with a little effort I was about to put my best foot in front of the public.

No matter how hard up we were in those days, there were always things I could do that didn't require money but would make a big improvement in our circumstances. And there was always something I could give, even if it was flowers from the garden, clothes the kids had outgrown, my time, my talents, or just plain hard work.

Although it's the nature of humanity for us always to want more than we currently have, Danny and I aren't struggling financially anymore. Pam and I are enjoying success in business now, and Danny has a secure, well-paying position with the police department. Some people would call us lucky, but we believe that luck is where preparation meets opportunity. I am absolutely certain that part of the preparation for greater prosperity is positive thinking. I also know that thought without action is only half the answer. Positive attitudes and expectations of greater good, combined with real, tangible action, is what finally brings success.

Since I have taken the time to organize our files, my desk, the bills, our receipts, and the mail, we have saved more money than I would have ever believed we could. In the month of April focus your attention on prosperity. Forget the past, except for what it's taught you, and try some of the things that have worked for me.

I like to separate prosperity into two parts: thought and actions. The thinking part is as important as actions are. In fact, it's more important because thought gives you the power to imagine and develop a plan or an idea.

In February's chapter I told about my friend whose husband built her a wonderful cedar A-frame cabin in a remarkably short time. The truth is, he had been imagining it in his mind for a couple of years, and had said to his wife on New Year's Eve, "Next year we will be celebrating this night at our beach cabin." She smiled a "sure we will" smile and he went on making his plans.

He went to the library and read everything he could find about A-frames; he asked experienced contractors questions about construction, and he watched them build similar homes. As he got more and more good ideas he applied them to the plans in his mind. Without worrying about the money it would take, he began to look for a building site. He found the perfect piece of property at their favorite beach, and because the price and terms were within their budget, they bought it.

Next, he took his ideas to an architect who, through the use of his own talents, was able to transfer the ideas from the realm of thought onto paper. Because the man's concepts had been so clearly formulated, the architect was able to draw the plans quickly and for a reasonable fee. Having built the cabin over and over in his mind, the man could anticipate problems and solve them mentally before they happened.

When the time came to take action he had the lumber

delivered, secured the necessary permits, and although he had never physically built anything before, he took his three-week vacation at the beach, where he began the construction he had rehearsed. Friends and relatives, amazed by his ambitious twenty-one-day plan, showed up to help with the work, and within three weeks the A-frame was a reality.

I think that one of the reasons his imagination led to the tangible cabin was that, while he was developing it in his mind, he kept it a secret (except from his wife). Even *well-meaning* friends and family members might have unintentionally cast a shadow over his vision and given him enough uncertainty to keep him from trying. Any lack of confidence would have stemmed from their *own* doubts, but they might have affected his decision to begin.

Keep your images of greater prosperity to yourself. Plan what you will do. Organize all the details in your mind, so that when you're ready to move you know exactly where you are going. Let the plans develop in your mind and your scrapbook as a baby grows inside before it can be seen. Like a full-term newborn, prosperous thoughts and images, nurtured and held on to long enough, will have a better chance than those that are released from the mind prematurely. A new idea is exhilarating, but if it hasn't been completely thought out before it's acted upon, it can become a disaster.

"People usually fail when they are on the verge of success so give as much care to the end as to the beginning," said Lau Tsu. Use your imagination to work out the details, and when your idea is ripe, share it.

Your imagination is such a powerful tool. Persist in picturing the standard of living you want, the balance you'd like in your bank account, the clothes you'd wear, the house you'd live in, the car you'd drive; but be specific about what you want. I once wanted some new plants in the house; the doorbell rang and my neighbor stood at the threshold, her arms full of plants for me to water and care for while she went on vacation.

Be optimistic about finances, but don't base your optimism of greater prosperity on physical events or tangible sources. Don't confuse the real source with a channel. There are hundreds of channels that can bring you money, but there is only one source and it is intangible.

Think about the source of the cash in your purse. Even if it's only change or a single dollar, take it out and look at it. Ask yourself where it came from: the mint, your husband, your employer, your customers, or the bank... then think again. The money came from an idea. It might be money you earned by working, payment in return for something you sold, or bills that came out of the cash machine at the bank (those are all channels). The true source of the money you see is an idea that took form because it was acted upon.

Use your creative mind to imagine your purse full of Hamiltons, Jacksons, and other large-denomination bills. Even dare to picture a Ben Franklin tucked in the paper money pocket. Then, while you have a mind full of money, ask your imagination where it came from. If the answer is something like "You earned it," ask yourself how. Keep narrowing it down and the answer will be clear; "You earned it because you are smart, talented, and energetic."

Banks, businesses, even cities, can fail, but what you have inside can't. Thoreau said, "Goodness is the only investment that never fails" and "A man is rich in proportion to the number of things he can afford to let alone... sell your goods and keep your thoughts." You could lose all your money but you wouldn't have lost your talent, your energy, or your ability to think and act.

When Pam first divorced, she went through a period of real financial worry. She was afraid that she wouldn't be able to meet her pressing obligations, and all of her attention was focused on lack and "what ifs." Yielding to her fears concerning money, she felt sick to her stomach, short of breath, and nervous, and she couldn't get a good night's sleep. All of her creativity, joy, and talent was swallowed up in a wild visualization of what the worst might be.

One day I said to her, "Okay, the absolutely worst thing that could happen is that your creditors would sign a warrant for your arrest and the police would come out here, surround the house, and tell you over a megaphone to put down that laundry basket and give yourself up. Then you'd lose your house, your credit cards, your home entertainment center, and your kids would all go to foster homes." Of course, she knew none of that would really happen. In fact, it was all so preposterous that it was funny. Then I asked her what would make her feel better and she said, "A check for about $85,000!" As we were laughing I took out my checkbook and wrote her a check for the full amount. I handed it to her and said, "You've got it!"

It was a joke of course, because I didn't have more than about $35 myself, and she knew it; but it was amazing what it did for her morale. Giving Pam a check for so much more money than I had or she needed put her financial situation into perspective. She was able to laugh at herself and she stopped feeling helpless. She began to think about what qualities she had that could be put to use and would in turn generate income.

Your subconscious mind can't take a joke. It believes whatever you tell it. Pam kept the rubber tender, and once in a while she'd look at it and tell herself she'd be all right financially because she had a check for $85,000. Meanwhile, she took her mind off the problems and focused her attention on her assets. Good ideas came to her that, when acted upon, brought her the money she needed to meet her financial obligations.

Along with thinking about financial prosperity, you have to take some action and work at it. Large sums of money in your bank account will do you no good if you don't know what your balance is, and having enough to pay the bills means nothing if you don't sit down, write the checks, and mail them.

Knowing the negative effect that my disorganization has had on our prosperity in the past, I chose to take the time to put order into all of our financial affairs.

I made a list of the tangible things that are associated with money: my desk, the file cabinet, the checkbook, and my purse. Then I took an honest look at each one.

Desk: You need a place to pay the bills, handle the mail, balance the checkbook, and keep office-type supplies. A table will do, but a desk is even better. You also have to have a comfortable chair, a wastebasket, and good lighting. If you don't have those things, add them to your notebook list of what you want and make them an A priority. If you already have a desk, it has to be clean and organized to be efficient. I decided that I would empty my desk of its present contents, clean it thoroughly, and refill it with only things that *should* be there. I stocked it with the following items:

Pens and pencils
Pencil sharpener
Tape
Scissors
Stapler, staples, staple remover
Paper clips
Ruler
Rubber bands
Typing paper
Carbon paper
Typewriter (optional)
Stationery and envelopes
Postcards
Supply of greeting cards
Stamps
Letter opener
Pocket dictionary

Now I make it a habit to put things back where they belong so that the desk never gets very messy and things don't get lost.

File Cabinet: There are several kinds of file cabinets to choose from. I have two. One is a chunky old metal two-drawer garage-sale eyesore that I keep hidden in a basement closet, and the other is a small modern bright yellow square box with a handle. I use the ugly file cabinet for the noncurrent stuff we want to hang on to, such as past income tax returns, home-improvement receipts, bank statements, and medical records. I also put a year's worth of canceled checks in one of these cheap plastic boxes made especially for that purpose, and I keep them in the closet with the file cabinet.

The modern yellow file is for the current year and contains folders for current home-improvement receipts, expenses for a rental house we have, medical receipts, bills paid, bank statements, and miscellaneous. There are two folders for warranties and owner's manuals; one for large appliances and one for small. Keeping the files organized makes income tax preparation easy, and when we need to find an important paper we know exactly where to look.

Checkbook: The most important part of the checkbook is not the checks but the balance. To keep a current balance I carry a solar-powered calculator in my purse along with a pen. When I write a check I subtract it from the balance immediately. Our checks have a carbon copy (which most banks offer now), making it easier for two people to share one checkbook. Danny usually uses cash and I keep the checkbook in my purse, but when he needs to write a check for something, he tears out both the check and the carbon and we have an automatic record of what's been written.

When the statement comes from the bank, I take a minute out (actually about ten minutes) to balance my check register with it. Pam and I have a rule: You don't get to go out to the mailbox until you have at *least* 10 minutes to handle what's out there.

In the same way that tight pants keep me aware of how much I can eat and when I have to turn away from a tempting meal, a current balance in the checkbook lets me know how much I can realistically spend at a clearance sale. It helps me avoid sudden, overpowering, unreasonable purchases I can't afford.

I used to be a panic buyer at sales because I was afraid I would never find another bargain as good as the one they were offering. Then I learned that there will always be another sale. When I was cleaning my desk I came across a "14-hour, preferred customer, prices slashed to the floor" sale announcement from one of my favorite department stores. I had saved it, thinking I should surely take part, even be there waiting when the doors opened. The announcement was more than a year old so I tossed it in the wastebasket, disappointed about what I'd missed. That afternoon I got the mail and there was another chance waiting in the mailbox, only this time it was a seventeen-hour, preferred customer, price slashathon...same merchandise, same store, but a year later. There will never be a sale to end all sales.

Now I have a list on a card of what month certain things usually go on sale, and it helps me plan my spending and get the most for my money.

> January—linens, refrigerators, freezers
> February—air conditioners, dishes, toys
> March—clothing, washers and dryers
> April—ranges, infants' wear
> May—televisions, tires
> June—building materials, lumber
> July—summer clothes, toiletries
> August—school clothes, drapes and curtains
> September—batteries, mufflers, new cars
> October—china, bicycles, silverware
> November—used cars, men's suits
> December—blankets, dishes

Purse: My purse is a receptacle for money, not a leather litterbag. If it is a mess, chances are good that my financial affairs are out of control too. It occurred to me that if I can't take care of what I've got, why should I be given more? Knowing that my purse is a reflection of my habits, I decided to weed it out and keep it in order. No more wadded-up currency and loose change in the bottom, and no more illegible deposit receipts or dog-eared store coupons jammed in there among all the other junk...just an organized wallet with some cash in it, a checkbook with checks, a calculator, a pen, and a pocket planner, plus a *few* other carefully chosen items I might need.

By organizing the tangible things as I did, you will be

more aware of what's coming in and how it's going out, and you can plug up the holes that are draining away your money while you establish a plan for spending and bill paying.

Here are some other actions you can take that will help you achieve the prosperity you desire.

Read books about prosperous people and how they've gone from rags to condos in the sun. There are books to help you understand the law of tithing, that will teach you the importance of giving back some of what you receive, and there are inspirational writings that can give you the faith you need to get through hard times. When you read something you want to remember, write it on a 3x5 card and put it in your inspiration divider. Make out "think" cards and put them in your checkbook, with your charge cards, and in your wallet to remind you to think about what you *really* want before you buy what you don't.

Make prosperous affirmations, as Pam advised in the January chapter, and work with them daily.

Develop your imagination of greater good by working with your lists of what you want to have and why. Cut out pictures of some of those things for a prosperity section in your scrapbook and look at them often. Imagine how you would enjoy them. (Thinking about a purchase is often more fun than the thing itself.)

Choose a time for bill paying and bookkeeping and get it scheduled on the Daily Routine Card.

Sign up for a payroll deduction savings plan, so that money will go into your account before you get a chance to spend it. When the bills come in, open them, discard the throw-away part, and put them in the desk in a "current bills" folder.

Keep a monthly list on a 3x5 card of all your fixed bills. On another card, list your installment payments and their balances. The cards will help you plan payoffs and establish a better cash flow.

Never go shopping without a list, and if you shop with a friend, don't be swayed by her purchases. I went to the mall with Pam a while ago and came home with everything on *her* list. Danny couldn't believe it when I walked in with a parakeet in a cage, a couple of pillows, and five pounds of nuts.

Finally I would suggest that you surround yourself with prosperous, positive-thinking people and that you remember what Thumper's mother told him in *Bambi* about watching his mouth. If you can't say something good about your finances—be quiet and, in your silence, do something about it.

As Booker T. Washington said, "Success is to be measured not so much by the position that one has reached in life as by the obstacles which he has overcome while trying to succeed."

Family Album

Mom and Dad, 1940

Grandpa Don't, Granny, and Pam

Pam before "The Rosebud" arrived

The generic dog, Ella Mae, and Pam

In between fights

A fishing trip at Silver Lake

Santa (age unknown)
Peggy (three years old)

Peggy (ten years old)

View of our house from the field we ruined

Our condos in the hay

The toe dancer and the toe picker

Cheers

Peggy's senior year in high school

Mirror, mirror, on the wall ...

Danny ready to hit the dance floor

The real world of Pvt. Dan Jones

May 13, 1967

Duke, The Wonder Dog

One last attempt to break into the costume industry

Left to right, our kids: Allyson, Joanna, Jeffrey, Chris, Peggy, Michael

The truth behind the rosy cheeks. Taken in August for a Christmas gift for Mom and Dad

Peggy and Danny—today

Five

May–Health and Beauty –From Pam

"Happiness lies first in health."
—GEORGE CURTIS

"There is no cosmetic for beauty like happiness."
—LADY BLESSINGTON

May is a happy time! May baskets are secretly left on porches, and doorbells are rung and answered as little girls giggle and vanish. Flowers are in full bloom, and folks open windows and bask in the sun that now shines more predictably.

We decided to have May be the health and beauty month, because it is a beautiful time of year, and it's a great month to start exercising and eating better.

I don't know George Curtis or Lady Blessington personally, but I sure like what they said. I felt a little shaky at first, writing about health and beauty (I'm not Linda Evans or the surgeon general); but once I got into it, I found that I had more to say than I had realized.

Webster defines beauty as "a person or thing that gives pleasure to the senses or pleasurably exalts the mind or spirit." Catherine Ponder said, "Beauty is a physical, mental, and spiritual necessity to our well-being." Physical beauty is often rewarded. It gets to ride on parade floats, do Ivory soap commercials, win trophies and bunches of roses, and catch the adoring eyes of interested bystanders.

The beauty that is mental and spiritual goes beyond the outer attraction. It is a quality that can't be enhanced by mascara, lipstick, or a pair of Calvin Kleins. That's because it's intangible. It's what gives real meaning to the saying "Beauty is in the eye of the beholder." It's also what baffles you when they crown Miss Ozone, instead of the one you were positive would win.

It would be an interesting experiment if you were to have a snapshot taken of yourself now, and then pose for one a year from today. If you have made the decision to work with the Happiness File for twelve months, you will be amazed at the changes in your physical appearance as a result of your new level of happiness.

Our mom is a wonderful photographer. She has been taking pictures of all of us for about twenty-five years. Like Kac Young, she has her snapshots developed and then puts them into photograph albums.

Because of Mom's hobby and discipline to follow through, we have been able to see that our appearances have improved since Peggy and I got organized. The drastic changes that followed June 16, 1977, took place not only in our homes, but also began to be visible in Mom's albums.

When I look back at her photographic collection of those horrible slob years, I wonder what we were thinking then. I know I was the unhappiest I've ever been, because I was out of control. I guess I thought somehow I'd get out of the whole mess. However, with every child I got a little bit fatter and farther away from what I wanted to be. In the depths of my slob days I weighed a hundred and sixty pounds and I felt horrible.

I quit looking at myself in the mirror when I was nude (I'd just pretend I wasn't there). Sex was embarrassing; I hated my husband to feel the folds of fat that drooped and flopped, and he didn't like it, either. I felt self-conscious walking past people. My pants cut off my circulation and caused sweaty red marks, numb feet, and shortness of breath from elastic that was too tight. It was depressing to be constantly tugging at my clothes, trying to get comfortable. I didn't like looking out of my face and seeing my cheeks, and I was embarrassed to run into old friends who remembered me when I was small.

Besides all that, I hated my appetite being out of control. All I did was think about food. When the family would go on a trip my mind was on stopping at Dairy Queen, Denny's, and Winchell's Donuts. I have fond memories of the Oregon Caves: not the stalagmites, but the deep-dish blackberry pie, à la mode, they served in the lodge. I craved mayonnaise, chocolate, butter, sugar, and bread. I sneaked food, lied about my weight, binged, and felt guilty, depressed, and discouraged.

I finally lost most of the weight by getting my house organized. (I was so busy cleaning that I didn't have time to think about food.) But now that I am at my ideal weight, I can see that there was more to the problem than I realized. Diet and exercise were both a part of it, but just as important was the unrealistic idea of what my physical goal should be.

Sensitive to the ideal that Madison Avenue created, I've tried to be slim, but I've wondered at what point they decided that "rail" was the "in" look. Maybe it started after the stock market crash in 1929, and all they could find were starving models who were skin and bones. Or maybe it happened when they discovered that the lens of a TV camera adds fifteen pounds to an innocent subject.

I think we should forget what the media tell us we ought to look like, and be honest about what we can achieve. If each of us took some time to evaluate realistically our own bodies, we would each come up with an achievable object to work toward.

Until I honestly looked at my body, I was always trying to be tiny. Molly Cutter was tiny. In high school she weighed ninety-five pounds. She wore a size four and a half shoe and a size three dress. I knew my feet could never shrink from a supportive seven and a half to fit into any of Molly's glass slippers, but I tried fiercely to be as petite as she was. Like a three-year-old who hasn't learned proportion and tries to get into her dolls' buggy, I was always trying to cinch my way into a smaller image.

Anorexia was not "in" when I was in high school; otherwise, I would have had it. I starved and Scarlett O'Hara-ed my waist from 1958 to 1961, in envious pursuit of a body like Molly's. I finally had to face the fact that I'm not tiny . . . I'm medium. Unrealistic goals cause us to make promises to ourselves that we can't keep. A broken promise to yourself is discouraging and sets up a pattern of failure.

You know that statue of the woman with no arms? She's Venus, the goddess of love and beauty, and she is *not* Molly Cutter! When the sculptor chipped out the famous lady in marble, I'm sure he was working with what everybody thought was "the perfect woman." I wonder what happened to using that heavier model as our picture of loveliness?

Recently I read an article in a health magazine that explained how to find your natural weight (I had to use my pocket calculator). It said to: (1) divide your height, in inches, by 66; (2) multiply the result by itself; and (3) multiply that result by your age plus 100. That weight would be in the middle of a range that is considered healthy. If you are within 15 pounds on either side of that figure, you are, according to Joel Gurin, editor of *American Health* magazine, in a very "safe" range healthwise. Using my statistics: 5'3" converted to inches is 63. Sixty-three inches divided by 66 equals .95. Multiplying that figure by itself: .95 × .95 equals .90. And .90 × 141 (my age plus 100) is 127 pounds.

Whenever I get below 120 pounds, I seem to catch colds more often. Above 135, I look stuffed into my clothes, but at 125, I look good to myself and I feel great.

What we weigh and how we look is an intensely personal thing. Research is coming in that is leaning toward Venus's shape as being healthier. The question soon may be "Fashion or health?" and ultimately, maybe all of our ideas of what looks good will change.

In the middle of raising babies, when I let myself go to

pot (I don't mean that literally), I didn't think I had time to do things for myself. That was a big mistake. For one thing, when I let my physical body go, I didn't like the way I felt mentally. I was depressed, which caused my family to get that way, so I wasn't happy with them and they weren't happy with me.

Until Peggy and I put health and beauty into the Happiness File, the only card we had for our own care was "shower and dress." That one card was a good start, but we discovered so many more ways to use 3x5s to help us improve our appearance and well-being.

I found an article that Peggy wrote several years ago for our newsletter, before we had developed the Happiness File. I can remember that day she wrote about, because when I got to her house, she was crazy.

From Peggy:
January 15, 1980 . . . I had slipped back into the pigpen. That morning I'd pushed the "snooze" button on the clock radio two or three times while the words "Get up a half hour before the mainstream of the family" haunted me.

My hair was bothering me! Maybe if it had looked cuter, I'd have felt more like getting up. "Where are my scissors?" I had yelled through the house. Everybody denied that they'd ever seen them.

"Jeff, when you made that deal for Ally's Barbie dolls out of one of my produce boxes, how'd you cut out the windows?"

"I used one of your steak knives."

"Oh, that's just great. . . . Not only do you wreck my knife, you could have cut off your hand."

"I'm sorry, Mom."

"Yeah, yeah, yeah . . . everybody's sorry, but nobody knows where my hair scissors are!

"Ally!" Whoa. Sometimes my voice is almost a yodel.

"She's right behind you, Babe." (When I get crazy, my husband gets so disgustingly calm. It only makes me more vicious!)

"Well, then, why didn't she answer?!! Did you use my hair scissors on Baby Cut 'n' Grow?!"

"No, Mom."

"Chris, what'd you do with my hair scissors?"

"Nothing, Mom, but didn't you lend them to Aunt Sissy to cut Peg's bangs?"

Oh, yeah . . . I guess I did . . . I forgot about that . . . mmmm.

I backed off and looked at myself in the mirror. I thought, *Why did I ever give myself this stupid permanent? "Body 'n' Bounce," ha! I need my scissors back so I can just cut off these ends. I can't go to Mr. Charles with this frizz. He'll wonder why I didn't get one of his "perms." I can't stand it when they call them "perms." Why don't they call them permanents? They probably don't because it sounds so final. I know why I didn't go to a professional—he couldn't take me till Tuesday and I wanted to look pretty for the weekend. Besides, I couldn't bear to spend $55 when a box of "Body 'n' Bounce" was only $3.95. Mr. Charles isn't so great anyway. These streaks he called highlights . . . ha! It looks like Garfield is sleeping on top of my head. I wonder if I should have used the "Body 'n' Bounce" for color-treated hair? I'll bet that's why it broke off in strips. When I get those scissors back I'll even it up and then call Mr. Charles. . . .*

When everyone was out of the house, I fixed some coffee and sat down to rest, but the doorbell rang. I crawled into the living room and peeked out the window to see whose car it was. Pam walked in.

"Oh, Sissy, thank goodness it's only you."

"What's wrong with you?"

"I don't know. . . . I'm mean and confused and I need my scissors. How soon can you get them back to me?"

"Why?"

"'Cause if I don't snip some of these hairs soon, I'll go mad! I mean it! I'm ready to use Danny's wire cutters or the pinking shears or—"

"Peggy, you don't want to cut your own hair!"

"Yes, I do."

"No, you don't!"

"I don't?"

"No. I'm taking you to see Mr. Charles. The last time I was in there he asked what had happened to you."

"Really? You mean he misses me?"

"No, he wondered what happened to your hair. He saw

you on television on *A.M. Northwest* and thought there was something wrong with his TV set. He said he was just praying you wouldn't say who does your hair. I told him you gave yourself a permanent and you're embarrassed to come in."

"You told him!"

"Peggy, he doesn't care. He deals with people every day who try to take beauty into their own hands."

"I feel like a fool."

"Well, you have to let him help you out of this."

Since the truth was out, I made the call. My hair had taken over my life, throwing everything out of balance, making me irritable, restless, and ugly. . . .

If one part of your body is bugging you, it throws everything else off. I have a white 3x5 card with Mr. Charles's name and phone number on it, filed under C in the ABC section. Since I have to get my hair cut every six weeks or I'll resort to self-whacking, like my sister almost did, I have a Reminder Card in the January through December section that tells the date of my last haircut.

If you don't have a good haircutter, start looking at people's hair on the street. When you see somebody with a haircut you like, stop her and ask her who does it. It's very flattering to have someone ask you and most people are pleased to tell. Once you find a good hairstylist, stay with him or her.

Peggy and I have learned the hard way not to entertain our stylist while he is cutting. Both of us have made Mr. Charles laugh so hard that we've come out of the salon lopsided. We have also learned to be the boss in the chair. We both used to be shy about what we wanted, but after years of going home and combing out the way "they" liked it, we have learned to stand strong against the somewhat condescending attitude that tends to pervade most of the beauty parlors that keep up with the styles.

Don't ever leave your look up to them. Be specific. It helps to have a picture of the look you desire. You can always find just the right "do" in magazines. Cut out the picture, tape it to the back of the Reminder Card, and take

184 / Pam Young and Peggy Jones

it with you. Before you put it back in the box for the next month, record the date of your cut.

Hair is an important part of your appearance, so take good care of it. Keep it out of the sun as much as possible and use a mild shampoo and a good conditioner.

You heard this part in seventh grade health class. You've heard it on television, and you've read it in magazines and books. "Eat right, exercise, and get plenty of rest, fresh air, and water." It's a cliché, but it is also the answer to good health and beauty.

Eating right is a big deal. There are hundreds of books on the subject, and more and more people are becoming diet-conscious. What you eat has a lot to do with your health and beauty. A well-balanced diet will give your body a healthy look that is so important to your appearance. A friend who went to Weight Watchers and lost 90 pounds on their diet plan said that, by eating right, she not only lost the weight, but her fingernails got strong, and her hair had never been shinier.

You can use 3x5 cards to keep track of what you eat. One of our Happiness File lab rats put a blank 3x5 card in the kitchen every morning. During the day she wrote down everything she ate, from a handful of Cocoa Puffs to the scraps from her kid's sandwich. She told us it didn't take long to see why she was overweight.

You can use 3x5s to stay on a specific diet. In our home executive cardfile system for organizing our house-work, we put all the jobs on cards, and when we completed a task, we moved it to the next day, week, or month, depending on how frequently we thought it needed to be done.

The diet cards can be used the same way. If you trans-ferred your diet menu to 3x5s and put them in the Monday through Sunday section of the Happiness File on the day you start your diet, you would have a revolving reminder of what you were supposed to eat each day, and as you ate something you would file the card to the next day. If some of the food was to be eaten every other day or once a week, it would be filed two days or a week later.

Ask your doctor to give you a diet that is just right for

you, and make an appointment for a checkup if you haven't had one in the last year or two.

Exercise is also vital to your health and beauty. I *am* an authority on exercise. When I didn't do it, I was fat and sluggish; I do it now and feel wonderful.

I go to an aerobics class two days a week, and I jog and walk for an hour three times a week. I don't like physical exertion, but I know it's important to my health and appearance. I had to ask myself what I'd have to do to stick with an exercise routine. The answer for me is music. I use my favorite songs to con myself into exercising. I bought a Walkman tape recorder, and I play tapes that inspire me to move.

I tried out several aerobics classes before I found the perfect one for me. I knew I would need a teacher who would encourage me to stick with the program and good music to keep me interested.

Peggy's answer was to get a bike. Mom and Dad's was the beach at Maui. "What can I do to keep fit?" If you ask yourself that question, you'll get the answer that is right for you. In your notebook make a list of the physical activities you like, and then get moving.

Get out in the fresh air as much as you can. If it rains where you live, get boots and a raincoat. If it snows most of the time, get snow clothes, but get out there. If you have been inactive, get a checkup before you start.

We hope we have already talked you into getting the right amount of sleep. Rest is one of the main things that affects my looks. When I'm tired, my face checks out. I lose my color and all evidence of life. When I get eight hours of sleep, for some reason, my makeup stays on my face and I look younger.

Laughter is another wonderful health and beauty booster. We rate it with diet and exercise in its importance to beauty and well-being. Studies have proved that laughter can heal. (Read Norman Cousins's book, *Anatomy of an Illness*.)

Chapter Ten, our laughter chapter, will get you started laughing and give you some good ideas to keep your sense of humor in tone.

To start getting your beauty and health care into the

Happiness File, make a complete evaluation of your body by standing in the nude in front of a mirror. (That might be something you'll want to add to the humor divider.) Look at the way you are standing. Good posture has such an effect on your appearance. Our friend Linda has wonderful posture. Her carriage is perfect and she looks elegant when she walks, stands, or sits. Peggy and I have to remind each other constantly to stand up straight. When we catch each other slumping around, a simple poke and the word *Linda* instantly sends the sloucher into correct posture.

Measure everything: bust, waist, hips, thighs, upper arms, and ankles. Put the notations on a card, date it, and project a reasonable date in the future that you want to see your goal reached. File the card in front of the month you expect to be looking like you want to look.

Get some graph paper and cut out a few 3x5 cards for charting your progress (see example on page 187). We like to measure and "weigh in" once a week, so we put the graph card in the Monday through Sunday dividers in front of the day that is best for us. You can use your quiet time in the morning to do all this figuring. It will be very helpful to watch your improvement.

Make a list of all the parts of you that you want to improve, emphasize, or play down. Leave space under each item, so that you can write what action you need to take (see example on page 188). Some things will go on the Immediate Action Card, like buy new tweezers." Some of the action steps will be put on the Daily Routine Card, like "walk an hour a day." Make out a daily (yellow) card with a twenty-minute regimen on one side for the time you have alloted yourself before bed, and your morning regimen on the other (see example on page 188).

Make a list in your notebook of all the things that will help you improve (see example on page 189). Look back in your clearing exercises and you'll find things that pertain to your health and beauty. Also look at the list of what was on your mind, and lists of what you want to be, do, and have, for more ideas.

Date	6/1	6/8	6/15	6/22	6/29	7/6	7/13
Weight	132						
Bust	37						
Waist	29						
Stomach	37						
Hips	39						
Thighs	22						
Upper Arm	12						
Goal	132	130	128	126	124	122	120

We post Think Cards in key places throughout our houses, to remind us of the reasons we want to improve. On my refrigerator I have a card that says, "size seven, bathing suit, 125 lbs": it reminds me to eat sensibly. I have the same card in my purse to remind me to grocery shop with health in mind. I also have a 3x5 by the kitchen sink that says, "Drink a glass of water"; one in the car that says, "Take a deep breath." You can put little reminders around to help you with things that you know will make you healthier.

I can remember looking at women who kept their fingernails manicured, their hair pretty, and their bodies in great shape, and if I found out they had kids, I thought they were selfish. I don't think that way anymore; in fact, Peggy and I call our new attitude enlightened selfishness. It's like the selfishness that is suggested by all the major airlines. If cabin pressure is lost in an airliner, passengers are instructed to put their own oxygen masks on first, and then assist their children. That policy confirms a fact that I hadn't thought of: you can't take very good care of others if you don't take care of yourself first.

When it comes to beauty, you have to be the final judge. You have to like your haircut, the shape of your body, and the style of your clothes.

FRONT (yellow)   BACK (yellow)

Morning Regimen

Exercise
Shower
Dress—hair—makeup
Take vitamin
Follow diet plan

Night Regimen

30 sit-ups
30 push-ups
30 leg raises
Bubble bath
Take off makeup
Moisturize
Brush teeth—floss
Brush hair
Hand cream—body lotion
Put clothes out for next
    day
Read
Say prayers
Lights out 10:00 P.M.

Emphasize	De-emphasize	Improve
Eyes—pluck eyebrows weekly/ eye makeup	Ears—wear hair over them	Teeth—whiten, call dentist
Hair—wash daily, cut every six weeks		Feet—toenails, pedicure weekly
Bust—wear good supporting bras, check monthly		Hands—nails, wear rubber gloves, hand lotion in purse, kitchen, and bathroom
Waist—cute belts, styles, with waistlines		

Freckles—get
    translucent
    makeup base
Calves/ankles—
    wear cute
    shoes, skirts
    just below the
    knee

Hips—exercise

Skin—use
    moisturizer,
    rubber gloves

Stomach—sit-ups

Things I Need to Do to Improve Health and Appearance

Hair

Good style   Immediate Action Card (start stopping people on street)
Appointment (every six weeks)
Shampoo and condition (daily)   Daily Routine Card
Hair spray   to buy
Brush   to buy
Comb for purse   to buy
Hand mirror to see back of head   to buy
Hat for sun   to buy
Hair dryer   to buy
Curling iron   to buy

Face

Moisturizer (use it morning and night) Night Regimen Card
Foundation makeup   use what you have
Blush   use what you have
Mascara   use what you have
Eye shadow   use what you have
Lipstick   use what you have
Tweezers   (tweeze every other day) to buy
Sun screen   to buy

Body

Body lotion   use what you have

Bath oil   use what you have
Body powder   use what you have
Scale (weigh and measure weekly)   to buy
Perfume   use what you have
Checkup (yearly)   Immediate Action Card

Exercise

Jogging suit   to buy
Running suit   to buy
Leotard and tights   to buy
Raincoat to buy

Misc.

Sleep (eight hours)
Vitamin supplement   Daily Routine Card
Health diet   Immediate Action Card
Laugh   see Chapter Ten—Laughter
Read books on health and beauty

May is a great month to start being more healthy and beautiful. Not the bathing-suit-body-by-June kind of crash course, but a practical plan to give you time to take care of yourself all the time. Your body is the only one you have, and if you take good care of it, you'll look better, feel better, and you *will* be happier.

Six

June–Parents and Kids
–From Peggy

*"When I was a boy of 14, my father was so ignorant I
could hardly stand to have the old man around. But
when I got to be 21, I was astonished at how much the
old man had learned in seven years."*

—MARK TWAIN

We chose June as the month to focus on kids and parents
because it's traditionally the time when school lets out, and
once again we're all thrown together for the duration of the
summer.

Don't you just love summer? We have so many wonderful childhood memories of that special time of year. As we
told you earlier, we lived on forty acres, in a century-old
farmhouse. Our bedroom was upstairs and in the summer,
while it was very hot, we'd get to go to bed extra late, after
our second-story room broke its fever. There were screens
on the open windows, and the sweet night air tangled with
the curtains and cooled us. We shared secrets and giggled.

Sometimes, after several warnings from their room below us, Dad would come up, giving us the final word to "settle down." Usually he'd end up sitting on our bed, telling us great stories of his summers in Illinois when he was little.

Mom was always up early (even in the summer) to make Dad a good breakfast. We had a big sun porch off the dining room and food (especially breakfast) always tasted better when we ate at the big patio table out there.

Never rushing, we'd sip our orange juice and nibble at the whole wheat toast. A seductive purple lilac bush near the porch sweetly lured every honeybee in Clark County. Their buzzing chorus promised "no rain today."

The smells, the sounds, and the feelings of those gentle summers are so clear even today. Every year early in June, Grandma Dot and Grandpa Buddy would come for their annual visit. We all looked forward to it, almost like a holiday. Thinking of Grandma Dot loading up Mom's grocery cart with Oreos and goodies while Grandpa Buddy cranked out a batch of homemade ice cream sent our taste buds into a frenzy of anxious anticipation.

Two weeks before their expected arrival date our "born organized" mother would announce the cleaning schedule. The house already looked perfectly acceptable to us, but it did not meet her standards. As soon as the furnace was turned off for the summer, Mom would start the "deep" cleaning, and we could almost taste the Oreos and ice cream. She would assemble all those good-smelling cleaning supplies, and room after room produced evidence of orderly accomplishment. Rugs were rolled up so that hardwood floors could be cleaned and waxed. Furniture was polished and rearranged. Windows were cleaned inside and out and curtains were washed, starched, ironed, and rehung. Cupboards were cleaned out and shelf paper was replaced. The oven and range were made spotless; the woodwork was cleaned and polished throughout; the bathroom was scrubbed. The fireplace almost shone, and every picture, ornament, book, and mirror in the house was cleaned thoroughly (she even did something to the lamp shades to make them look brighter).

And the guest room where Grandpa and Grandma would stay was so clean and bright, it made us want to sit in there for no reason. Window screens had been washed and put back on all the windows so that warm summer breezes freshened every room in the house.

After two weeks of organized, systematic cleaning, the house was "ready" by Mom's standards. We had thought it was clean before she started, but there was no denying the difference. When everything was immaculate she would say, "Now, you see, girls ... *this* is what I mean by clean." The rest of the summer we played, and Mom put the housework on hold. We loved knowing that no matter what she was doing, Mom always had time for us. She was a motherhood model who made Margaret Anderson look like a failure.

Robert Schuller said, "Consider your child's request to tell him a story or read him a book not as an interruption, but as the most honored invitation you will ever receive."

My daughter is still young enough to ask for a story once in a while, but I've seen my other two and my sister's three kids grow up past that kind of interruption. Now Pam's eighteen-year-old is asking her what to pack for college, and her sixteen-year-old is begging for the car. It's such a worn-out saying that "kids grow up too fast," but it's true.

I didn't think it could happen when mine were all three and under. Our two boys were thirteen months apart, and they were at the height of their escapades as toddlers when Allyson was born. One day as I was painting the nursery in expectation of the new baby, Chris came to me and said, "What happened to the balls, Mom?" "What balls?" I asked. "The 'frigerator balls ... come see." I followed him to the room he shared with his crimemate, Jeff, and was just in time to see the last of a dozen eggs sail through the air from the crib onto the green shag carpet. The rug looked like a Caesar salad.

Anyone who tells me that those were the great years wasn't aware of what was going on at our house. Village people (not the rock group but the little Fisher Price guys) were flushed down the toilet frequently. I seemed always to be trying to get gum out of someone's hair, bark dust out of somebody's shoe, a sliver of wood out of one of their fingers, the ring from around the tub, pens out of the sink, and grass stains off their pants. And there were diapers, diapers, and diapers...

When the kids were all very little, I had a cheap tape recorder that I'd use to record the newest baby learning to talk. I'd leave it on, hoping to catch something darling, with the intention of mailing the tape to Pam, who lived in Fresno. Usually I'd forget the thing was on, and all I'd end up with was a cassette of me yelling at the boys to "Get out of that!" or "Put that back!" Anytime the baby did say something, it was inaudible over the sound of pots and pans crashing, someone crying, the dog barking, or the phone ringing.

I have a tape that I made back then that says it all. Once again I'd forgotten I was recording because my voice wasn't as formal as it was when I was "on." I sounded exhausted. I must have been nursing Allyson because you can hear a distinct sucking noise in the background. Then Chris, my three-year-old said, "Wookit, Mom." ... No answer.

"Mom, wookit dis." ... No answer.

"Jeffy gots wektwicity in him." No answer.

"Mom."

"Huh?"

"Wookit Jeffy's wektwicity." That time he got my attention and you could hear Jeff starting to fuss.

"Oh, no, no, Chris! Don't rub his head on the rug like that."

Jeff had snow white curly hair that Chris had a fascination for, and standing on end, it was even more of a wonder.

Throughout the tape there were loud commands to "Stop that," "Get down from there," "Spit that out," and "Be nice."

The final blow to my nerves came when Chris said, "Mom." ... No answer.

"Mom." No answer.

"Mom, somebody camed here."

"Huh?"

"Somebody camed here."

"Camed isn't a word . . . it's somebody *came* here. . . . Somebody was here?"

"Uh-huh."

"Who!? When!? Where was I!?"

Finally after several minutes of interrogation I got to the bottom of it all. The garage door had been left up, and with all the big wheels, wagons, trikes, and mess in there, some guy assumed we were having a garage sale and had stopped to inquire about the price of the lawn mower.

The greatness of those days of hard work and fatigue is captured only in photographs when my darlings were momentarily at their cleanest, in their Sunday best, and being entertained by the antics of the photographer at Penney's, so that they were too engrossed to be teasing each other.

Today I can honestly say that these *are* the great years. Our kids are twelve, eleven, and nine and they are a delight! Thanks to the earlier years of teaching, tending, and tempering, they seem to know the difference between what is acceptable behavior and what isn't. Bob Lagler, our neighbor, said after a four-day ski trip when we all stayed in one condominium, "I don't usually like kids, but yours are happy, friendly, and considerate human beings."

"They're smart, too," I added proudly.

My sister tells me to enjoy my children's preteens because once they become adolescents, their bodies grow faster than their reasoning ability, and they turn into lanky renegades who won't accept your counsel. I don't believe it will happen to me; but then I didn't believe her when she told me you could get pregnant even when you're nursing.

Dr. James Dobson, child psychologist and author, said in his book, *Dare to Discipline,* that the only way to defuse the teenage time bomb is to start when the child is two. My sister followed his advice, but when Michael turned fourteen she felt as if she were standing in the fumes below a Cape Canaveral liftoff. The six-foot teenage missile refused to cooperate and help with the yardwork. There was a loud exchange of words, and then my tiny 5'3" sister raised her hand against the smart-mouthed arguer to stop his disrespect. He blocked her intended swing with his forearm, covering his face, and made it impossible for her to strike the target. Catching him off guard, she lunged forward and bit his arm! "And if you get smart with me again, I'll bite you *harder* next time! Grow up!"

I don't know what the moral is to that story. Maybe it's that you should start biting your kids when they're two, or maybe we should all remember how hard it was to be teenagers ourselves. A subscriber to our bimonthly newsletter, *S.H.E.s on Track,* shared her exasperation and an interesting idea she had for a teenage "minipunishment." She said, "When my teenager does something wrong that needs punishment or a reminder that it was wrong, I hate to say 'You're grounded' as much as she hates to hear it. For things such as coming home past her curfew, I have her turn the stereo on at the volume she likes, place a straight-back chair three feet in front of it, and I have her sit down. Then I play 'Mom's music'—be it forties, fifties, polka, religious, western, classical, opera, or whatever I'm in the mood to hear. I can hear it all over the house and she now realizes how loud her rock 'n' roll is to me. While she is sitting in the chair she is not allowed to fix her hair or nails, read, or do anything but listen. One hour of music for each fifteen minutes she's late has made her very prompt."

Our friend Dee Anne told me about the time she yelled at her son, "Stop that, you're acting like a two-year old!" and the poor kid *was* two. Raising kids isn't easy, but then growing up isn't either.

As an adult, I can finally appreciate my parents' combined efforts in raising my sister and me. They worked it out so that at least one of them was always available when either of us needed them, and they stuck together on everything.

Since Pam was older, she was the first to be a Brownie (Mom became her troop leader); the first to go to school dances (Mom chaperoned); the first to have a boyfriend (Mom counseled); the first to be a cheerleader (Mom was one in high school, too); and, of course, the first to do everything. My time was coming. Mom was especially involved with Pam's activities because hers were more demanding than mine. I was almost five years younger, and still having a ball with my bike, the dog, my dolls, Granny, and the simple things in life you don't have time to appreciate again until you retire.

Dad spent a lot of time with me. He taught me to fish and hunt, and I was as good as Rudy Lockinmeyer (the local TV sportsman). I went with him on his work route on Saturdays, and all the time in the summer. One day, riding in the cab of his huge oil truck (I wasn't a bit ashamed of it when I was eight), I asked Dad, "What would you do if The Millionaire came to our house and gave you a million dollars?" He thought for an instant and said, "I'd pay off this truck." Then he started to laugh. "Heck, if I had a million dollars I'd drive this thing into the Columbia River." He told me about the time when he was young and worked for the City of Manhattan Beach, California, delivering water bills. He received a check from an inheritance and felt so rich and smart-alecky that he took the bag of bills to the post office, bought hundreds of stamps, mailed all the statements, and put the bag in the garbage can. We laughed hard. In fact, we laughed all the time, and I could always get a story out of him.

I loved being with him. I watched him try to fix things, helped him in the garden, played cops and robbers with him while he mowed the lawn (he'd pretend to chase me with the Toro), and generally hung around him. He always made me feel smart. He said I was a wonderful helper. He'd say, "My hand's way too big; see if you can get yours inside this hole in the wall and grab this plastic tube while I feed it through." I'd be able to get it every time and he'd rave about how clever I was.

One Halloween, Pam and Mom were involved in a deal at Shumway Junior High, called "The Halloween Fair." Pam was there to flirt and Mom was there to chaperon. Dad and I were going to watch, but one thing had been forgotten. . . . I was still at the trick-or-treating age and the night was growing old. The two of us slipped away to the cafeteria, took a lunch tray, gave me big cheeks and lips with Mom's lipstick, and trick-or-treated our way around the neighborhood. When the people dropped the candy on my tray, we thanked them and moved on to the next house. I made a haul that year like no other year (probably because I looked so pathetic trick-or-treating with a tray).

By the time I was in junior high I was preoccupied with boys and Dad wasn't one of them. That's the way it was for a long time until I married and started my own family.

When the kids were little I was so busy with them that I didn't have much time for anything else. I'd invite Mom and Dad over for dinner regularly, but I'd be up and down serving the meal and taking care of the babies, so it was hard to carry on a good conversation. I let the pressing demands of a young family bury me in dishes, diapers, and meals, and I kept thinking about the "someday" when things would slow down and I'd have more time for visiting. Things never did slow down.

By the time the kids were in school, Pam and I had begun to give workshops all over the country and we'd started writing books and going on promotional tours. I loved it, but it took us away from our families, and when we were home I wanted to be with my kids and husband. I didn't see Mom and Dad as often as I would have liked, but they understood our busy schedule, and often, after an all-too-brief phone conversation, they would say, "We'll let you go, sweetie. We know you're in a hurry."

In December 1983 Pam and I made a big mistake. We agreed to leave our families for the three weeks just before Christmas to do some television appearances for a large company. The money tempted us, and we thought of the tour as a good career opportunity. Going against our own rule that December is a time to devote to our kids and family, we packed up and headed out.

The decision proved to be disastrous, both in terms of our work (we couldn't concentrate) and the strain it put on everyone back home.

One night, two weeks into the fiasco, I called home (as I do every night when we're away) and my housekeeper answered the phone. "Dail, why are you still there? It must be seven o'clock," I questioned. "Well, Danny asked me to stay with the kids. He and your Mom took your Dad to the hospital. He was having chest pains this afternoon," she said, trying not to alarm me. From the look on my face Pam

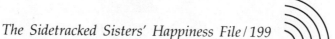

knew something awful had happened. Almost afraid to ask, I said, "Is he all right?" "Who? What?" Pam yelled. "Dad's in the hospital, he had some pains in his chest." My voice was shaking. Then Dail said that Danny had just come home and she would let me talk to him. Pam and I both put our ears to the phone, and Danny told us that Dad had had a heart attack and was in Intensive Care. I felt weak in my legs as we listened to the details.

"Your Mom is fine. She's going to stay here with us." As he continued to talk my mind flashed, trying to grasp what we were being told. I wished I'd gone over there to say good-bye in person. I thought about Mom facing this crisis alone. I thought of things I wanted to tell Dad about how much I loved him and how great he was as a father. I felt sick, thinking about how far away we were and what might happen before we could get back home. I prayed, "Dear God, take care of him until I get there," as if I could take over from then on.

Pam and I were so glad we had each other. We clung together like two lost souls in Philadelphia, and we thought about how hard it must have been for our mom (who's an only child) when she was faced with losing her parents. Each of us understood exactly what the other was going through.

Of course, we cut our trip short and took the next plane home. When we got there, Dad underwent quadruple bypass surgery.

Mrs. Nevin, Kathy's mom, and our longtime family friend, stayed with us all day in the Intensive Care waiting room. Mr. Nevin had come through the same surgery eighteen months earlier, so she was a tremendous comfort to us.

We were all relieved when they brought Dad out of surgery and the doctor reported that things had gone well. He said it would be a while before we could see him and suggested that we get a bite of lunch. Mom wasn't hungry but insisted we go ahead. Danny, Pam, and I decided to walk across the street and have a sandwich in a little restaurant we knew. Mrs. Nevin wanted to stay with Mom. As we left we all felt light and happy and positive everything was fine.

When we returned about a half hour later the chaplain was there. Mom was lying down on a couch, her head in her hands. Mrs. Nevin met us at the door and said, "They're having some problems with bleeding. They're taking him back into surgery now, and the doctor will come and talk to you when it's over."

Finally, strained and exhausted-looking, Dr. Krause came to the waiting room and told us that everything had been done medically that could be, and we would just have to wait to see how things developed in the next few critical hours. Those were the most agonizing few hours we've ever had to endure. At 11:00 P.M. we learned that Dad was conscious and the bleeding had stopped.

Mrs. Nevin had stayed with us throughout our eighteen-hour vigil, helping us every minute with her strong presence and positive attitude. When the crisis was over and we knew Dad would fully recover, she told us, "I believe that when we go through these negative experiences, if we don't share what we've learned with others, the experience is worthless." I can tell you that we learned a lot about priorities: *nothing* is more important than time spent with the people we love.

Danny and I have the special privilege of having both sets of our parents living in the same town as we do. Unfortunately, there have been times where their nearness actually made us put off getting together. It was as if we thought, *We're so close, we can always see each other next week,* but we let weeks go by without actually getting together. I think we were worse at planning visits with Danny's parents than with mine. I talk to my mom and dad on the phone every day. Sometimes we only chat for a couple of minutes, but each day we say hello and share a bit of news or humor.

Danny is not one who likes to chat. He doesn't call his parents every day or even once a week. He doesn't ever think to invite them for dinner, either, but he loves it when I tell him they're coming. He thinks it's great that I've taken care of the plans, the invitation, and the meal. What he doesn't realize is that I have a Family Dinner Card, so that I make a point to have each set of grandparents over for dinner once a month. On occasions such as holidays and birthdays, we include all the grandparents at once. Even though they are not otherwise close friends socially, they do have a great deal in common: they all love their children and grandchildren.

I never used to think it would be comfortable to throw both sides of the family together to celebrate an occasion. Our traditions are different, and each set of parents really doesn't know the other very well. I thought maybe each side should have a separate get-together. Then one Easter, as I was juggling both our families, making two meals, brunch for one set and supper for the other, Danny made me realize the futility of it all. He said that none of our parents would want me to work so hard, and he was right. For years I had made two cakes and dinners for each of the kids' birthdays; there were separate Christmases where we'd stuff ourselves twice; there were double the pots and pans, twice as many tablecloths to iron, and extra time and energy spent to pull it all off.

When I began to dread special occasions, Danny persuaded me to offer an open invitation to both our parents (as well as all the brothers and sisters), and since that decision we have had some of the nicest celebrations as one big happy family that you could imagine. Since we do get together separately once a month, that gives us an opportunity to talk closely and stay current with each of our parents alone. In the November chapter, about hospitality, friendship, and giving, Pam will give you some more specific ideas for remembering parents.

During the years we were growing up our dad was self-employed. He worked long hours, especially in the summer; and because it was his busiest season, he could never take time off for vacations. Because he ran his own business, it was difficult for him to get away. It seemed that if the money was there, he was working too many hours to take the time. And if the time was available, the money wasn't.

In September when we went back to school and were assigned the standard "How I Spent My Summer Vacation" paper, there was no doubt that our adventures made wonderful reading. True, other kids wrote their papers detailing a fun-filled trip to Disneyland or a long-distance car trip to visit family relatives, where, along the way, it was one tourist attraction after another. Occasionally someone could boast of spending the whole summer at the family's beach cottage. There were always boating trips and camping trips, excursions on the train, or tales of an exciting flight to some exotic vacation spot. But our vacation was always the best.

Poor Dad. He still feels guilty thinking that his work cheated us out of our summer fun, because he wasn't able to take the family away on vacation. We can't understand why he feels so bad because in our eyes, every summer was magic.

As organized and immaculate as Mom was, when school let out, she let up. There were picnics, water games in the backyard, special craft projects, lazy days of sleeping in and special nights for staying up late. There were porch camp-outs, barbecues, and sometimes friends stayed overnight.

You won't have to travel this summer to have a great vacation. It isn't necessary to make a family pilgrimage or treat your kids to a glorified amusement park to have their memories of summer be wonderful. Ease up from the hectic school time schedules you've stuck by for nine months.

Relax your standard of cleanliness to allow for temporary summer dirt tracked through the house on the bottoms of small feet. Put a sign on your front door—"Housekeeper NOT on duty; please excuse our mess or call again in September." Let there be a feeling of being "on vacation" even if you never leave the driveway.

To help make the next three months an intermission instead of an interference, it's a good idea, though, to adopt a summer schedule. Let the kids relax in the morning, but have a certain number of jobs they need to complete before they head outside for play. Implanting a good work ethic into their little minds will pay off in a lifetime of dividends. Besides, while they are working each morning, they will have "play" as something to look forward to.

Get away from it all without going away. Spend valuable time with your loved ones instead of with your housework. This summer, let your kids play. Let them sneak past you and go outside with your Scotch tape, Tupperware, blankets, and snacks. Let them go barefoot and play in the sprinkler. To spark their imagination, tell them about what you did when you were little. Offer your Jell-O molds for special mud pies and let them camp out in the backyard. Put the housecleaning on hold and take this time to have fun with your kids.

There is no excuse to let summer turn into one boring day after another. Take the extra effort to plan some special activities. Start brainstorming; put some real gusto into these three months and make this summer the best ever.

The following is an "idea" list to get the family thinking and planning. The activities don't all have to be restricted to summertime. Many of them are good weekenders any time of the year. As you read the list, if something sounds good to you, write it on a 3x5 card and file it within the next few days, the next month, or schedule it farther into the next year, but don't let it get away from you like good intentions gone by. Kathy Liden, the co-author of *The Compleat Family Book*, said, "Ideas are like rainbows, we need to record them with a pencil or they soon fade right out of sight." Get your good ideas on 3x5s, on your wall calendar, and in your pocket planner so that you can enjoy them.

—How about buying a new pet? A parakeet, for instance. It needs to be kept in a draft-free place; it needs a dish of seeds and water daily. If you take care of it, the bird can be part of your family for fifteen years (unless you have a cat).

—Would your older kids be interested in starting their own business? The following books should be available at your library or bookstore: *Extra Cash for Kids* by Larry Belliston and Kurt Hanks—Writers Digest Books; *Good Cents— Every Kid's Guide to Making Money*—Houghton Mifflin Company; *How Kids Can Really Make Money* by Shari Lewis— Holt, Rinehart, and Winston; *Working Kids on Working* by Sheila Cole—Lothrop, Lee, and Shepard Books.

—Consider a subscription to *WORLD* by National Geographic. It's a wonderful kids' magazine full of beautiful pictures and stories and an excellent combination of learning and fun. About $8.95 for one year, National Geographic Society, P.O. Box 2330, Washington, DC 20013.

—Spend a week or two learning all you can about a certain animal or plant and then go search it out. For example, study about eagles, vultures, ospreys, hawks, etcs., and head out for the woods or zoo and spot some.

—Make this the summer you teach one or all of your kids to sew. Or take one at a time each week and teach him/her to cook several easy meals.

—Enroll the kids in swim classes, gymnastics classes, karate classes, day camp, etc.

—Daily, go for a walk or bike ride. Really enjoy the outdoors this summer as you never have before.

—Go camping, even in your own backyard. Study the stars and read about our universe; watch the moon's shape each evening. Select an especially scenic spot and make an event of watching the sunset. Or if you are really adventuresome, select a scenic spot and watch the sun come up. Take along an easy breakfast of hard-boiled eggs, muffins, and hot chocolate.

—Pick strawberries, blackberries, etc., and make jam together. (Peanut butter sandwiches will taste great with *the kids'* homemade jam.)

—Plant a garden together. It doesn't have to be forty acres; even flower beds will do. Enjoy harvesting and eating the fruits of your labor.

—Make cheese or grow mushrooms.

—Hatch your own butterflies. Write to Insect Lore Products, P.O. Box 1535, Shafter, CA 93263 for a free booklet and order form.

—Go skating; make bread together; visit a fish hatchery, the newspaper, or a cheese factory; or build a birdhouse.

—Save your aluminum cans and newspapers; ask your friends and relatives to save theirs and collect them regularly. It is so much fun to take them to a recycling station and collect the money. There are several good lessons involved here.

—Sell worms for a money-making venture or start a neighborhood dog-walking business.

—Go fishing—you'll need tackle box, poles, line, sinkers, bobbers, leaders, hooks, stringer, knife, nail clipper, screwdriver, bait, life jackets, and a snack.

—Go for a "night" walk as a family. The neighborhood looks and smells different on a warm summer evening.

—Go hiking and let everyone carry his or her own pack with lunch inside. Have the kids help prepare those lunches.

—Get a jump on the holidays and make some Christmas gifts, candles, etc.

—Play school with the kids and make improving or maintaining their scholastic skills a game.

—Play board games or card games, or have video game competitions.

—Go window-shopping and out to lunch.

—See a matinee together.

—Take a bus ride; go to the park or the zoo.

—Meet Dad for a lunch-hour picnic near his office or work.

—Have a letter-writing time and let the kids draw pictures, send photos, and perhaps bake some cookies for a relative who lives far away.

—Mail away for freebies. Look for corporate giveaways in magazines or write to the state capitals for colorful, education, and *free* information.

—Make a "summer memory" wall hanging. You can do this project with your kids the next time you go to the beach. Gather: rocks, seashells, small pieces of driftwood, leaves, grasses, feathers, etc. Into a bucket pour:

> 3 cupped handfuls of patch plaster
> 1 cupped handful of sand
> 3 cupped handfuls of sea water

and mix. Add additional plaster or water if necessary. This is a very forgiving recipe. Pour into three paper plates and arrange your treasures. After a short time sprinkle a little sand over the top and allow to dry. Peel off the plate, paste a hook to the back, and it is ready to hang.

Once a week do a good deed for someone else, and be sure to get the kids involved. With a little planning, you can make warm memories and have more fun with your children. Involve the grandparents in lots of your activities, and the family rewards will be multiplied tenfold, along with the wonderful memories.

We are so grateful to be mothers! How better could we learn patience than to tie and re-tie three small pairs of shoes 45,000 times in one week, and listen to the screen door slam 46,000 times in one day? How could we understand unconditional love, if we had not seen it in the faces of our children? They have shown us how quickly one can forget an injustice or an admonition against picking the neighbor's tulips. Our children teach us simplicity in a complicated world; they are reminders that great wisdom often comes in very small packages. Learning all these lessons of patience, love, forgiveness, simplicity, and wisdom, we are sure that, when our kids are grown, we will be sainted women with glowing halos. *Our* mother, however, assures us we will probably carry the glorious marks of "motherhood" as she has...several gray hairs and an uncanny sense of humor.

Seven

July–Freedom
–From Pam

"Ye shall know the truth and the truth shall make you free."

—JOHN 8:32

July sparks the feeling of freedom in me. It makes me want to get out and run barefoot, turn cartwheels, roll down grassy hills, and skinny-dip. (I got to do that only once as a child, when Mom, Peggy, and I slithered into Spirit Lake while Dad promised to look the other way.)

July brings with it spontaneous departures, suspended routines, music in the park, children's laughter, the sweet night air, and, of course, the Fourth.

When Peggy and I talked about what this chapter on freedom would include, we agreed it would be appropriate, because of the Fourth of July, to write about patriotism. This would be the place to tell about how we had become better Americans (one of our goals that we left on the train).

Starting with a brief history of our country's break from England, I would write about the Declaration of Independence, talk about the Fourth of July, and give specific things to do to get some red, white, and blue into the cards. At the end of the chapter anyone who had read it would almost be able to picture Peggy and me in that group of marines raising the American flag on the top of Mt. ? (I know it wasn't Rushmore).

I got a C in American History, so my recollection of the events surrounding our battles was sketchy. I reluctantly agreed to do a little brush-up research on the subject. Mom loves history, and she suggested a fun way to read about it would be get John Jakes's *The Kent Family Chronicles*. She claimed his accounts of historical events were extremely accurate, even though the characters were fictitious.

I don't think I've ever gotten so sidetracked as I did when I bought Jakes's eight volumes. They were fantastic! The romance and adventure left me spellbound, and the end of one book pulled me eagerly into the next. (I forgot all about Chapter Seven.)

Aside from my inadequate knowledge of history, I can't write about how to become a better American by using 3x5 cards, because I haven't done it.

I had *planned* to get involved with the party of my choice, keep abreast of current events, and take the kids into a few courtrooms. But last year all I did that was even close to that was date a guy who works at the Republican headquarters, subscribe to *Time* magazine, and watch several episodes of *People's Court* with the kids.

With nothing left to write about except my own freedom, I decided I'd share the two experiences in my life when I felt utterly helpless, yet managed to break free, and offer suggestions to help you find freedom from similar circumstances.

My fifteen-year marriage, which was as hopeless as my passionate courtship, was doomed before we ever said our vows.

We fought about the wedding; where to have it, who to invite, and when it should be. The honeymoon plans ended up in a big brochure fight, and we battled over where to live after the trip.

We argued about how much we would spend on food, entertainment, and transportation. We waged a month-long cold war over whose church we'd go to, and we hit a stalemate on whether to get a puppy or a kitten.

The minister who married us insisted on premarital counseling and, in his lecture to us, said there were three main things couples fight about: religion, sex, and money. He was right about that, but he forgot to mention the fights over my cooking, his driving, my housecleaning, our incompatible sleeping habits, and our different interests. He didn't warn me that before getting married I should observe my future mate in a traffic jam, being put on hold by United Airlines, filling out a tax return, or changing a flat. Our kindly advisor didn't say that I should see my fiancé through a year's worth of holidays, or try out what it would be like to stand with him at the end of a "wait to be seated" line for a Mother's Day breakfast.

No warning was given to stay away from trying to drive his stick shift, help him back an RV into a camping slot, assist him in docking a thirty-foot boat on a roaring river, or read the map while he was fighting his way on an L.A. freeway.

One other thing the minister neglected to advise against was moving fourteen times in thirteen years.

After each of those transfers I intended to get organized, but efficiency somehow evaded me, and I turned every new and bigger house into a shambles, plunging our marriage deeper into the pits.

Our last move was from Fresno, California, back to our hometown. I was delighted! Now Peggy and I could play together, after fourteen years of separation. But when I found out where I'd have to live, I was shocked and appalled.

My husband had always told me that I didn't deserve to live in a nice house, and he threatened, more than once, to buy a dump in the slums the next time we moved. With this move, he did it!

He bought the place from a buddy in real estate; and because the children were still in school, I hadn't been able to travel to Vancouver to help make a choice.

When we drove into the driveway I couldn't believe it. The house was worse than I had imagined. I thought maybe he was making a cruel joke and that he'd back the car out and take me to my *real* new home. But it wasn't a joke.

The neighborhood had previously been a two-acre pear orchard that had attracted some struggling subdivider, who promptly turned it into 248 lots, catching the eye of a sleazy contractor with a bunch of prefabs.

Our house was dirt-clod brown. It had a sheet of fake brick siding glued to the front, and a large living room window with a distortion in the glass. (The kids loved to watch their deformed reflections every time they passed by.)

In the yard were three dead pear trees. Some quicko landscaping outfit had come in with a large roll of black plastic and not enough bark dust to cover it. They had rolled out a piece of grass the size of a double bed, and had left their card in the mailbox.

The interior was no surprise. (I never quite knew if the sunken living room was part of the plan or not.) The carpets were gold shag throughout. My furniture didn't match.

The neighbors on both sides drove me nuts. The one on the right had a logging truck, which he parked right in front of our house. (The front of his house was taken up by his auto body repair work.) Every Saturday he'd drag home a tree, and all through the night he'd slice it up with a chain saw. Sunday morning, he'd heave the logs into a rickety old pickup and take off in search of people with fireplaces. Business was great, and we got very little sleep on weekends.

The neighbor on the left was very industrious, too—until "the raid." I just assumed she had a lot of men friends with fancy cars. Not so.

I was miserable. The marital fighting was now worse than it had ever been, and I wanted to be free; but I was scared to think about being on my own because I never had been before. I had married when I was twenty, and had gone straight from a very sheltered and protective home to a very powerful and domineering husband.

I was not only insecure about myself but also financially frightened. I was afraid I'd have to live in one of those motels that get left in the tourist dust when a new freeway is built. I pictured myself having to go on welfare. I thought about keeping track of food stamps when I couldn't even use coupons to my advantage. One day I realized that my present situation was far worse than anything I had to fear. Peggy and I have always asked the question "What's the worst thing that could possibly happen?" and usually it's something we could handle. The worst thing that could happen had happened to me. Seeing how ridiculous it was to be afraid, I finally considered the possibility of being on my own. I knew that I was in a really bad situation; but if I could summon up every ability I had, maybe I could change things.

If you are discontent with something in your life, and you know you are ready to make some positive changes, ask yourself what is the worst thing that could happen. If you can handle that, you are home free. Give yourself a reasonable deadline, and then make a list of everything you can do, right now, to improve yourself. If you are unhappy in your marriage or you don't like the house you live in or the job you have, get your mind off the problem and start working on a solution. If you work on your own self-improvement, you won't have any time to worry about anybody or anything else.

It was in that house with the dead pear trees that I got organized. It was ironic that after wrecking thirteen houses across the country, I would turn a disaster like that one into a castle.

The improvement I made, by cleaning and organizing my house, gave me a great deal of self-esteem. I had conquered a problem that had plagued me all of my life. In my unhappy marriage I always had focused my attention on what was wrong with my husband. When I turned my attention to what I could do to change myself, I stopped trying to get him to change. I was too busy with my own work to be concerned with his faults.

A year after Peggy and I got our lives under control with our 3x5 system, I had enough courage to stand up for myself for the first time in my life, and I divorced.

Giving yourself a deadline is such an important decision that it bears repeating. A deadline will keep you from wandering through life holding on to something for too long. Perhaps if I had imposed a deadline on myself earlier, I wouldn't have stayed for fifteen years in a relationship that was so personally defeating for both of us.

Several years later Peggy had to hit me with a deadline when I didn't realize I needed one; but because she did, I was helped out of the crush of a broken heart. His name was John. He didn't want to be married, but when I found out that his intentions were not the same as mine, it was too late; I loved him. Since I couldn't compromise such a serious difference, I broke off the relationship, but I was heartbroken. I felt as if I were under water for months.

All I did was talk about him. Everywhere I went, I would see men who looked like him. Every restaurant I dined in reminded me of meals we had shared. I thought I saw his car everywhere (even though he lives six hundred miles away); and when the phone rang, I would leap to answer it, hoping it might be John saying he'd decided to settle down.

Songs made me cry; movies made me cry; just about everything made me cry. Even Peggy couldn't help me...until she gave me a deadline.

We were having lunch together one day. When the waiter brought our food, I looked at my plate and started to cry.

"What's wrong?"

"Oh, nothing. It's just that John loved jumbo shrimp like these."

"Sissy, you know what?"

"What?"

"I'm tired of hearing about John."

I almost choked on my mouthful of coleslaw.

"What do you mean?" I sniffed.

"I think you've been feeling bad long enough." (She tried not to sound too hard on me.)

"But I've tried!" I cry-babied.

"I know, but you're not getting any better. Whatever happened to that book you bought, *Letting Go?*"

"I lost it."

"You need to get another copy, and you need a deadline to get over this. I am going to allow you to talk about John until February 3rd, and then after that date, I don't ever want to hear his name again!"

"Well!" I was crushed.

She continued, "If, after February 3rd, you so much as *mention* the J word, I am going to take you to get professional help. I'll drive you there, take you in, wait for you, and take you back home."

"Professional help?"

She was serious!

It was in January that I was given my ultimatum, and I went home with twenty-six days until the deadline. Peggy was right. More than a reasonable amount of time had passed for the average person to get over another average person. On February 2 I talked about John all day and said his name every chance I got, but on the 3rd, he was off my lips. (He wasn't out of my mind, but at least putting a plug on my mouth was the first step to getting over him.)

To get him off my mind I had to figure out a way to distract my brain. Telling myself not to think about him didn't work. If somebody said to you, "Don't think about Cheerios," you'd instantly picture the yellow box. You'd see a bowl of Cheerios with milk and sugar on top, and you'd even be able to smell and taste a spoonful of them.

If somebody said, "There's a new cereal out. It's called Vitamin-Flavored Machos and they're shaped like little dumbbells," you'd forget about Cheerios and start picturing little honey-coated barbells.

That's what I did with John.

I decided to study French. Every time I started to sink into thinking about him, I'd make myself study vocabulary, conjugate a verb, or practice a sentence. When I realized two months after my silence deadline that I was free from John, I also discovered I knew enough of the language to go anywhere in France!

Freedom is such an intangible thing. It's really a state of mind. I had felt caged in the little house with the dead pear trees, and yet it was in that house that I eventually felt free! The imprisonment of my feeling for John was an emotional kind of bondage, but just as gripping.

The only thing that blocks your path to freedom from anything is the self-imposed rut you can think yourself into, and the only way I know of to get out of the rut is to get busy changing your mind.

I sew a lot and I have a huge box of patterns, some dating back to 1953. One day Peggy Ann (my daughter) and I were looking through the box, and she said, "You made a dress like *that*, Mom?"

"Yeah, it had a boat-neck and a skirt with six yards of taffeta in it."

After she had a good laugh, I took another look at the patterns I'd saved. They were not my size anymore; most of them were completely out of date, and I wouldn't want to use any of them today. If I bought some lovely new material in the latest texture and color, and I pinned an old outdated pattern to it, cut it out, and sewed it up, with all the skill of a tailor, I would still create an old, outdated garment.

Every moment of our lives is like a piece of new fabric. Each moment holds the possibility of meeting interesting people, finding fresh ideas, better ways, happy times, new songs, love, laughter, and opportunity. Every moment is open for us to be, do, and accept what we desire, but so often we slap an old pattern of rut-thinking, like that boat-neck dress, down on that precious new material of "now," and we miss the potential of the present.

If you keep repeating the same mistakes, attracting the same kinds of hanging, moaning, drooping people worrying about the same sorts of things and basically turning your new moments into an anxious, vengeful, and bitter series of failures, then you can be sure it's because of a mind full of old patterns.

If you want to be free of something that is keeping you

from being happier, you *can* do it. You may need a professional to help you, or maybe a loving friend or relative. Maybe this book will be the stimulus that helps to change your state of mind.

In Part II we had you prepare a place for inspirational words. We suggested posting the little uplifters in places where you could read them often. In this month you might want to make some affirmations that state, in a sentence, what is it you want to be free from.

An affirmation is a short positive declaration that you choose to write and repeat routinely until the desired result is produced.

Take the problem and invert it so that it is solved in one sentence. For instance: if the problem involves *fear,* the affirmation needs to have the feeling of *security* in it. Some good antifear affirmations are:

I feel safe.
My source is God.
I am secure.
Peace is mine now.

If the problem involves *lack,* the affirmation needs to have a feeling of *plenty.* Some examples of antilack attitudes are:

The universe has abundant wealth.
I am financially secure.
All my needs are met.
God supplies me with everything I need.

If the problem is *loneliness,* the affirmation could be, I am *loved.* If the problem is *sickness,* the powerful sentence, I am *healthy,* needs to be attached to the door of the medicine cabinet, kitchen cupboard, dashboard, refrigerator, or ceiling over the bed, if necessary.

Notice that the affirmations are in the present tense. If you write them in the future tense, they'll be no more powerful than wishful thinking.

Most of the negative thoughts that you have stored in your head were put there before you were four years old. They were usually told to you by your parents, and it's probable that they used your name when they programmed them into you.

Try writing your affirmation several ways. Write it as if someone is telling it to you: "Pam, you are free." Write it as if "they" (whoever they are) are talking about you.

"Pam is free." Sometimes just changing the voice will give your affirmation more meaning. Use some of your quiet time in the morning to make some Affirmation Cards. So that reading them will become a routine, write a reminder on your Daily Routine Card and keep the affirmations in the Monday through Sunday dividers. Make out a monthly card (white) that says, "Put up new Affirmation Cards around the house, in the car, and at work." File that card in August and then move it to September and on through the year.

You might get a little resistance when you write an affirmation like "I am rich" when you are unemployed. You can wear down the resistance by doing this exercise:

In your notebook date a page and number it from one to ten, leaving a few lines under each number. Write the affirmation you've chosen and wait for a few seconds; then see what thoughts emerge. Write the thoughts in the space you have provided. You will discover that there will usually be several negative thoughts surrounding the main idea you chose to produce results (see my example below). The only thing that stands in the way of your good is negative thinking. This writing exercise will expose some of the barriers that are keeping you from experiencing what you want.

This is an affirmation I used to help me with my weight. If you do this exercise every day for twenty-one days, the results will be absolutely incredible to you.

1. My body is the perfect size God created it to be.
    Response: Boy they're sure making big rear-ends these days.

2. My body is the perfect size God created it to be.
   Response: Liar, liar, pants on fire.
3. My body is the perfect size God created it to be.
   Response: Dreamer.
4. My body is the perfect size God created it to be.
   Response: It could be, if I didn't eat so much.
5. My body is the perfect size God created it to be.
   Response: Maybe.
6. My body is the perfect size God created it to be.
   Response: It's a possibility.
7. My body is the perfect size God created it to be.
   Response: I love that idea.
8. My body is the perfect size God created it to be.
   Response: I'll think about it.
9. My body is the perfect size God created it to be.
   Response: OK.
10. My body is the perfect size God created it to be.
    Response: Yes.

In our first book we worked out a weekly plan. Each day was devoted to a certain kind of activity. Included was a "free" day in which we could do whatever we wanted to do. But we've since realized that to tell a basically disorganized person just to do whatever she wants is meaningless.

When we developed the Happiness File we made a list of all the things we loved to do, the simple things that made us happy. We want you to make your own list of "love to do" things. (It will be different from the list of things you *want* to do.) It is the same as the list of things you made for your spouse in the February chapter, only this is a list of your loves. Sometimes we get so busy that we don't take the time to do the things we love to do. It helps greatly to make a list (see mine on page 218).

Decide how often you would like to do each thing and incoporate this frequency factor into your cardfile so that you can follow through.

Start thinking and feeling free right now. I loved the definitions for freedom in *Webster's Collegiate Dictionary*.

Some of those that popped out at me in the three inches of description were: independence; relieved from something unpleasant or burdensome; not bound, confined, or detained; having no restrictions; not taken up with commitments; not hampered, fastened, or held. I felt free just reading about it.

Enjoy this lovely month and use it to break free so that all though the coming year you can experience greater happiness in everything you do.

What I Love

Sitting in the sun
The smell of freshly cut grass
The sound of those sprinklers that jerk
  around
Puppies
Baby anythings
75° weather
Long walks in the country
Window-shopping
Christmas music
Cooking
A fresh hot cup of coffee in the morning
A nap at 2:30
Eating in a restaurant
Singing in a group and harmonizing
Playing the piano
Playing the guitar
Gershwin's "Rhapsody in Blue"
The ballet
Reading a good novel
A crackling fire
Baked potatoes
Dancing
Going barefoot
Parties
Having a barbecue

Eight

August–Appreciation –From Peggy

"Happiness grows at our own firesides, and is not to be picked in strangers' gardens."

—DOUGLAS JERROLD

August is usually the hottest time of year. The scorching heat can make you restless and send you in search of anything cool. You can find what you're looking for in an air-conditioned mall or by walking down the frozen food aisle at the grocery store. To get relief you can run through the sprinkler, take a cold shower, sit in front of a portable fan, find some shade, or retreat to the basement. But it's hard not to be envious of the rich folks with swimming pools, when the only way you're cooling off at your place is by putting your face inside the refrigerator.

August seems like a good time to talk about appreciation (or making the most of what you have). The old deal that the "grass is always greener" seems especially true when your lawn is brown and the guy next door has his sprinkler system going. "Keep up with the Joneses" ha! We *are* the Joneses and we still want more.

In the past I have struggled with being envious of my neighbors and their possessions. At our first apartment there were the managers, Anne and Gary Skordahl. They were an adoring couple with two darling, well-behaved young boys. All four of them were immaculate. I was a slob. I watched the couple wash their car together, leave on dates, and walk with their children, hand in hand, and I was jealous.

On our first wedding anniversary, as I was washing a week's worth of dishes and gazing out my kitchen window into the street, I saw a flower van pull up in front of our apartment. I dropped my rag and ran to the front door to greet the delivery man as he rang my doorbell. He held a huge, tissue-paper bouquet in his arms, which I grabbed excitedly. "Mrs. Skordahl?" he asked, keeping a grip on the flowers. It was quiet. "She's over there in the front apartment." I pointed to the one with the manicured lawn and let him have the bouquet. I felt so sorry for myself. Danny had forgotten our first wedding anniversary, but Gary Skordahl just wanted to send Anne some flowers for no reason.

I was so selfishly wrapped up in my own wishes that I actually thought my paratrooper husband should have been able to find a florist shop in the Vietnam jungles and FTD me an anniversary bouquet, "if he really cared."

In our next neighborhood there were Dan and Genevieve. They didn't have children and lived in a four-bedroom house next to ours. The houses were similar, so I wasn't jealous about that, but what killed me was the way they got to travel! He worked out of the country half the time and she went with him whenever she pleased. (I watered their lawn and picked up the mail.)

I ached to go someplace. I begged Danny to take me on a trip just for the sake of getting away, but with two toddlers and a baby in the car, it wasn't any fun. By the time we packed the playpen, walker, and diaper bags, and hooked the kids up in their little car chairs, one of them had to go back in the house to go to the bathroom, the baby was crying, Danny was perspiring, and I was wishing I were Genevieve. Every place we've ever lived I've found someone to envy, whether it was a couple's togetherness, their fuller life-style, or their beautiful house.

The house we live in now is more than forty years old. Danny and I have been remodeling it since we moved in eight years ago. Although we've never regretted buying it, at times we've gotten so discouraged that we've considered giving up and moving on.

The remodeling process is boring, while everything about a new house is so exciting. They smell of fresh paint and new carpeting. Even the cement in new garages smells good, and everything, everywhere, is clean. Old houses have old smells, like the inside of a Goodwill truck on a hot, rainy day. It's very depressing to take a tour of a new model home and then have to come back to the reality of an old house. Every once in a while I'm intrigued by an "Open House," and I persuade Danny to take me by, telling him that we can get some good remodeling ideas, and every time we return home depressed. It's not that we don't love our home; it's just that remodeling is hard work, and everything we do seems to take so much time and money.

At the time we found our house, we weren't even in the market for one. Actually, we were relatively content in a basic colonial-style three-bedroom ranch that we had built just before our first baby was born. It was so much bigger than our apartment had been. But right away we had a second baby, and all at once the rooms were filled. When the third baby came soon after, we seemed a bit cramped.

Danny was working nights and going to the University of Portland in the daytime. Money was tight, and we left hopes for a larger home unspoken. One day while Danny was away at school, I opened the newspaper to the Classified section to see if I could find any good deals on family-room furniture. I forgot what I was looking for because I got sidetracked reading the Personal column (I love to read that stuff); and while I tried to remember what I had opened the newspaper for, my attention drifted to the Homes for Sale section. That's when I spotted it...

"5-Bedroom Rambler!" *Oh, boy,* I thought, *wouldn't that be great!* I went on to read that it was a solid brick, older home with a basement and more than 3800 square feet. It had a workshop, three fireplaces, three bathrooms, and a view, and the price seemed extremely low. I made the call.

The agent said it was a new listing that had just gone on the market. It was the first time it had been advertised. Hearing the address, I was even more thrilled. It was in an area I had always loved. "It's a great buy for a handyman with a growing family." *Perfect!* I thought. *That's us!* My voice trembled with excitement as I tried to talk and breathe at the same time. I didn't want to sound too anxious, so I told the agent we would drive by, and if we were interested, we'd give him a call. He suggested that he might as well meet us there and show us the inside. "This one won't be around very long. Somebody will grab it fast at that price," he warned. I got panicky and decided Danny would never forgive me if I didn't make the appointment and we lost the chance of a lifetime.

When he came home, I met him at the door and talked so fast that I had to sit down. (I was beginning to hyperventilate.) He didn't share my extreme enthusiasm (he never does); but he was willing to go look at the house. When we drove down the lovely winding street, I watched the house numbers and looked for For Sale signs; I could hardly keep from squealing. All the houses looked wonderful. It was an old, established neighborhood, with fully grown trees and well-maintained yards.

Before we got to the end of the street, we saw it. From the outside it looked just like what the ad said, a five-bedroom rambler. It was big, and it was definitely brick, but it was odd brick. I had pictured used brick in the colonial style. This was Roman brick without style.

We went inside. The carpet was the only thing with personality, and even it was rather dull. The living room was huge (they had two full-size davenports in there, facing each other). Almost as an afterthought, the agent pulled the drapes open and suggested that we might find the view pleasing. It was a spectacular sight! We looked directly down into a wildlife refuge. Geese floated on the water, and more were circling on their landing approach. Beyond the pond was a huge lake lined with stately fir trees, and far in the distance we could see the outline of two ships moving down the Columbia River. It was the most breathtaking view I had ever seen from any living-room window. It was the kind of view you take out-of-town visitors to see and pay a park entrance fee for the privilege. I was sold!

It was lucky I saw the view before I saw the kitchen. The woman of the house was frying a chicken on a 1950s Philco stove. It was of the same vintage as the ones Betty Furness used to demonstrate. Grease spattered onto the wallpaper, but it seemed to blend right into the roosters-and-teakettle pattern. The cabinets were birch (orange with age) and had round chrome handles the size of wide-mouth jar lids. The floor was dark green linoleum with a contrasting yellow line all the way around it. Baseboards weren't necessary because the flooring curved and went up the wall about six inches. The countertops matched the color of the floor, but gave the illusion of green marble. There was a nice sunny window over the sink, and I could see the view again. Somehow even the kitchen had possibilities.

We moved on to the main bathroom. They must have found a good deal on fake marble because the bathroom was done with the same stuff as the kitchen, only in pink. This time they had chosen mermaids with glitter bubbles coming out of their mouths for the wall coverings.

Danny asked why they were selling the house, and we learned that a divorce was pending. When we got to the master bedroom we could see why. It was done in black and gray. The carpet was black and the walls were gray. The draperies were of black rubber-backed fabric with metallic gold pagodas woven on top.

There was an abundance of storage and closet space throughout the house. The ugly orange birch was everywhere. In the basement there was more cement than I had ever seen (except at Bonneville Dam) and there was a huge laboring oil furnace right in the middle of it. Even down there I thought there was hope. It was big and open, and the kids could skate and ride their trikes all around the furnace in the winter.

While I was mentally stripping wallpaper off every wall, Danny was checking out the structural soundness of the place. He was very pleased to find a sixty-foot steel beam as support in the basement, and although the birch had discolored, he pointed out that it was *solid* birch. "This place is built like a rock," he whispered behind the agent's back. "What do you think?"

"I think we could sure use the space, and I don't think they realize the value of the view!"

"We better get something on paper before they find out it's a steal."

Only a few hours after I had wandered into the Homes for Sale section of the newspaper, we had signed an earnest-money agreement and put our three-bedroom home up for sale. We talked about it all the way back home. Were we moving too fast? Could we really do all the renovation the rambler needed ourselves? Could we sell our home fast enough? Were we crazy? Together we agreed that if it wasn't the right thing for us, the deal would fall apart. We agreed that our impulsive decision would be overriden if it was not in our best interest or for the good of all concerned.

We pictured the perfect buyers who would live in our home and take good care of it. We imagined them to be prosperous and wanting a home just like ours. We agreed to give them a fair price so that it would be a good deal and a simple transaction. We further agreed that if the move was right, all things would work together toward that end, and if it was not, we would release any feelings of disappointment, knowing that we would find something better.

The divorcing couple were eager to sell their house and get away from each other, so they accepted our ridiculous offer. Within seven days of posting our For Sale sign in the front yard, we had sold our home, and by the end of the month, everyone had moved. Quickly and without manipulation, we had found our rightful place. But the work was just beginning.

Instead of relaxing in the evening, Danny came home and put on his handyman clothes either to paint, putty, plumb, plaster, or patch something. It was hard work, and it was also frustrating when we'd reach a point where the next step required money, but the funds weren't available. One time Danny put an eight-foot hole in the wall to allow for a huge view window, but when the hole was ready, we couldn't afford the glass. We sat around our dining room table, straining to see the autumn landscape through flapping plastic taped over the hole. Two paydays later we got the window, just in time for the holidays.

Another time we tore off a decaying deck from the back of our house to make way for a magnificent new deck. Thoughts of an easy-living summer of turning T-bones and sipping cool drinks on the deck made us work quickly as we ripped away the old wood and hauled it off to the dump. Although we had both disliked the old deck, it had served a purpose—it kept us from stepping out the kitchen door and dropping out of sight. When we found out how much the new cedar would cost, we were shocked. The deck had to be put on hold while we saved enough money for lumber. For three years we lived with a six-foot drop-off, warning guests to "watch that first step" as we leaped out of the door and onto the grass with a tray of hamburgers for a backyard barbecue.

Entertaining can be difficult when you're in the middle of remodeling, but we had to face the fact that what we had undertaken was not a quickie do-it-yourselfer's weekend-type project. If we had waited until everything was finished before inviting people over, we would not have had company for eight years. We learned to relax and be more like the Pusebombs. They live between my house and Pam's in Hazel Dell. Their place is continually torn up, but judging by all the cars there, they always have company.

We decided to entertain in spite of the confusion. We handled it as they do at the airport or a department store when they tear out an escalator or knock out a wall. We asked our guests to pardon the mess while things were under construction. We gave tours of the house and let our company enjoy the developing stages of our projects. Invariably our friends would get enthused about what we were doing and we collected some good ideas from them along the way. We realized that our friends didn't come over to see our house, they came to visit us.

If Mrs. Pusebomb could throw a party and not worry about what the people thought of the surroundings, then we, in the midst of our mess, could surely entertain.

Passing the Pusebombs' house always made me feel better, but the house next door to ours made me feel worse. It was an estate. People say that it's better to buy a house in a neighborhood where the surrounding houses are worth more than yours. Maybe it's better in terms of resale value, but egotistically speaking, it's really tough.

Protected by an eight-foot black wrought-iron security fence and two bull mastiffs, the mansion next door could be seen only in the winter after the surrounding trees lost their green. It was a contemporary two-story home with walls of glass in the back and massive stonework in the front. Pam bought us binoculars for Christmas; not so we could watch the river traffic and wildlife, but so I could keep her abreast of what was going on over at the mansion. For five years we monitored the comings and goings. Who were the owners? How did they feel over there, living like kings? Where were their kids?

We were so jealous. It wasn't fair! When they'd have a party, Pam and I would get out some garden tools and pretend to work the ground at the fence line. We'd crane to get a whiff of the action. Like two second-string football players, eager to run onto the field if the coach would only invite us, we hung around the arborvitae hedge in party clothes, waiting for an opportunity.

We knew they had a pool (we heard laughing and splashing as happy guests cooled themselves). We could smell the aroma of hot charcoal and sizzling steaks (served medium rare on fine china, no doubt) and we ached to be in the game. There's nothing more painful than being left on the sidelines when you've suited up. It was worse than living next door to the *Love Boat*.

We were almost sick with curiosity. It wasn't the good kind of curiosity that kids with thick glasses on commercials for Apple computers have, and it wasn't the kind that leads to scientific or sociological breakthroughs, either. It was the sick kind of curiosity that makes scandal tabloids thrive. We had to know their story. We had to meet *her.* What did she know about the law of abundance that we didn't? Finally it happened. We were troweling along the wrought iron when her guard dogs caught our scent and bolted toward the fence.

She called after them, "Here, Gable . . . Come back here, Flavia . . . Don't you recognize them yet?" She apologized for the would-be attack. "Hello, there. I'm Boardra Waycliff Lakewood." She extended a slender manicured hand decorated with gold and precious stones.

"Hi, I'm Peggy Anne Jones."

"I'm Pamela Irene Young."

Why were we talking like that? We wondered. We didn't use our full names ever. We exchanged smiles.

"The doctor and I were pleased to see that you have youngsters."

"The policeman and I were pleased to have them, too." I caught myself before I said it.

"Better stay back away from the fence now. . . . The dogs can become quite aggressive at times." We stepped back.

"Well, it's been refreshing to meet you both," she said over her bronzed shoulder as she swanked back toward the mansion.

"Thank you," we called after her.

Even her dogs were ritzier than we were. It was our big chance to make friends and get through the gates, and we had let her get away without an invitation.

We talked about it all the time . . . about the responsibilities that go with a name like Boardra. She walked like a Boardra and spoke and dressed like one. She drove a foreign car, and she was tan even in winter. She had a gardener and somebody to wash her windows and probably someone to draw her bath—a life-style right out of the movies. She was clearly different from us, and even our kids recognized it.

"Mrs. Lakewood is real sporty, isn't she?"

"Sporty? What do you mean?"

"You know . . . she looks real sporty."

"You mean athletic?"

"No, like top-down-on-the-car sporty."

Maybe her tan made the difference. Maybe it was the gold jewelry glinting against her tan. . . . Maybe it was her sun-streaked hair that hinted of a leisurely and luxurious way of life. We studied her from my kitchen window, taking turns with the binoculars.

"She even has rich hair."

"I know. . . . How come she can put that sweatband around her forehead and still look great? If I tried that I'd look like Willie Nelson."

"That's because you'd sweat and she doesn't."

"I'll bet she's never carried a garbage can to the curb in her life."

"She's getting some kind of exercise. . . . Look at that waist."

"Yeah . . . but she's never had kids. . . . She's still got that fresh look you lose in labor."

Thinking of how much easier her life was than ours was torture. It was hard not to believe that her grass was greener. Back then we had six children between us to tend (four of them were toddlers), and we never took time for a sunbath or a manicure. I think that after the Tenth Commandment—"Thou shalt not covet thy neighbor's house, nor his wife, nor his manservant, nor his maidservant, nor his ox, nor his ass, nor anything that is thy neighbor's" —there should have been an eleventh: "Thou shalt not buy an ordinary house that's next door to a mansion."

We continued to covet all of my neighbors' stuff for years. Without any more direct contacts, we had decided their lives were perfect. Life seemed to be one big party after another over there. We imagined them to be passionately in love with each other, free from financial concerns, and getting happier with every barbecue. We thought they must be as thrilled as we would be if the mansion was ours.

Meanwhile, we continued to live our own lives. We decided to get organized and we were successfully enjoying our newfound freedom from chaos and confusion. We were also enjoying the financial success that accompanied the sharing of the 3x5 cardfile system we'd invented to organize our homes. Book advances and royalties came in and large deposits from seminars we taught. For the first time in our lives we had a taste of what it was like to have a bank balance.

We went crazy. We bought two sets of matching Hartman luggage (fourteen pieces in all), thinking we looked like jet-setters. Actually we looked more as if we'd been on *Family Feud* and won. (Jet-setters travel light, but we didn't know that.) Pam was single and we wanted her to have a wonderful home, not so she'd be comfortable, but so we could show everybody how great she was doing on her own. We bought her a brand-new smarty-girl house in a prestigious neighborhood and waited eagerly for her ex-husband to have to come to the new address and pick up the kids. We were very immature and impractical and no happier than we had been when I sold cosmetics door-to-door and Pam lived in the dead-pear-tree house.

We were so busy in our business that we only occasionally got out the binoculars, but things still looked great over at the mansion. Then one Fourth of July there was a For Sale sign on the gate. Gable, Flavia, Boardra, and the doctor were gone. We got as excited as when we were children and found out we might have enough money in the club-house dues jar to go to the Jantzen Beach Amusement Park. Could we possibly pool our money and buy the mansion together? It would be like the Kennedy compound.

We poured Danny a glass of wine and hit him with our proposal of buying the property and dividing it between the two families. Projecting an optimistic cash flow, we convinced Danny of our ability to handle the estate, and we all decided on an offer. We were very excited when it was accepted. While eagerly waiting for the deal to close, I began making extensive plans to join the two properties with a common driveway. Danny and I had often complained about the crumbling condition of our old driveway, so I thought it would be a perfect time to change the whole layout. (Besides, I'd always wanted a circular driveway like rich people have.) There was, however, one problem: moving the driveway would also mean moving the garage door to the other side of the garage.

I scrawled the new plan on a piece of notebook paper and approached Danny. As usual, he pointed out the drawbacks of such a scheme. For one thing, the house was solid brick. (Evidently he anticipated the difficulty of making a drive-through hole big enough for two cars.) Then there was the problem of what to do with the hole that would remain when the garage door was moved to the other side. I got the *Better Homes and Gardens* remodeling books out from under the bed and riffled through them for ideas.

Before he could think of more reasons why we shouldn't do it, I'd torn out as an example a picture of a brick home with a side-entry garage. It had three lovely shuttered windows in the front.

"We'll put windows in the hole and brick up around them!" I was delighted.

"And where will we find matching brick? They don't make this kind anymore. We'd have to wait till they tear down some old library to get any more of this stuff."

I had to sleep on that one, but in the shower the next morning the idea leaked into my empty head. We could tear the bricks off the walls in the breezeway, and with those we'd taken from the new garage hole, we could plug up all the holes. . . . Then we could make a little mudroom out of the breezeway with a door going out the back . . . and Danny could move my washer and dryer out of the basement and into the breezeway. That way I'd have a nice laundry room with a garden window.

"What garden window?" Danny said as I handed him an ad from the magazine, picturing a beautiful bay window. Danny thought the whole plan was insane. He posed difficult questions I couldn't answer about plumbing, electricity, and possible brick shortages.

In time I wore him down. I think he began to see the project as the ultimate challenge. Against his better judgment, he set aside the baseboards he had been refinishing (all the woodwork in the house was in the process of being stripped, sanded, stained, sealed, and sanded again), and on the following Saturday he began work on the garage.

He started early with a hammer and chisel on the outside where the new go-in would be. The wall of brick looked like an impossible obstacle, and after the first few hours of hard labor, there was only a small pile of mortar-bound bricks at Danny's feet. I wanted to say, "Never mind. It was a lousy idea," but he had a wild look in his eyes, like a psychotic chisel-murderer, that warned me not to speak. I went back into the house.

Two weeks later the hole was perfect, and he was ready to begin stripping the breezeway. After all the bricks were wheelbarrowed to the side of the house, he still had the terrible job of cleaning them by chipping away the old mortar. Danny's wild look was softened now by monotony and fatigue. Every day he gave me the brick count, like a prisoner notching off days on his cell wall. Of course, the numbers were relatively meaningless, since we could only estimate the finished hole sizes which we would eventually brick around.

Meanwhile, as he continued to clean the old bricks, Danny had a guy come in with a big Cat and chew up the whole front yard, erasing the old driveway and the cement walk. He began soliciting bids for concrete masonry work and custom windows. The driveway, we learned, would be the major expense. In an effort to recreate the driveway on *Dynasty* and recapture the charm of the wooded road to Camp Julianna, I had routed the concrete so that it would meander past every tree on both properties, regardless of cost and confusion.

"It's a straight shot from the street to the house, lady. . . . How come you're gettin' so carried away?" a smart-aleck cement man asked as he happily tapped his pocket calculator.

As so many of my "money is no object" plans had, this new one went sour with reality; the bids were all too high. We divided the project into phase one (the circular part and garage entrance) and phase two (the winding connection of "estates"). Even by cutting the project in half, we still had to conserve further with Ken's U-Cart Concrete (a do-it-yourself outfit). Ken's motto of "Helping pave the West . . . and beyond" seemed to fit.

Danny took down the garage door and laid it against the house in the back. Then he made arrangements for the garage-door-opener people to come and replace it over the new hole. "There's no real hurry," I heard him tell the man over the phone. "We're not concerned about security." Security was a joke. . . . We had a drive-through garage. For a while it must have looked to passersby as if we'd eaten some bad mushrooms and, in the resulting fit of insanity, had attacked our home with a jackhammer.

The rains came, making the torn-up ground a mud rink. There was no way out of the house except through the brown-pudding yard. School was about to start. The house deal still hadn't closed. Nevertheless, Pam enrolled her children in our district, using my address. It was agreed that after school they would get off the bus at the stop near my house, and Pam would pick them up there. That way no one would have to change schools after the move.

One afternoon Peggy (Pam's oldest daughter) came in the door, laughing. On the bus she had been sitting with a girl who lived down the street several blocks. They were getting acquainted, and as they approached Peggy's bus stop, the girl said, "So where do you live?" Peggy said she was going to move into the house with the wrought-iron fence around it, and the girl said, "Oh . . . you mean next door to the crazy people?"

On Halloween (four months after we'd made the offer), we went to our attorney's office, thinking he had called us in to sign the papers. His face was gray. "I have to advise you not to do this," he said. "There are more liens against the property than the place is worth." We were shocked. Everything had looked so rosy over there. How could it be that they were facing bankruptcy?

By coveting someone else's property, we had almost manipulated ourselves into a legal mess that would have shadowed our fun, our work, our future with heavy indebtedness. We rescinded our offer, and it cost Danny and

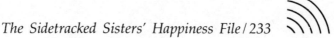

me only our reputation and $8,000 for the brick work, the windows in the garage, the driveway, the lawn, the walkway, the garden window, and a new washer and dryer. (I didn't want to move the old set into my spiffy new laundry room.)

Our house has never been my dream house. (It isn't Tara.) There are no white columns or winding staircases, no crystal chandeliers or tennis courts. It is simply our home. As eight years' worth of remodeling nears completion, we spend more and more time walking around complimenting each other on what a good job we've done.

"Remember how this used to look?"

"Yeah..."

"Would you do it again if you had to do it over?"

"In a minute."

"Danny, how would you feel about taking the roof off and building a master suite up there?"

"????"

Our $8,000 second mortgage was the result of covetousness and manipulation. Although the project turned out beautifully, we had put ourselves through some pretty rough times getting it that way.

You don't need to take out a loan to make your home more attractive and comfortable. Go over what you wrote down during your January clearing. Really take a good look at what you wanted to be able to change in the month of August. Maybe you were overly optimistic a few months ago, thinking you'd be able to afford some big home improvements. Suppose you had hoped to have enough money by now to get new wallpaper and carpet for the den, but unexpected bills have used up your nest egg. Don't get discouraged and just do nothing. And don't get impatient and buy everything on credit. Look at the den again (through the clearing) and take some actions that don't require a large amount of money.

We have some good friends who were willing to be guinea pigs and help us test the Happiness File and then share their experiences with us. One friend had written in her clearing section in January that by August she wanted a new light fixture in the kitchen, modern canisters, and a tile backsplash above the counters.

She knew that the kind of light fixture she wanted would be quite expensive, and she'd seen the canister set she liked for about $50. The tile was a question mark, since she thought it would have to be done professionally and she'd need to get estimates. In her mind she'd put a $350 price tag on the whole project, and felt sure that when August came she'd have saved the money. In June her husband had to have some unexpected and costly dental work done. Although their insurance helped with the bill, there was still an outstanding balance that gobbled up the kitchen money.

Our friend was momentarily at a standstill. We told her to go ahead with the estimates and at least get a real dollar figure on the exact cost of what she'd hoped to do. We thought she'd get to the light fixture place, spot the one she wanted, and find out it was only half as much as she'd imagined.

She was off on the price, all right. The one she'd pictured cost *twice* as much as she'd estimated! While she was staring at it, she began to notice how it was put together. Its base was similar in shape and size to the outdated metal fixture she already had. The main differences between the white, high-tech designer one at the store and the old one in her kitchen were the color and the modern globes. She bought three of the globes (the store carried them as replacements) and picked up a can of white spray paint at the hardware store.

When she got home she took down the old light fixture, threw away the glass light-diffusing bowl that covered the light bulbs, and replaced the one-hundred watters with the modern soft-light globes she'd found at the store. She spray-painted the aluminum rim white and replaced it. When she stood back and looked at the finished fixture, she was thrilled, and even more so because she'd only spent a few dollars.

Since she had leftover paint, she took a look at her old metal canisters. They had brown lids and all the bottoms had tan and rust-colored mushrooms on them. The mushrooms were the only real problem for her; after thirteen years she was sick of looking at them and wanted a change.

Because the sizes and shapes of the canisters suited her needs, she decided to make use of the leftover white spray paint and do a makeover on the mushrooms (she left the lids brown). When she saw them lined up on the counter, they had become as attractive and modern as her "new" light fixture and she had saved $50.

Next she went to a do-it-yourself tile store and picked out the tiles she wanted. She needed only one row, the length of her counter, so the cost was practically nothing. The man gave her pamphlets on how to lay tile; and since Danny and I had recently finished a do-it-yourself tile project ourselves, we gave her our leftover grout, and supplies enough to complete her project. We lent her the tools we'd used, and in one afternoon the job was done. The $350 estimate had been reduced to a pittance because of her creativity and willingness to take whatever action she could.

When her husband saw how much effort she was putting into the kitchen, he surprised her by making a stained glass border, framed in oak, to encase the metal range hood. When the light above the stove was turned on, the leaded glass was especially beautiful. The whole thing was made of pieces of glass and oak, left over from other projects.

By using the materials they already had on hand, the two of them were able to fix up their kitchen without spending much money at all.

Webster defines appreciation as "an expression of gratitude; to increase in value." When you appreciate something you take care of it and it becomes more valuable. Pam once considered buying a house that had five acres and lots of potential, but it hadn't been taken care of, so its value had depreciated. The house was a real mess inside. Paint was peeling, the wallpaper had yellowed, there were cracks in the ceiling, and belongings were scattered everywhere. Outside, the conditions were even worse. The yard was overgrown and out of control; trees needed pruning and blackberry vines had taken over what once must have been an impressive greenhouse. In a leaky shed there were all kinds of garden machinery and tools—a rusty Rototiller, a filthy hand mower, a riding lawn mower in pieces, and various gardening tools, all rusty and broken.

"Why are you selling the place?" my sister asked the owner.

"Because it's just too small for me. I'm a nurseryman, and I need more room to really do what I want to. I'd go all out if I could find about twenty acres."

My sister didn't buy the place. It was priced right, but it was just too much of a wreck. We never knew exactly what happened to the seller, but it seemed obvious that if he wasn't able to take care of and appreciate five acres, having a bigger place would just mean he'd make more of a mess.

When you plan a home improvement take "before" and "after" pictures so that you can enjoy the results even more. Use some of your free time to cut out pictures from magazines, showing "good ideas" for the future. Put the pictures in your scrapbook and put the idea on a 3x5, filed in a special divider for home improvements. If you know in which month you would like to schedule the project, file it within the monthly dividers. File your completed projects in the success divider.

Affirm often, "I appreciate my home and my belongings enough to take good care of them, and by doing so, I increase their value." Even if you want something better, appreciate what you already have and it will be worth more when you are ready to move up. And don't forget to appreciate the things money can't buy . . . like a beautiful day, an unexpected hug from a child, or having a sister you can really talk to. It's those blessings that, in the end, mean the most.

It's easy to get sidetracked by the world and assume that material things are most important. If you stop to think about it, our survival on this physical earth depends on four basic elements: food, water, oxygen, and whatever the energy force is that keeps the heart beating. Food is the most perceptible of the four things. It has color, texture, taste, shape, and smell. Science says you can go approximately six weeks without food, if you have water. Water is less perceptible than food, but it can still be seen. You can only go six to ten days without water. Oxygen (less perceptible than water, because we can't even see it) is even more vital to our survival. You can live only five minutes without air. The fourth essential cannot be tasted or touched, smelled or seen, yet without "it," there wouldn't be *anything* to appreciate. It is life itself.

Nine

September–Work
–From Pam

"The world is moved along, not only by the mighty shoves of its heroes, but also by the aggregate of the tiny pushes of each honest worker."

—HELEN KELLER

Whether the summer was filled with exciting trips or long, lazy days, we're ready to reorganize when September comes. The kids go back to school and resume their routine, things get back to normal at home, and the mornings are suddenly cool. It's a great time to put our attention on work.

Remember the old story about the grasshopper and the ants? The grasshopper goofed around while the ants worked. While he was socializing, they were organizing. He danced and played his fiddle while they stored up food for the winter. The organized ants warned the procrastinating grasshopper that he'd be sorry when winter came.

Before Peggy and I were organized, September gave us the false sense that with the kids back in school we had loads of time to kill. As we relaxed in the autumn sun the good news went out to swarms of fruit flies and yellow jackets that there was a heaping box of decaying peaches in the garage. Swollen zucchini, too big to use for anything, lined the deck with cookie sheets of pumpkin seeds, meant for fireside treats, grew mold in the sun.

The painful proof that procrastination doesn't pay always came when it was too late for us to do anything but regret that we'd put things off again. Thoughts of a crackling fire on a stormy night made us wish we'd ordered a cord of firewood. Knowing that thinkers-ahead had pantries bulging with gifts from the harvest, and freezers pregnant with packaged and labeled beef and homemade goodies, only added to our frustration.

In September our organized friends had tried to remind us that the holidays were coming, telling us we'd better get to work; but, like the grasshopper, we continued to play. Content to live for the moment, we'd set aside our good intentions as thoughtlessly as the pillowcase we'd stuffed with delicate hand-washables and never put into the washer.

Now that Peggy and I are organized, we use September as the month to regroup and get things done on the homefront. It's the time when most of our heavy, once-a-year, deep cleaning gets done. In other words, we spring-clean in the fall. It makes more sense to have the house cleaned really well after the summer is over and before the holidays. Then we're free to enjoy the season, without having to worry about what needs to be scrubbed or polished.

By the time we created our 3x5 Happiness File, our houses had been clean and free of clutter for more than six years. If your house is a mess, and it's bothering you, we suggest you try our basic household cardfile system. It is explained in detail, with charts and illustrations, in our first book, *Sidetracked Home Executives*.

We want to give you a concentrated summary of it right now, however, because in a very practical way it reflects the essence of our philosophy of life. Obviously we're only going to go over the main points of our 3x5 system, but we hope we can give you a basic knowledge of the way it works.

The basis for our system and the tool for organizing our houses and our lives is an Activity List—a room-by-room master catalog of *every* household job, all family-related jobs and errands, plus personal things that need to be done. It includes everything from filling the dishwasher to reading stories to children; waxing floors to painting nails. Our own complete personal list is in our first book.

We took each task on our list and decided how often it should be done: daily, weekly, monthly, yearly, etc. Then we made a time estimate of how many minutes, hours, or days each activity should take to complete. We knew we needed to be aware of time, because losing control of time—sometimes months and years—is a problem for people who are easily sidetracked.

We also decided whether a job could be delegated to a husband or child, and whether it was a Mini-Job. A Mini-Job is any project that takes ten minutes or less to complete. We emphasized Mini-Jobs on the Activity List because, if you're, by nature, a sidetracked person, you can go through each day unaware of how you could have used those small blocks of time.

Our next step was to draw up a Basic Week Plan. This flexible guide helped us spread our work and activities through the week. We set up a free day for ourselves, free from housework, elaborate cooking, and errands. It was our reward to ourselves for being so well organized. Then we designated: a moderate-cleaning day; a quiet day for paying bills, balancing the checkbook, clipping grocery coupons, writing letters, and tying up loose ends; a grocery-shopping day; a heavy-cleaning day; a family day; and Sunday, which we would keep free.

Next we transferred the Activity List to color-coded 3x5 cards. For example, we used yellow cards for all daily jobs, one job to a card. Blue cards were for all weekly jobs. White cards were for monthly and seasonal jobs. Pink cards were for all personal things, the things we loved to do, and jobs and errands outside the home.

On each card we wrote the job's title, whether it could be delegated, a description of the job, its estimated time limit, whether it was a Mini-Job, and how often it needed to be done.

When we started our system we made cards for everything, because we knew we'd neglect to do a job if we didn't have a card for it. But now that we've been on the system for so long, we've found that many jobs have become so automatic that we've been able to throw away many of our original cards. Probably you'll need to start your own file with fewer 3x5s than we did, because we were the ultimate slobs.

Next in our setup came the one through thirty-one dividers, which became our rotating monthly "calendar" in the file box. We numbered the first divider with the current date, then filed the rest of the dividers, in order, behind it. Each night we rotated the date just ended to the back of the box, so the current date was always at the front. (Since the development of the Happiness File, we have simplified this part by using Monday through Sunday dividers instead of the one through thirty-one, keeping everything together in one cardfile, and it works beautifully.)

Then we were ready to start filing. We made four piles of cards, separated by color, and filed individual cards from each pile (pink, yellow, blue, and white) in front of the appropriate day, date, or month.

We filed the daily, weekly, and monthly cards according to our Basic Week Plan, depending on whether the job fit into moderate-cleaning, heavy-cleaning, quiet, grocery-shopping, family, or free day.

In the first few weeks of using our system, we tried desperately to do what was scheduled on every card in our file at the appointed time. We made it through the daily and personal cards without much trouble, but some of the weekly and monthly jobs—like waxing floors and washing windows—were real dogs.

After trial and error and lots of guilt, we came up with a way to give the system flexibility and freedom, and still prevent jobs from piling up beyond our ability to cope. We called the system's fail-safe device "File It and Forget It." We permitted ourselves to skip a job twice before it had to become a priority item.

We found that sometimes it was necessary and possible to skip a whole day or week of cards. When an old friend came to town on what should have been our heavy-cleaning day, when we went on vacation, or when we canned pears for a week, we just skipped all the cards and filed them for when we would be back to normal. Why? We wanted our get-organized system to reflect our philosophy of life: People, and our love for them, came before vacuum cleaners and dishcloths.

We loved the system. We had never felt so well organized or so much in control of our lives. Our houses were clean, our families were happy, and we had time for ourselves.

As the months passed we grew with the system, expanding it into every area of homemaking to include meal-planning and kitchen organization. When you're ready to go beyond the basics, you might want to read our second book, *The Sidetracked Sisters Catch-Up on the Kitchen*. It covers those subjects.

Be sure to take before and after pictures of your home when you start working on it. The sense of accomplishment you'll feel when everything is clean and organized will be so satisfying; and you will be able to enjoy the fruits of your labor all over again through the photographs.

Maybe, as you read each chapter in Part IV of this book, you felt you'd like to switch some of the themes around to suit your particular circumstances. That will work just fine with any of the months but September and December. As a matter of fact, if you're reading this work chapter in December, and you're tempted to try to get organized and set up a household cardfile before Christmas, we have to warn you against it. Relax and accept the fact that you're not going to have time to shop for gifts, cook, bake, wrap, decorate, and have the house thoroughly cleaned in a couple weeks.

If your house is a mess, there's not much you can do. If you're feeling desperate, you might consider buying some spray cans of artificial snow. Start at the front door and flock clockwise. (A three-bedroom ranch-style will take about a case of spray snow.) You could decorate right over the dirt and distract your visitors' sense of sight by tantalizing their other senses. Holiday music, a fire in the fireplace, candles

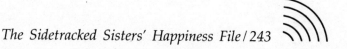

glowing, the scent of pine and bayberry, and a simmering kettle of chicken necks should warm even the most discerning houseguests; and if they do notice, perhaps the generous spirit of the season will make their comments kinder.

Think back to the grasshopper we talked about earlier. In the end, everything turned out well for the fun-loving bug. Because of his good humor and talents, he was invited by the organized ants to join them. In exchange for his entertaining them with laughter and song, the ants provided food and shelter through the winter. I like to believe that by the following September, the grasshopper had worked to make a nice, clean, comfortable, organized home of his own. I think he'd have even more fun if he were able to entertain the ants over at his place once in a while.

For fun-loving people, the word *work* can imply something negative. I looked up the definition of *work* in the dictionary and could see why I'd had trouble dealing with the word in the past. There are nearly three pages of depressing derivations: words like workaholic, workbook, work camp, worked up, work farm, workhorse, workhouse, working class, working order, work load, workmen's compensation insurance, work out, and work over. The word *work* has a lot of meanings, many involving physical labor, drudgery, and exertion. I was thankful finally to come upon this positive definition: "something produced or accomplished by effort, the exercise of a skill; or expenditure of creative, artistic talents." *I felt better.* If all work and no play made Jack a dull boy, all play and no work would make him a careless playboy.

Work doesn't have to be like an evil giant hanging over you. Thomas Edison is quoted as saying, "I never worked a day in my life, it was all fun." Peggy and I feel as Edison did about our work. We love to write and we're fortunate to be able to earn a living doing something we enjoy. Once, while we were at Peggy's house writing a humorous article for our newsletter, we found ourselves consumed by the kind of uncontrollable laughter that hurts your stomach. Danny had been busy watching all of the kids and had just finished up the lunch dishes when our prolonged laughing session finally got to him. "I know you're working," he said, "but does it have to be so much fun?" The beauty of our work is that when we're laughing and having fun, we're doing our best writing.

I have been criticized for my work philosophy and told that I live in a dreamworld. If it's true, all I can say is that it's a great place to live. I believe that if you don't enjoy your work you're in the wrong business. I also think that if you looked hard enough, you'd find a happy worker for every job. I wouldn't be happy as a garbage man, but I know one who is.

One morning I met my whistling trash collector out at the curb (I had to run with my can so I wouldn't miss him), and as he hoisted my garbage into the smelly truck, I felt as if I should apologize for my part of the stink.

"I'm really sorry about that horrible smell. I let a red snapper get away from me, and then it sat out in the can for a couple of days . . ."

After removing his Walkman headphones he said, "What'd ya say, ma'am?"

"I said I feel bad about the smell."

"Oh, heck, lady, I don't smell a thing. It's all part of the job." He continued his whistling.

"You seem to like your work."

"Sure, I like it. I wouldn't do it if I didn't!" He went on to tell me how great it was performing a service for his fellow human beings and how he felt he personally knew each home owner by his garbage. "I could tell you things about your neighbors that only the garbage man would know." He chuckled.

"I'll bet you can."

I wondered what he knew about us from what we'd put in our can.

"Did you know that the only true way to measure the state of the economy is to look at what people throw away?" he continued.

"You're kidding."

I snugged the neckline of my bathrobe up around my throat and glanced to see if any of my neighbors were watching.

"Heck, no, I'm not kiddin'. I saw the recession coming a good six months before it hit the *Wall Street Journal*."

"Wow!"

"Oh, yeah! I'm tellin' you, for a while I wasn't seein' any two-ply trash liners and nobody could afford double-can service."

Leaving me on a positive note, he said that things were looking up, and judging by the amount of convenience-food cartons and disposable diapers he was seeing out at the dump, it was going to be a great year!

I have always made it my goal to do only the things I love. That doesn't mean I haven't had to do some work I didn't like, but whenever that happens, I make a point of figuring out a way to change things. I can do anything that has to be done, if I'm sure it's temporary. I could work at a cannery, sorting snakes out of the green beans, as well as anyone, but I'd make sure I had a plan so that it would only be for one season. I would take any work I could find if my family's existence depended on it.

I am in the difficult position, as many women are today, of being a single working mother. It's not only hard emotionally and physically to have sole responsibility for three children, it is financially a heavy burden. Although it's true that I do enjoy my work, there is always the underlying reality that I must make enough money to support my family.

Fortunately, I have learned how to rise above my circumstances and use my talents to earn enough income to take care of my children. Mary Kay started her multimillion-dollar cosmetic business based on that same purpose, and combining her own need with her desire to help other women reach their potential, she became a success. My family is my first priority. To have a job that would take me out of my home for forty hours a week has *always* been out of the question. Consequently, I've never suffered the strain of being torn between my children and a nine-to-five job.

Before I had children I worked as a bank teller in a small town in Oregon. Marge, my supervisor, had three children and one husband. For a whole year I got to be a part of

their family, thanks to her frequent conversations over the
phone.

"Hi, Tony! How was school?"

". . . . ."

"We'll talk about it later. Did Bobbie get off the bus
okay?"

". . . . ."

"What do you mean you haven't seen him?!"

". . . . ."

"All right, go answer the door and come right back."

". . . . ."

"Bobbie, where have you been?"

". . . . ."

"You're kidding. The Blue and Gold Skill-a-ree was today
after school?"

". . . . ."

"Well, I hope you thanked Doug's mother for bringing
you home. Put Anthony back on."

". . . . ."

"Hi, Tone. Listen, I need you to peel some potatoes for
dinner."

". . . . ."

"They're either under the sink or still in the garage."

". . . . ."

"Don't argue with me! You need to get them out and peel
them now!"

". . . . ."

"No, you can't!"

". . . . ."

"Just because I said no!"

". . . . ."

"You'll have to ask your dad, but don't bother him at
work." (Mr. Griffin was a troubleshooter for a bus company.)

The rearing of the Griffin children took second place to all
deposit and withdrawal transactions. Marge was tired! When
she saw the morning plane leave the Medford airport and
pass over the bank for San Francisco, she was mentally
on it, and said so. She was a smart woman. The best person
in the bank at figuring things out.

All of us brought her our questions and she always had

the solutions, when it came to banking. But when it involved her own family, she was baffled.

Marge had originally taken the job on a part-time basis so that she and her husband could turn their carport into an attached garage. Yet fifteen years later she was still in cage one at the First National Bank of Oregon, and her kids were raised by telephone. (Jokingly she once said, "The only way I can get my kids to mind me when I'm at home is to go next door and call them on the phone.")

If a person is working so that she can get a new davenport, remodel the kitchen, or buy new carpet for the family room, then the work is based on materialism. If that is the case, she needs to stop and think about what she is doing . . . especially if she has children. No material thing can be a reason for raising your children via Ma Bell. No hot tub, second car, cabin in the mountains, or swanky motor home will compensate for lost time with your children. No other person has the same involvement as you have. What child-care attendant has one-on-one time to read your small child a special story? Who can find the time to work your self-conscious youngster out of a cutesy lisp? Who would care enough to get to the bottom of your child's lie? Why would anyone care whether your child (among all the other full-time day-care children) lost a kitten or got a new tooth?

A kindergarten teacher once told me, at my child's first conference, that she could always tell the difference between full-time day-care children and those who has been nurtured at home by their parents.

Live in a tent, ride bikes, eat macaroni and cheese, do what you have to do to stay with your kids before they get into school, and once they're in school, be home when they get home.

There is only one exception to how I feel on this subject, and it's directed to the mother who should never have had kids in the first place but does. To her, my heart goes out. She's got one, two, maybe more and she has neither the patience nor the desire to handle the complicated and often hectic job of raising children. In that extreme case she needs to find a loving atmosphere in some other mother's home for her children.

A loving atmosphere is hard to find in most overcrowded, understaffed, nonregulated day-care facilities across our country. A person who can open her home and her heart to take in someone else's child is providing a service that should receive payment equal to its importance. There is *nothing* more valuable than the care and rearing of our children. If you have that gift (whether you're raising your own kids or someone else's), it's worth money. Even though the world isn't ready to pay you what you deserve, you must know that your contribution to society makes every minute of your time worthwhile; and in the end you will be recognized for what you've accomplished.

In the spring of 1983 Peggy and I were on a promotional book tour that took us to twenty-six cities. While we were being interviewed on a live radio talk show, some guy called in to complain about what a slob his wife had been (they were divorced). He said that the house was always a wreck, and she was a good-for-nothing, lazy broad.

I asked the man if they had had any kids. He replied, "Four, but they are all grown-up now." He didn't have the slightest idea that I was getting ready to strike at his jugular.

"How did the children turn out?"

"They're great. One's a teacher, the two boys are in the grocery business together, and the youngest just graduated from Illinois State with a degree in sociology."

"Who would you say raised the children?"

"Well, she did. I'll have to give her credit for that."

"Sir?"

"Yeah?"

"Do you have any idea what it takes to get four children out of diapers, into teeth, over their fears, under your thumb, through their teens, behind the wheel, and graduated from college?"

Click . . .

It was too much for him. If he had been a part of it all, he would have called in to say how grateful he was to have been married to someone who had carried the responsibility for raising the children (even if the house had gotten away from her). There is no higher calling than motherhood.

Peggy and I have what we call our mother's creed, and although it is printed in one of our other books, I think it is important enough to repeat.

When someone at a party asks either of us, "What do you do?" We reply, "I am responsible for creating a climate of love, peace, joy, beauty, and order in my home. I am raising future citizens of the United States of America.... What do you do?" If you are doing the same thing, be proud of it and say so. Don't let anyone (even in ignorance) diminish your life's work.

On that same book tour television talk show hosts constantly asked us, "So who's taking care of your children while you are gallivanting around the country?" Gallivanting around the country? I was trying to earn a living to feed and clothe my three dependents. Was this same question asked of male authors, or was it assumed that fathers on the road had a woman at home to care for their children?

My reply was that my mother and father were taking care of them while I was working. My sister's indignant answer was to the point: "The children have what is commonly known as a *father*; the other half of a two-part reason why they're alive."

Balancing my career with my home is a real challenge. Giving each area of responsibility the right amount of my time and attention takes organization and sensitivity. How to run a successful business and still maintain a happy family life could be a book by itself.

Peggy and I know that that balance is a crucial struggle for most of us today. One day I realized that cleaning my toilets didn't make me a better person; it didn't mean that I loved my family any more, and it didn't prove that I was a hard worker. That was the day I hired a housekeeper and began using my time to develop my own talents.

I realized that it didn't matter whether I did the cleaning myself or hired someone to help me with it. The important thing was that everything at home was taken care of so that when I was busy earning a living, I could keep my attention on my work.

One day I was over at Peggy's house and she was ironing Danny's long-sleeved dress shirts for work. She was wrestling to get the cuff area right and complaining that ironing his shirts for the last seventeen years had become a hateful job.

"Why don't you *have* them done?"

"You mean pay someone to do it? It'd cost a fortune."

"Have you asked the cleaners what they charge?"

"No."

I persuaded her to call, and we found out that it would cost $1.05 to wash, starch, and iron one shirt. For $5.25 a week Peggy could put away the ironing board and make better use of her time. The money wasn't a problem, but she still resisted the idea. "I don't know, Sissy. I'm a homemaker; ironing shirts is part of my job."

"Your job is to be a good wife and mother, and to manage the affairs of the household. Ironing isn't your talent, Peggy. Look at that shirt you just finished. You're not doing Danny any favors."

Sometimes we work at things we don't like just because that's the way it's always been done, because our mother did it, or because we aren't aware of our options. If you dislike doing something to the point of complaining about it, hire someone else to do it, trade your services with another person, simplify it, delegate it, or eliminate it altogether.

Ask any high-level executive, "When was the last time your business was affected by one of your employees' disorganization *at home*?" You'll find out that business is constantly hampered by the domestic problems of scattered and sidetracked workers (perhaps even those of the boss him/herself).

If the executive is honest, you'll hear that her own disorganization at home has pulled her attention away from her work at one time or another.

For women who have a job outside their home, there is a double challenge. A lot of those women are victims of the chauvinistic thinking of an earlier generation. Their spouse sees housekeeping as woman's work and, unfortunately, in many cases so do the women themselves. From speaking to them in workshops across the country, Peggy and I have recognized the struggle these people go through as they try to do it all and be all things to all people. There is an excellent book, written by Marjorie Hansen Shaevitz, called *The Superwoman Syndrome* that explains this problem better than I can, and sheds light on the stress these women are going through. I think it is a book that every woman (and man, too) should surely read.

In the area of housekeeping I believe that everyone who lives in the house should take part in keeping it up. For our 3x5 cardfile system we timed each job. For example, emptying the dishwasher takes approximately ten minutes, sweeping the kitchen floor takes five minutes, and vacuuming the family room takes fifteen minutes. We fed all the jobs and their estimated times into a home computer. Then we totaled all the manhours involved in keeping the average house clean.

We found out that it takes two hundred and twenty-one hours a month to maintain a three-bedroom, ranch-style home with a family room, garage, laundry room, and a couple of bathrooms. (The figure also includes personal maintenance such as washing combs and brushes, doing the laundry, etc., and it even takes into consideration chores such as bathing the dog and emptying the Kitty Litter).

Next we figured out how many hours there are in the month and came up with 720 hours. If you work outside the home full-time, subtract 240 hours. If you get 8 hours of sleep a night, subtract 240, and if you're still trying to do all the housekeeping yourself, deduct 221 hours. That leaves you nineteen hours a month for leisure (unless, of course, you subtract the time it takes to eat, drive the kids back and forth, attend a PTA meeting, go to church, take the dog to the vet, help your daughter with spelling, and make it to your son's track meet).

If you fall into this kind of desperate situation, you can see that it must change. The answer lies in learning to delegate and deciding that you aren't doing your family any favors by trying to do everything yourself. Expect help. Ask for it. Accept it. Let 3x5 cards be the taskmaster. Write down what you want done, give each job a time estimate, give each family member an equal amount of chore time, and see how much better it feels when everyone works together as a family rather than you doing it all like a slave.

Teach your children (and your husband, if he's a reasonable man) the way to load a dishwasher, sort wash; dry, fold, and put away laundry. Show them how to vacuum, dust, scrub, polish, and scour. Let them experience the good feeling that comes from a completed task.

Next time ask your husband to take the Labrador to get his shot. Then he will appreciate how it feels to have hairs all over his suit, and he and the dog can experience the close bonding between man and dog on the happy return trip home. Write important dates in your husband's appointment book so he won't forget that he has a PTA meeting the second Tuesday of every month, and he'll make it to the children's school conferences when he's supposed to. Give him a grocery list, put an apron on him while he's in the kitchen, hand him a knife and stand him at the cutting board to chop vegetables for tacos. While he watches the Monday night football game, he can crack walnuts, stir cookie dough, peel potatoes, or clip coupons.

When your kids want to go to a friend's house, or go ride bikes, have some little mini-job for them to do first. They'll do it quickly and automatically when they know it's expected. "Sure you can go for an hour, but empty the garbage first."

All of these delegations take more organization than authority. The written word has much more authority than a mother's nagging voice. Each family member should develop the habit of keeping his clothes hung up or folded and put away, making his bed each morning, getting his laundry in the right basket (according to color) in the laundry room, clearing his own dishes and rinsing them and putting them in the dishwasher, and making sure all of his belongings are put away at night. On the weekend it works well to schedule a family work day. (Why should one person work for five hours when five people can work one hour so that everyone will be free to have fun?)

Peggy's family has had success using a point system. Jobs are timed, and the point value of each task is equal to the time it takes to do the job. A ten-point job is worth ten cents and takes ten minutes to do. Peggy has a list of prizes on the bulletin board with the number of points it will take to earn each prize. The values range from a 150-point roller skating trip (the exact amount it costs to skate), all the way to a deluxe 10-speed bike worth 18,500 points. She says she doesn't worry that anyone will ever earn the ten-speed. It would take 18,500 minutes worth of work, and by the time any of them finished that many jobs, he or she would be old enough to want a car. Each kid has a 3x5 card posted with the total number of points accumulated. Extra bonus points can be earned for a good attitude toward helping, getting along with siblings, notes of praise from school, and good grades. (An A is worth a hundred points, Bs seventy-five and a C just means the child gets to live in the house for another semester.) The points can be cashed in for prizes at any time.

If you do any job with purpose and dedication, you can look back on it with a feeling of accomplishment and joy. Few pleasures in life can equal the good feeling that comes with a job well done. The difference between drudgery and fun is measured in the heart of the worker. Let your work speak of your talents, your humor, your efforts, and your willingness to share with others. Whether you're a butcher, a baker, or a homemaker, make your work be a pursuit of happiness. Let it be the gift you give to the world around you; and finally, when you go to that great retirement party in the sky, you'll be able to say that your work in life was one of your greatest joys.

Ten

October–Laughter
–From Peggy

"Laugh and the world laughs with you; cry and it's not going to change anything but your mascara."

—PAMELA I. YOUNG

October is one of my favorite months! I liked it when I was younger because my birthday falls on the 23rd. The older I get, the less thrilled I am to add another year to my age, but I still look forward to October.

It could be that it's a special month because we live in the Pacific Northwest, where there are four seasons, and October marks the change from fall to winter. The warm days and cold nights make the leaves on the trees brilliant. (If I didn't know differently, I'd swear Mother Nature drinks once in a while and gets carried away with her paint set.) Looking out my kitchen window, I can see a view in October that is absolutely glorious! I hear the wild geese and ducks honking from their refuge below our property and realize that soon they will head south to spend the winter. It's a signal that the holidays are coming. Our family always makes a big deal of Thanksgiving and Christmas. (We even decorate the bathrooms.) In October, I start going to holiday bazaars and flea markets, and I start playing my Christmas albums. I love it!

After Pam and I had finished writing about most of the twelve themes that would make up the chapters in Part IV, I spoke with Danny about my subject for October. It was to be called "Preparation." "I don't know what to write," I complained. "I'm not an authority on readiness; I was born three weeks late, and I wasn't even prepared when I was a Girl Scout."

Danny is always calm and rational when I get nuts.

"Who decided what the chapters would be about?" he asked.

"Pam and I did."

"Then change the theme to fit what you know about. Write about something funny."

"I can't do that."

"Why not?"

It almost seemed sacrilegious, like taking Revelations out of the Bible and putting in limericks.

As we were talking the phone rang. It was Mom. She said, "Dad and I were talking today, and we think you ought to have a whole chapter about laughter." Throughout their life together they have had the greatest time laughing, she said, and it had pulled them through even the hardest times. She told me she'd heard about a book a man had written about his recovery from a crippling disease because he was able to laugh.

I understood the value of preparedness, but I felt more comfortable writing about laughter, so I called my sister and told her to scratch Preparation; we were going for Laughter.

Sometimes when unpleasant things have happened to me, people have told me, "Someday you'll laugh about that!" They were right. I want to share two of those incidents with you in this chapter. Even though, at the time, I was horribly embarrassed, I can look back on them now and see that the episodes were really funny.

The first incident happened when Danny and I were

going to move across town to a new apartment. We planned to rent a truck and move all the prepacked stuff one night after work. We'd been married only a few years and had no children yet, so it should have been an easy move.

A couple of weeks before U-Haul night I noticed that my organized husband had begun to gather packing boxes for his belongings. For several evenings in a row I watched him systematically fill the boxes and log their contents on a master guide sheet. The neat boxes were all the same size, and they were alphabetically coded to correspond with the guide sheet. I silently saluted his ability to analyze a job and organize it. In my mind I copied him.

At work I sat at my desk visualizing the move. I saw myself stopping at the Safeway that very evening and carefully picking out the perfect boxes for my stuff. I'd get those nice heavy ones with lids. I'd use the ones with a big orange on them for bedroom and bathroom items; the ones with a yellow lemon would be for kitchen things. I'd pack living room and miscellaneous objects in the apple boxes. I got excited. *I'll run by the print shop and get a set of colored felt pens so I can color-code my master guide sheet*, I thought. Instantly, in my imagination, I was in the print shop selecting a dozen or so bright-colored pens. I could hear Danny saying, "Great idea! Why didn't I think of using those?" For days I packed . . . mentally. I thought of ways to use colored stickers and colored envelopes for special items. In my mind I was a creative moving master.

Too tired to do the actual packing (I was all packed out from thinking about it so much), I'd go home from work and flop into a chair. Meanwhile, Danny's boxes were starting to line up against one wall of the living room. The guide sheet was taped to one of them. I felt nauseated. On my lunch hour the next day I bought the pens. They cost more than I'd estimated. Actually, I hadn't visualized myself at the cash register, paying for them. My imagination had stopped at the point of selection.

After work I was starving (I'd skipped lunch), so I headed for the Won Ton Gardens to pick up some Chinese food for dinner. It was a good idea, but on the way I realized that, having egg foo yung on my mind, I'd already sped past the Safeway. *Oh, well*, I thought, *you can run back by after you eat. . . .* I liked that idea.

At home I took the pens into the house. Danny was numbering his boxes and sealing them. I refused to look.

"Tomorrow's moving day, you know," he warned.

"I know," I said, as if I had no concern.

"So how are you going to be ready? You don't seem to be grasping the moving concept . . . you have to *pack!*"

I flashed the pens in front of him and said with arrogance, "Never mind. I have a plan."

After dinner I tore over to the Safeway for the special boxes. There weren't any. I settled for several of the biggest toilet paper and dog food boxes that were left. The next day I simplified my packing plan and opted to label each box "Miscellaneous." With the U-Haul in the driveway pressing me to hurry, I went in and out of every room, putting whatever I found there in a box; and when each box was full, I sealed it up and Danny hauled it away.

I rationalized that I'd sort everything out at the other end of the move, but when we were through, I was exhausted. I told Danny I'd have to unpack later, and we went to bed.

The next morning, rushing to get ready for work, I ran into a slight problem. I couldn't find my underwear. It was getting late. I looked over at my organized husband as he confidently unsealed his box labeled "U" and took out a pair of undershorts. My options were running out. "May I borrow a pair of those?" I asked casually, as though we'd often traded shorts.

"What?" he said. (There was a look on his face that was a cross between contempt and disbelief.)

"Just give me a pair of those. I'll get 'em back to you."

"I can't believe you would actually stoop to wearing my underwear to work."

"Well, it's *that or nothing!*" Against his better judgment he handed me a pair. As we continued to get ready to leave that morning, I could feel Danny's scornful stare, but I pretended not to. I kissed him. "Good-bye," I said.

"Good-bye . . . I hope you don't have an accident." He couldn't resist.

"Well, now, isn't *that* a pleasant parting thought," I said as I whirled and made a haughty exit.

In the car on the way to work I was haunted by my mother's presence, as if she were sitting in the backseat. "Always wear nice underwear. It speaks well of your family background, and you never know when you may have to be taken to Vancouver Memorial." I was grateful finally (and without incident) to make it to my job on time. My secret secure, I worked all morning until it was time for a coffee break. With a Coke in one hand and my purse in the other, I started to go down the stairs to the employee lounge, but my high heel caught in the carpet on the top step and threw me. Coke and change flew everywhere.

My frightened boss, who had been going down the stairs just ahead of me, turned and tried to catch me, but I had already come to a stop at the bottom of the steps. "Oh, Peggy, are you all right?" he asked in shock.

"I'm just fine! All that ballet training as a child finally paid off," I said jokingly, as if the fall were nothing. (I wondered if he'd seen my shorts.)

He helped me up. "I'm so glad you're not hurt, but it's company policy that when something like this happens, you need to be checked by a doctor...you know, Washington State Industrial Accident Insurance and all. I'll take you right now to your family doctor just to be on the safe side."

We went from the bottom of the steps out to a company car, and he drove me straight to the doctor's office. On the way I wanted to say, "Could we just buzz by Penney's for a second? I could be in and out in no time." But there was never the opportunity; and besides, I was a little afraid he might say, "What do you need? I'll get it!" Sitting in the waiting room, I prayed for a miracle. "Please, Father, change these shorts into panties." It didn't work. When my name was called, the nurse (the sharp one I'd never cared for even as a child) said, "Strip down to your underwear and get on that table."

There I was, lying on a stainless steel X-ray table, in my bra and Jockey shorts, when the old woman returned. She looked right at my shorts and then at me.

"Hey, I know you must be wondering why I'm wearing men's underwear."

"Quite frankly, my dear, it's your own business." She snatched my chart and left the examining room in disgust. I was never able to explain that I didn't have a thing for men's clothing and that it was just a one-shot wearing, a desperate measure. It was a long time before I could laugh about that one!

The second incident happened nearly a year later. I was expecting our first baby (in fact, I was almost ready to deliver). As I waited in the same examining room to see the doctor, I got very bored. It seemed as if I'd been in that doctor's office more often than I'd been at home. I'd already snooped in all the stainless steel containers on the counter and read the pamphlets about diabetes and menopause, and the doctor still hadn't come.

Resting on the examining table, covered by a skimpy little gown, I noticed the window at the foot of the table. I thought about getting up to see what the view from there would be, but it seemed like too much of an effort. Lying there, I began to fiddle with the drapery cord. Using my foot as if it were a baseball bat and pretending the cord was the ball, I made a little game out of kicking the cord. It would swing back and I'd smack it again. Back and forth, I played footsie with it, until I noticed that it had been tied in a hangman's noose. Some kid, probably as bored as I was, must have done it. Challenging the knot with my big toe, I stuck it inside the noose and I pulled it back out. In and out...in and out...I dared the cord to catch me. It did! The third time, the noose tightened around my unlucky toe, capturing my foot in the air. It struck me funny. I thought about how Pam would get a kick out of it if she could see me hanging there.

After I'd rested a second I decided I'd better get out of it before the doctor came. I tried to sit up and undo the knot with my hand, but my huge stomach was in the way and my arm wasn't long enough to reach. I tried to jerk my toe out of the hold, but as I pulled down on the cord, the drapes started to open! Not knowing what or who was outside the window and taking into consideration my compromising position, I chose to hang there until help came. Winded from the struggle, I put my head back and tried to relax. (I was afraid I might go into labor if I had any more excitement.)

Soon the door to the examining room pushed open and I saw the familiar face of the crotchety old nurse I had always disliked. "Hi," I said nonchalantly. She stared at me for a moment as though she could not comprehend my predicament.

Finally, she said, "Well, *now* I've seen everything!"

She turned and, after opening the door, yelled into the hall, "Hey, Carol, come in here. You've gotta *see* this one!"

By the time all the other doctors and nurses in the office had a chance to come by my room for a look and a laugh, my big toe was purple and throbbing. Finally a *true* angel of mercy let me down and I was free to go on my way.

Throughout my life I've enjoyed my ability to laugh at myself. I have made some ridiculous mistakes, but thanks to a well-developed sense of humor, I have been able to see my mishaps as funny. When I let people laugh at what's happened to me, I can laugh too.

Nobody wants to look like a fool, but we all have done or said foolish things at one time or another. Being able to laugh at ourselves is a healthful release of tension. I have watched people who are unable to see the humor in their mistakes and I've seen the pain they go through. Once in an airport when Pam and I were waiting at our gate for our flight to be called, the ticket agent (microphone in hand) announced, "Please extinguish your boarding passes and have your smoking material ready to show the flight attendant." We got hysterical. The announcer didn't find her mistake one bit funny. She was too embarrassed to laugh (as if, by laughing, she would lose her dignity and the respect of the people around her). When she saw us laughing, she took it personally. I told her, "We're not laughing at you. We're laughing about how you got your announcement mixed up." She looked us straight in the eye and said, "I did not!" We felt sorry for her.

If you haven't been laughing enough (it's important to do

it every day), then it would be a good idea to take some of your free time in October and get your sense of humor in shape.

Look for funny anecdotes in *Reader's Digest*. Cut them out and tape them to a 3x5 to file in front of your humor divider. Cut out cartoons and comic strips, and put them in your scrapbook. Find funny pictures of animals, babies, tourists, and politicians and put them in your scrapbook.

Look in the section of your newspaper that lists upcoming events and enter the dates of musical comedies, plays, and personal appearances of comedians you'd like to see in your pocket planner, on your wall calendar, and on a 3x5 card for a specific month (if it's in the future).

Get a comedy schedule out of the television section of the newspaper and make a TV Comedy Card. Some of the great classic shows, like *I Love Lucy, Jack Benny,* and *I Married Joan* can bring back a laugh every time, no matter how often you've seen them.

Read humorous books, listen to a tape of laughter, or read your humor cards. Use your camera and try to fill up a roll of film with humor. Surround yourself with people who make you laugh. Have lunch with amusing friends or just call them regularly. Do everything you can think of to put more happiness in your life by laughing.

Eleven

November–Hospitality, Friendship, and Giving –From Pam

"It is more blessed to give than it is to just think about it."

—PEGGY A. JONES

"Happy is the house that shelters a friend."

—EMERSON

The holidays are almost here! I know because the kids' trick-or-treat sacks are empty except for wrappers and rejects. Lint-covered jelly beans and tipless candy corns are the last remnants of Halloween past, and the winter holidays are next.

With the season comes an almost universal urge to be more friendly and giving. Part of the tradition of this time of year is to think of others by sharing our love, opening our homes to friends and relatives, and giving gifts and cards to show our caring.

Organized people have a definite advantage over those of

us who get sidetracked easily. Before we got a hold on ourselves, we suffered from HBO (Holiday Blow-Out). As we stood in line to pay full price for Christmas cards and gift wrap, we felt cheated. We kicked ourselves for not getting in on the half-price sales the year before.

With no plan of action we'd spend the entire holiday season at the mercy of our moods. The mere mention of crimson ribbons, calico, or patterns for old-fashioned any-things would send us over the holiday edge. The sight of decorated store windows, the aroma of evergreen boughs and bayberry votives, or the voices of Steve Lawrence and Eydie Gormé pounding through the snow on a wild sleigh ride (recorded in a sound studio in Burbank) would drive us in search of holiday merriment. The Osmonds, skating on a Teflon pond, could throw us into reaching out and touching 'way more than we could afford.

Without direction our loving holiday intentions ended up being gift-wrapped in anger, stuffed into stockings with resentment, and sent in greeting cards with haste and no feeling.

It's true that whether we are prepared or not, none of us is denied the wonderful blessings that go with this time of year. The celebrations do not depend on candy canes and plum pudding. You don't have to be organized to sing Christmas carols or kiss under a sprig of mistletoe. Laughter cannot be charged on a Visa. Forgiveness can't be strung on a Christmas tree or poured into a Tom and Jerry. Love, joy, and understanding are gifts of the spirit—gifts that are not dependent upon decorations, feasts, or even a certain time of year. However, having a plan will turn all of your great intentions into tangible results that reflect your feelings.

Disorganized people are the *most* thoughtful people in the world, but usually all they *do* is think. Emerson said, "We have a great deal more kindness than is ever spoken." The reason it's usually never spoken is because we don't have a plan of action. Plans have a miraculous effect on an idea. Plans give big ideas little steps to follow. Without the path that plans provide, we end up leaping, usually in a frenzy, from the initial idea to a slipshod result. Disorganized people's brains do not see a process. They see only beginnings.

With a system we've been able to be more thoughtful, entertain more, and follow through with our good intentions. In our first book, *Sidetracked Home Executives*, we wrote an entire chapter on how to get organized for the holidays, beginning in January. We buy gifts all year. (When we buy a birthday gift, we buy a Christmas gift for the person, too.) We keep Christmas wrapping paper handy so that we can wrap presents as soon as we buy them. (Then they aren't given away before Christmas.)

There's a great song about the holidays that says it's not the decorations, the gifts, the foods, or any of the holiday trappings that make the season so terrific, but it's the little things you do all the time.

So that you can do the little things all year, use this month to take inventory of the people you love and care about. Make a list, in your notebook, of everyone you want to acknowledge in the next year (not just during the holidays). Your Christmas card list might give you a good start, but this list also needs to include your immediate family.

When you did the clearing exercise in January, we asked you to write down all the names that came into your mind, and now is the time to add those names to this list. Once the list is made, you can keep adding names you may think of later.

The next step is to set a priority for each name. The most important people in your life will be the As. The A people in my life are my children, my parents, and my sister and her family; the B people are my close friends; and the C people are business acquaintances, the children's teachers and friends, my hairstylist, my aerobics teacher, etc.

Once you've established those priorities put each person's name, address, and phone number on a white 3x5 card.

Starting with January, make out a white 3x5 card for each month. On each card write the names of all your A priority people. (You'll be writing that list on all twelve monthly cards.) Each monthly card will have all the birthdays and special occasions that you want to remember. In January three of my A people have birthdays, so I will need to buy three gifts. One of these people is Allyson, my niece. Since I want to do something special each month for all of

Peggy's children, this is a good month to get Chris and Jeff a small gift when Ally gets her birthday present. I think it's nice to see them all get something.

I am assuming that you will want to do something special each month for the VIPs in your life. The monthly card provides a monthly reminder of what you can do for them (see example below).

<u>January</u>
New Year's Day—1st
Mom's Birthday—9th
  gift and card
Ally's Birthday—16th
  gift and card
Dad's Birthday—20th
  gift and card

Peggy Anne—French book
Joanna—New crayons
Mike—Send cookies and a
  book to college

Aunt Peg ⎫ Bottle of
  and   ⎬ champagne for
Uncle Dan ⎭ having Ally

Chris—small gift
Jeff—small gift

Steve—28th
  birthday card
John and Susan—29th
  anniversary card

The people you have categorized as B people will be put on the monthly cards also, but probably not on every one. Maybe you'll just send a birthday card once a year. Having their names and birthdays on the right monthly card will remind you to send a card.

The C people probably will not be on the monthly cards. They are most likely people you will want to send a Christmas card to, and having their name on a 3x5 will be sufficient.

The cards with your people's names on them will be filed in the ABC section of the Happiness File, alphabetically by the person's last name. The twelve monthly cards will be filed in the January through December section.

At the beginning of each month you pull out the card for that month and take it with you on your shopping day. You already have a Tickler Card to tell you to pull the monthly Reminder Card.

In Chapter Four of Part IV Peggy talked about getting your desk organized so that you would have an efficient place to keep your finances in order. Your desk is also the place to follow through with cards and letters to friends and relatives. She suggested that you stock your desk with greeting cards, thank-you notes, stationery, and stamps. Sometimes the only thing that stands in the way of your thoughtfulness is an evenlope or a stamp.

The thoughtful people I know, the ones who never miss my birthday, think to cut out an article in the newspaper and send it, or call just to see how I'm doing, are either born organized, have a Rolodex on the left side of their brain, or have a system. They also take time to listen and care, and then they follow through.

If you think about it, the mailbox is pretty important to everyone. There isn't a person I know who would forget the daily hike to the box to see what's come in. Children love mail. Grandmas and Grandpas love mail. Lovers love mail. Astronauts, doctors, and attorneys love mail. The pen *is* mightier than the sword, and the power of an envelope and a stamp is awesome.

Gift-giving can be a tricky thing. A gift that delights one person may depress another. All it takes to make a gift a winner is a little thoughtfulness, the desire to please, and the willingness to work at it.

First determine the recipient's attitude about gifts. Does he or she like surprises, practical or personal presents, nostalgia, humor, etc.?

Listen. You should be able to pick up clues in everyday conversation. Draw out information about hobbies and collections, favorite colors, and pet peeves.

Be observant. Do the people you care about have a weakness for anything? Some people can't walk past a bookstore, cosmetic counter, jewelry department, or garden shop without admiring the merchandise.

All gifts carry a message. They should convey your good wishes and affection. Presents that express a compliment are always welcome. Ones that indicate a hint at the need for change or express criticism are not. Overweight people, for example, are not amused by exercise equipment or diet cookbooks.

Take notes on the back of the person's card you have filed in the ABCs. Don't rely on your memory. Keep a 3x5 pad of paper with you, in your pocket or purse, to jot down notes to be transferred later to the person's card.

Gifts don't have to cost a lot of money; in fact, they can be free when they come in the form of a kind deed or gesture.

Here is a list of ideas from my dear friend Vicki Frey. Vicki is the *most* hospitable person I have ever known, and her list reflects her warmth and caring. You might want to circle the ones that you think would be appreciated by the people in your life.

1. Tell someone he or she is special.
2. Give someone a hug.
3. Give someone a shoulder to lean on.
4. Ignore a rude remark.
5. Call a friend just to chat.
6. Forgive an old grudge.
7. Pat someone on the back.
8. Wash your teenager's car.
9. Make your child's bed.
10. Laugh when the joke's on you.
11. Drive within the 55 mph speed limit.
12. Mail a letter to your grandmother.
13. Tell someone how nice he or she looks.
14. Bake cookies for a friend.
15. Run an errand for a shut-in.
16. Don't wait for a reason to give someone a kiss.
17. Say you were wrong when you were.

18. Take the kids for an ice-cream cone.
19. Buy the wine your spouse likes.
20. Squeeze the toothpaste tube from the bottom.
21. Send a product manufacturer a nice letter.
22. Take your mom to lunch.
23. Take your dad to lunch.
24. Crawl in bed with your child for a few minutes at bedtime.
25. Keep a secret.
26. Laugh at an old joke.
27. Leave a loving note on a friend's windshield.
28. Buy your spouse a tank of gas.
29. Play catch with your child.
30. Offer to keep a friend's children for a weekend.
31. Take dinner, prepared, to a new mother.
32. Write your child's teacher a note of appreciation.
33. Let someone ahead of you in line.
34. Pass on some good news.
35. Put a note in your child's lunchbox.
36. Let your children watch cartoons for as long as they want one Saturday morning.
37. Feed your spouse breakfast in bed.
38. Serve ordinary dinner by candlelight.
39. Tell your mother-in-law what a special person she raised.
40. Type a term paper for a friend.
41. Offer to help your friend clean her house when you know her mother-in-law is coming to visit.
42. Fix your spouse's favorite dinner.
43. Put the mail in the same place every day so your family can find it.
44. Return a book to a friend.
45. Look at both sides of a story.
46. Try to understand your kids.
47. Write a nice letter to an editor.
48. Spread a little laughter around.
49. Take your grandmother shopping.
50. Mow the lawn.
51. Leave a tip for the newspaper boy.
52. Tell a store manager he has the cleanest store in town.
53. Take your teenager out for a Coke.
54. Leave a funny card for the mailman.
55. Share your umbrella.
56. Give someone a flower you have picked yourself.

57. Take an apple to your boss.
58. Rub a sore back.
59. Read to your child at bedtime.
60. Wake each member of your family with a kiss.
61. Do a kind deed anonymously.
62. Sing happy birthday to a friend over the phone.
63. Wash your spouse's back in the shower.
64. Plan a surprise weekend for your spouse at a nice motel.
65. Don't cut coupons out of the newspaper before your family has looked at it.
66. Take your parents out to dinner.
67. Use the good china when only your family is there.
68. Tell someone you are praying for him or her.
69. Share your lunch with someone who forgot to take one.
70. Let your spouse use the shower first.
71. Send someone you know very well a letter of encouragement.
72. Let your child have a friend stay overnight.
73. Say "I love you" often.

As you can see, most of the things on the list don't take much time and yet can mean so much to both the giver and the receiver.

Opening your home to your friends and relatives can be a joy if you are organized. There's nothing worse than having the doorbell ring if you're not ready for your own party.

The party should be for both you and your guests. A hostess who thinks of her party as a gift can't go wrong: a gift of people enjoying each other; a gift of food everyone will like; a gift of herself.

The more detailed and thorough your planning, the calmer and more self-assured you'll be on the day of the party. Begin by asking yourself the following questions:

—What kind of party do I want? Brunch, sit-down meal, buffet, cocktail party, dessert and coffee?
—Whom do I want to entertain? Women, couples, friends, family, business associates, etc.
—How many do I want to invite?

—How much space will I need? Not just for people, but for cooking and serving. For a large group, an open house with staggered hours will stretch your entertaining ability.

—Do the guests know each other? If they know each other well, plan a leisurely sit-down meal where there's lots of time to talk. If your guests are strangers, a party with movement is better.

—What time of day? Weeknights are fine, but don't expect guests to stay late.

—What date should I set? Avoid planning dates that conflict with other activities or interests of your guests—or plan to incorporate the activity (brunch before a sporting event, late-night party after the theater, etc.).

Use your 3x5s to make out a detailed guest list, menu, shopping list, and time schedule. Specifically itemize "to-dos" for the week ahead, days before, and day of the party. Plan to have thirty minutes to an hour before your guests are due to arrive—for yourself.

The Betty Crocker book, *Home Entertaining*, is a great help if you are just getting organized enough to enjoy having people visit. Your local library may be an excellent source for more books filled with recipes, menu plans, themes, and centerpieces, too. Decide to subscribe to *one* magazine this year, for example: *Bon Appétit, Good Housekeeping*, or *Better Homes and Gardens* to get yourself in the mood.

For unexpected guests keep an emergency shelf in your cupboard and/or freezer with party crackers, ingredients for fix-it-fast foods, or ready-make items. It is also wise to have a few cookies or snack bars on hand to serve with coffee for friends who stop by for a short visit. Keep these items hidden from hungry children and husbands.

As important as menus, recipes, guest lists, invitations, and organization is your warmth, cheer, and gracious welcome to the people you love.

This is a good time to start being more thoughtful. One of your greatest happiness factors is the time you spend thinking of others and then doing something about it. In the coming year you will feel the joy that comes from following through—revealing what's in your heart so that the people you love don't have to read your mind.

Twelve

December–Faith
–From Peggy

"Blessed are they that have not seen, and yet have believed."

—JOHN 20:29

December is the month we chose to represent faith. It is traditionally a time when two of the world's greatest religions, Christianity and Judaism, celebrate their faith.

Being a Christian, I already knew well the story of the birth of Christ with its subsequent miracles of faith and salvation, but I wanted to know about what Jewish families were celebrating on Hanukkah in December.

I found that as they light each candle in the menorah (a nine-branched candle holder), it is in remembrance of an act of faith that happened more than 2,000 years ago.

According to the story (loosely translated), after an impressive fight to recapture their Holy Temple in Jerusalem, the Jews wanted to relight the menorah at the altar and keep it going twenty-four hours a day. They didn't have candles back in those days so they had to use oil, but only the purest olive oil would do. Unfortunately, they had only enough of the good stuff to last the first day, and they knew it would take eight days to prepare some more. Nevertheless, they lighted the lamp, fueled by faith, and hoped that a one-day supply of oil would burn for eight days and not run out until the new oil was ready. Against all odds it was so, and the menorah did not go out.

What is it that changes things miraculously and meets our every human need? I think it's faith. St. Augustine said, "Faith is to believe what we do not see; and the reward of this faith is to see what we believe."

My good friend once told me about the hard times her family went through when she was a child. There were six children to feed, clothe, and support, and it was through the strong faith of her mother, a devout Catholic, that somehow the necessities were always provided. She said, "Just when we were at the end, something would happen every time and pull us through. My mother said she is absolutely certain that many times our huge, gas-guzzling station wagon operated on 'empty' just as if the tank were full."

I love it when logic and intellect can't explain something. It tickles me to hear or see miracles, no matter how small they seem in comparison to the walking-on-water kind Jesus had enough faith to demonstrate.

A few months after my marriage I discovered that, with God, I could handle a situation that appeared impossible. I found that my faith is strong and I have an inner security that can never be taken away from me.

While Danny was stationed with the 173rd Airborne Division in the central highlands of Vietnam, I was living with Mom and Dad and working as a chemist's assistant in a nearby paper mill. I kept myself busy spending money on hope-chesty things for our first home. I also saved enough for a trip to Hawaii to meet Danny on his rest-and-recuperation leave.

The reunion was wonderful to anticipate. We were going to stay at the Ilikai Hotel, right on the beach in Waikiki; and although we knew it would be expensive, we were planning to live in paradise for six glorious days and nights. All of our letters to each other were filled with our dreams of how fantastic it would be. I sent him travel brochures, and we counted the days until we would leave to meet each other. Ecstatically Danny wrote, "Just thirty-three days till Hawaii!" That was the last I heard from him.

There were no more letters. Every day I'd run to the mailbox; and when there was nothing there for me, I grew more and more desperate. Two weeks passed with no word from him, and then one day (I was almost afraid to open the mailbox), I spotted familiar handwriting on one of the envelopes. I grabbed the letter, only to see that the letter was one I'd mailed to Danny. I had the same sickening feeling I'd had as a child when I got lost in a department store and, seeing myself in a mirror, felt for a second that I'd found somebody I knew.

The envelope (returned to me unopened) was dirty and crumpled and was stamped with the horrible words "FOUND IN ABANDONED EQUIPMENT."

When I had last heard from him, Danny was in a place called Dak-To. The evening news assaulted my faith with pictures of the brutal beginnings of the Tet offensive. Dak-To was the subject of every piece of journalism and every "film at eleven." I had to stop reading the paper and stop watching the news to keep my sanity.

Another two weeks passed and still there was no word from Danny. He had said that he would send me a copy of his travel orders so that I could get a reduced airfare, but nothing came and time was running out. I had to face the fact that without the orders I didn't have enough money for the trip. I wished I had saved more and bought less. I didn't know what to do, but then I remembered my free-way theory: Once you're on the freeway, you have to keep moving, even if you don't know where you're going. If you stop, you'll get knocked off the road, but if you keep moving, the worst that can happen is you'll go for a little extra ride.

With that in mind I quit punishing my brain for not being able to work out the solution to my problem. Quietly and calmly I kept moving. I got out a suitcase for myself and one for Danny. While pressing and folding his things I pictured us laughing on the beach together. In my mind I saw him strong, tan, and healthy. I mentally hugged him while I packed, and then a thought came to me: I had to go to the Army and make them draw something up so that I could get the reduced fare.

With three days left on the countdown, I told Mom that I had to go find a general somewhere and get things moving. I got all fixed up, went to the Army Induction Center in Portland, and found the perfect parking space right in front of the door. I asked the sergeant at the desk if I might speak to the general about a personal matter. I was told that he wasn't in, but that perhaps a lieutenant would be able to help me. We bartered ranks and I settled for a major. I can't remember anything else about the man except that his voice was kind and friendly. When I showed him the letters and told him the problem, he stood up and left the room for a moment.

Alone in his office, I looked at Danny's handwriting and felt sure that a rush of tears would overtake me. "Don't you dare cry!" I commanded, and the tears went back to wherever tears go when you pull yourself together.

The major returned with several folded papers. Travel orders! The Red Cross had been contacted, and I was assured that they would find Danny and let me know his whereabouts. I told the major that I would be leaving on schedule and that I would just wait for Danny in Hawaii, however long it took. We shook hands and I left the building.

An older man in a big car was double-parked behind my car and was staring at me. His window was open, so I said, "Are you just waiting for someone or would you like my parking spot?"

"I'd like your spot," he answered.

"Okay, I'll just be a minute," I said. As I was backing out of the space I saw a small sign that I hadn't noticed before: RESERVED FOR THE COMMANDING GENERAL. I looked over at the man in the car. He was still staring. "Good-bye, General," I called. He nodded.

With my travel orders I bought the airline ticket, and with

the last of our savings I had enough money for food, six nights at the Ilikai, and a tiny cushion for an emergency. Still without word from Danny or the Red Cross, I went to the airport as planned. I had absolutely no idea what I would do if Danny didn't come and the money ran out. I prayed that maybe I'd find a wallet with no ID (great prayer, huh?), and I looked on the floor for cash the way I had when I was a kid at the fair and my money ran out.

Just before my flight I was paged for a phone call. It was Danny's mom. She read me the telegram over the phone. "Soldier did not make it to forwarding area. Advise wife not to travel." Her voice was shaking when she read it.

"I know he's all right, and I'm just going to wait for him. I know he'll come," I said with a confidence that went beyond anything I could conjure up on my own. She seemed relieved by my unshakable faith.

On the plane I said those same sentences over and over, as if by repetition it would be so. I wavered in and out of believing it.

When I got to Hawaii, Danny wasn't there. The beautiful room at the Ilikai with all its elegance and breathtaking views meant nothing to me without him. I had dreamed of such luxury, but in my sadness I could enjoy nothing.

Remembering the freeway, I decided to move. The Holiday Inn would be cheaper. I spoke to the assistant manager at the Ilikai about my circumstances. The remainder of my week's lodging was refunded, and I said I would return with my husband as soon as he arrived. I quickly realized that even at the Holiday Inn, my money wasn't going to last. I prayed. Either I needed a job or a handout, but I needed an answer fast. Once again I went to the Army and asked them for help.

I was taken to a dormitory-type building where other wives in my predicament were being housed while they waited for their missing husbands. I shared a room with a quiet, dignified woman much older than I. She didn't talk about it much, so neither did I. Secure and safe in my economical new home, I waited and prayed. Thanksgiving came and went. I ate turkey dinner, Army-style, and refused to believe that Danny wasn't coming. I expected him every day.

The chaplain arranged it so that I could ride the Army bus to the airport every time a planeload of soldiers landed. There were three flights a day. For the next three days I met each plane, and every time I rode back to the barracks in the bus without Danny. Then on the 1:00 A.M. pickup, I saw him. Taller than most, he stuck out in a moving confusion of khaki. He was looking in my direction and he smiled hard when he saw me. Most of the soldiers carried big duffel bags, some even had luggage, but Danny had nothing except a small rolled-up combat blanket about the size of a soccer ball. When we finally reached each other we hugged and hugged and hugged, but neither of us could say anything.

Once on the bus, Danny told me that he knew I'd be there. He didn't know I'd be at the airport, but he just knew I would be in Hawaii. He apologized for being late. I said it was all right, and then we laughed. It sounded as if he'd come home late from the office and missed dinner.

He told me that after their airfield was hit by mortars and two cargo planes were destroyed, no other planes were allowed to land. With just what he could easily carry, Danny spent the next several days hitchhiking his way to another airstrip in Phu Cat, where he waited for a small plane that could take him to the airport at Cameron Bay. When he finally got there, he had to wait again for a flight to Hawaii. It had been a tremendous ordeal.

He wondered how I'd managed to get there without the orders, and when I told him about the major, he said that what I'd done was impossible. I still had most of the money I'd started out with, so we checked out of the barracks and into the Ilikai. To our surprise we were given the bridal suite for the same rate as a regular room.

The suite was spectacular, the weather was warm, the ocean was beautiful, and we had plenty of money to do whatever we wanted...but we were miserable. Six days was only enough time to reinforce our sadness at having to be apart again. The impending separation hung over our heads like a hangman's noose. Danny was quiet and unsettled. There was a gloominess about him that I had never seen before. He knew what he would be going back to, and no amount of luxury could change the way things were.

When we said good-bye and he left Hawaii to go back to Vietnam for the rest of his thirteen months, it was just short of being unbearable. The war had us both frightened. Those months of separation required our unswerving faith; strong enough in its conviction to keep away the influences that would weaken it.

Christmas passed and so did winter. Spring came and we celebrated our May anniversary apart. I had rented an apartment and moved in with all the stuff I'd collected over the year. It was a cute little nest, just waiting to be filled.

One morning in early June the phone rang. It was Danny. "Hi, I'm home!" I'll never forget the joy in his voice. I was thrilled, but I had thought he'd be coming home four days later. I had been fixing up the apartment, painting and cleaning, and although it was almost ready, I was a real mess. Anne Skordahl (the apartment manager's wife) was over having coffee when I got the call. "I'll be *right* there!" I shrieked and hung up the phone. Anne finished putting things back for me while I changed my clothes. I couldn't take time for a shower . . . I just wanted to get over to the airport.

"What about your hair?" my spotless friend asked. She had a look of mortification on her face.

"Maybe I oughta put the scarf back on," I said.

"No!" she insisted. "That's really bad!"

I resorted to an old trick I'd learned in the theater (actually it was when I was in my high school play and I needed white hair—the fact that the flour neutralized the grease had been a side benefit) and I dusted flour throughout my hair to absorb the natural oils. I brushed it hard and it almost returned to its natural color; the grease was gone. My friend couldn't believe it.

When I got to the airport, Danny was standing alone outside. He looked tall, tan, tired, and wonderful! He said I looked beautiful. (He never knew my flour secret.)

I share this story with you because of what it taught me about faith. Webster says faith is "belief in something for which there is no proof," and "complete trust without doubt or question." Use your early mornings to schedule daily time to keep in touch with God and grow in your own faith.

For me, faith is having enough conviction that a power greater than I am exists that I can control my second thoughts. Without those crippling second thoughts I can continue in the firm, unwavering belief that, with God, everything will be all right.

I am not talking about blind faith where one sits in a rocking chair and hopes that something good will happen, but faith bold enough to face negatives and keep moving. I am speaking about an active faith, greater than any circumstance; that *still-small voice within* that urges us to keep going, to try again, to ask for help and *believe* that there is an answer.

Afterword

The Happiness File is yours now. Use it as you see fit. Let it serve you. Let it reflect who you are and it will have within it the possibility of a happier life.

In thinking about how we would end this book we wanted our final words to be exactly perfect; but endings are always hard for us so we thought we'd let Ralph Waldo Emerson do it.

> "Finish every day and be done with it. You have done what you could. Some blunders and absurdities no doubt crept in. Forget them as soon as you can. Tomorrow is a new day; begin it well and serenely and with too high a spirit to be cumbered with your old nonsense. This day is all that is good and fair. It is too dear, with its hopes and invitations, to waste a moment on yesterdays."

Pam and Peggy present motivational lectures for churches, clubs, and conventions throughout the country. If you are interested in more information or would like to order their various home study courses on video and cassette tape, call (206) 696-4091 or send a self-addressed, stamped envelope to S.H.E. Inc., 401 N.W. Overlook Drive, Vancouver, Washington 98665, for a free brochure.